THE SLAVERY OF SEX
Feminist-Abolitionists in America

Blanche Glassman Hersh

Building on the acknowledged historical link between abolitionism and feminism, Hersh examines the beginnings of organized activity for women's rights, concentrating on the antebellum women's movement of the 1840s and 1850s rather than the much-studied period after the Civil War.

A portrait of Lucy Stone, Elizabeth Cady Stanton, and Susan B. Anthony, the movement's three major leaders, illuminates the abolitionist roots of their common ideology. Hersh delineates the shared characteristics of fifty-one leaders in the struggle leading from abolitionism to the campaign for women's rights. Comments on their childhoods, family backgrounds, educations, religious beliefs, personalities, husbands and marriages, and involvements with reforms other than abolitionism provide a social and intellectual profile of the first generation of feminists and explain how common patterns contributed to their united efforts.

Hersh's study is firmly rooted in the cultural milieu of nineteenth-century America and offers an appealing new interpretation of feminism as an outgrowth of antislavery protest. Her discussions of egalitarian marriages, role models, and the ways in which these outstanding women reconciled their commitments to domesticity and equality are of special interest.

Blanche Glassman Hersh

The Slavery of Sex

Feminist-Abolitionists in America

University of Illinois Press *Urbana Chicago London*

Library of Congress Cataloging in Publication Data

Hersh, Blanche Glassman, 1928–
  The slavery of sex.

  Bibliography: p.
  Includes index.
  1. Feminism—United States—History. 2. Women's
rights—United States—History. 3. Feminists—United
States—History. 4. Abolitionists—History. I. Title.
HQ1423.H47   301.41'2'0973   78-14591
ISBN 0-252-00695-X

This Book Is Dedicated to
HERB HERSH,
to the Memory of
GILBERT OSOFSKY,
and to Future Workers in Women's Studies

Preface

THE FIRST GLIMMER of the idea for this book came to me when, as a graduate student in the mid—1960's, I studied the antislavery movement with the late Gilbert Osofsky. Among the many interesting abolitionists included in his research were several remarkable women who appeared also to be strong feminists. The connection between abolitionism and feminism has since been well established, thanks to the recent work of scholars of women's history, but at the time I had the pleasure of discovering it for myself: all of the women, and the men, who first spoke out and organized for women's rights were abolitionists!

I came to realize that feminism was a logical outgrowth of antislavery because the abolitionists' argument for human rights transcended both sex and color, and because the obstacles which women faced in working against slavery made their efforts a feminist consciousness-raising experience. The questions I began to ask about these feminist-abolitionist women became the basis for my own research. The title "Slavery of Sex" was chosen early because of its double connotation. It was used in feminist-abolitionist rhetoric to denote the parallel positions of women and slaves: black women were enslaved by chains and codes; all women were the slaves of creed and custom, imprisoned within the traditional concept of woman's sphere. The phrase also suggests the close historical link between abolitionism and feminism.

The growth of the women's movement during the course of my academic work served to reinforce my interest and excitement. Much

vii

of my own feminist consciousness-raising over the next few years, however, resulted from reading nineteenth-century women's letters and speeches, proof to me of the power of their ideas. It also became apparent to me, after immersing myself in their lives, that those women had left other important legacies. They viewed the cause of human rights as a divine mission and adopted it, in effect, as their religion; their devotion to this cause, the most important force in their lives, led them to fight a multitude of battles. The temperance movement, for example, although generally viewed by historians as a conservative social phenomenon, was to them a radical crusade for the protection and emancipation of women. Perhaps most interesting to me was the fact that their "reform religion" touched even their private lives and resulted in the creation of models of egalitarian marriage that would still be remarkable today.

In the course of my research, I also became aware that the antebellum feminist-abolitionist movement, which came to exist independently of the parent antislavery crusade and the postwar suffrage movement, had not been identified as such before. Because the lives of so many first-generation feminists spanned the entire century, the importance of their roots in the earlier era of religious fervor and radical reform has been overlooked. A few women, like Lucretia Mott and Abby Kelley, have been discussed within the antislavery context; their importance as prototypical leaders of the women's movement has not been fully examined, however, although they and others were arguing for female equality years before the Seneca Falls meeting of 1848. Most feminist leaders, like Susan B. Anthony and Elizabeth Cady Stanton, are usually associated with the later suffragist period; insufficient attention has been given to their abolitionist origins and the cultural milieu from which they emerged. Other important leaders go almost completely unmentioned in historical studies. Would not a portrait of Lucy Stone—so typical of her generation of feminists—offer new and valuable insights into the entire group? One goal of this study became to bridge the historiographical gap between the two movements, and to restore the feminist-abolitionists, as a group, to their proper place in history.

Chapter 1 looks at the beginnings of organized activity for women's rights and examines the "woman question" in antislavery from the viewpoint of feminism, rather than abolitionism. The

Garrisonian women in the 1830's are seen as laying the groundwork for a feminist ideology, developing new styles of female leadership, and creating models of new social roles for women. Chapter 2 overviews the antebellum women's movement of the 1840's and 1850's and points to a crucial transition: from seeking equality for women in order to free them to work against slavery, to working for women's rights as an end in itself. The major demands of the period as expressed in newspapers and conventions are examined, as are the tensions and conflicts which led to the split in the movement. In Chapter 3 a portrait of the three major leaders, Stone, Stanton, and Anthony, is offered; this chapter attempts to counter stereotypical images and misleading interpretations of those women, as well as to illuminate the diverse facets of a leadership that shared a common ideology but differed in personality, style, and priorities.

The remaining chapters present a profile of a larger, more representative group of feminist-abolitionist women, to delineate the shared characteristics that define them as a special group. Why did feminism develop as it did? And why did certain women become feminists? Of special interest here are similar cultural origins, common world-views, and parallel life patterns. Chapter 4 explores early influences—religion, class, family, education—and suggests, among other things, that emancipation from religious orthodoxy was a crucial element in the development of a feminist leadership. The elitism and nativism that have been identified in the next generation appear here as well, though in a more innocuous form. The broad scope of this group's reform efforts is described in Chapter 5, as is the unique feminist perspective they brought to their universal crusade to make the world better. The sources of feminist-abolitionist ideology and its principal tenets are the subjects of Chapter 6. The women's roots in nineteenth-century culture are here apparent, but so are the ways in which they modified prevailing doctrines. Their belief in human rights appears as a dominant theme in their lives, uniting their public efforts for human liberation and their private attempts to reform marriage and family life. Here, too, the seeming contradiction between their radical goal of broadening woman's sphere and their conservative defense of home and family is explained by their theory of overlapping spheres, and by a closer look at their idea of marriage. In Chapter 7 the feminists' own unusual marriages are described and compared with the ideal. Important historical questions are raised about why men became feminists, and about men's role in the women's movement—questions which this study can only begin to answer.

A number of people have helped throughout the long process of writing the dissertation and adapting it to book form. My greatest intellectual debt is to Gilbert Osofsky, who encouraged me as a late-blooming graduate student, taught me how to think about history, and propelled me into the serious business of becoming a historian. He also guided the early stages of my research. Other members of the history department at the University of Illinois, Chicago Circle, were crucial in enabling me to complete it. I am grateful to Robert V. Remini for taking on the supervision of the work at midpoint and seeing it through to the end. Marion Miller and Leo Schelbert were much-needed sources of support and also offered invaluable criticism of the entire dissertation. Melvin G. Holli, Daniel Scott Smith, and Michael Perman also read the entire manuscript and offered useful comments and advice. I also acknowledge the aid of the interlibrary loan department of the library, especially William D. Thrasher and Antonia Valencia, who managed to locate even the most obscure source materials.

Many others have also made helpful contributions. My colleague at Northeastern Illinois University, June Sochen, read the entire manuscript at several stages and offered important insights and suggestions. Another colleague, Nancy Green, helped with the chapter on ideology. Kathryn Kish Sklar, Joseph Pleck, Kirk Jeffrey, and Rosemary Keller provided useful comments and perspectives on earlier versions of the chapter on feminist marriages. The suggestions of all of these people have served to improve the book; its failings, of course, are my responsibility alone.

My greatest personal debt is to my husband, Herb, who read the book patiently and critically through all of its stages, and who provided every conceivable other kind of support. I have relied on his advice more than any other (though not always graciously!). My daughter, Joan, provided critical comments and moral support from an early stage, as well as lots of typing and editorial help. My son, Mark, has been a continuing source of encouragement and has provided a variety of useful editorial services. The support of Reynold Feldman, director of program development at Northeastern Illinois University, for my efforts in history as well as in women's studies, has been crucial. Joan Allman typed the final manuscript with professional efficiency and competency. Finally, I am grateful for the assistance of the editors at the University of Illinois Press, and acknowledge especially the helpful editing of Ann Lowry Weir and the patient support of Frank O. Williams.

Northeastern Illinois University —B. G. H.

BLANCHE GLASSMAN HERSH is coordinator of the women's studies program at Northeastern Illinois University. She has written a chapter, "Am I Not a Woman and a Sister?: Abolitionist Beginnings of Nineteenth-Century Feminism," for a forthcoming book entitled *History and the Abolitionists.* She was one of the founders of the Great Lakes Women's Studies Association and is a member of several organizations for professional women.

The Fifty-one Women Included in This Study

MATHILDE FRANZISKA ANNEKE (1817–1884)
SUSAN BROWNELL ANTHONY (1820–1906)
ANTOINETTE LOUISA BROWN BLACKWELL (1825–1921)
ELIZABETH BLACKWELL (1821–1910)
AMELIA JENKS BLOOMER (1818–1894)
ELIZABETH BUFFUM CHACE (1806–1899)
MARIA WESTON CHAPMAN (1806–1885)
LYDIA MARIA FRANCIS CHILD (1802–1880)
ELIZABETH LESLIE ROUS COMSTOCK (1815–1891)
BETSEY MIX COWLES (1810–1876)
PRUDENCE CRANDALL (PHILLEO) (1803–1890)
HANNAH CONANT TRACY CUTLER (1815–1896)
CAROLINE HEALEY DALL (1822–1912)
PAULINA KELLOGG WRIGHT DAVIS (1813–1876)
ABIGAIL KELLEY FOSTER (1810–1887)
FRANCES DANA BARKER GAGE (1808–1884)
MATILDA JOSLYN GAGE (1826–1898)
ABIGAIL HOPPER GIBBONS (1801–1893)
MARY GREW (1813–1896)
JOSEPHINE WHITE GRIFFING (1814–1872)
ANGELINA EMILY GRIMKÉ (WELD) (1805–1879)
SARAH MOORE GRIMKÉ (1792–1873)
LAURA SMITH HAVILAND (1808–1898)
SALLIE HOLLEY (1818–1893)
ISABELLA BEECHER HOOKER (1822–1907)

JULIA WARD HOWE (1819–1910)
EMILY HOWLAND (1827–1929)
HARRIOT KEZIA HUNT (1805–1875)
ABIGAIL HUTCHINSON (PATTON) (1829–1892)
JANE ELISABETH HITCHCOCK JONES (1813–1896)
MARY ASHTON RICE LIVERMORE (1820–1905)
HANNAH E. MYERS LONGSHORE (1819–1901)
CLEMENCE HARNED LOZIER (1813–1888)
ABIGAIL WILLIAMS MAY (1829–1888)
ELIZABETH SMITH MILLER (1822–1911)
LUCRETIA COFFIN MOTT (1793–1880)
CLARINA IRENE HOWARD NICHOLS (1810–1885)
ANN PRESTON (1813–1872)
SARAH PUGH (1800–1884)
HARRIET HANSON ROBINSON (1825–1911)
ERNESTINE POTOWSKI ROSE (1810–1892)
CAROLINE SEYMOUR SEVERANCE (1820–1914)
ABBY HADASSAH SMITH (1797–1878)
ELIZABETH OAKES PRINCE SMITH (1806–1893)
JULIA EVELINA SMITH (1792–1886)
ELIZABETH CADY STANTON (1815–1902)
LUCY STONE (1818–1893)
JANE GREY CANNON SWISSHELM (1815–1884)
MARY FRAME MYERS THOMAS (1816–1888)
AMANDA M. WAY (1828–1914)
MARTHA COFFIN PELHAM WRIGHT (1806–1875)

Contents

Introduction:
Prelude to Feminism

THE SURGE OF ABOLITIONIST ACTIVITY in the 1830's served as the catalyst which transformed latent feminist sentiment into the beginnings of an organized movement. This sentiment had existed before, as had the grievances it reflected, without causing the development of a public activism. In the early nineteenth century, however, several historical developments coalesced to create a setting in which a women's movement was possible. This setting provided the preconditions for social reform: a group able to provide leadership, a set of issues around which people can be organized, and an atmosphere in which social change is possible.

The growth of industrialization played a key role in the development of a feminist leadership. Burgeoning factories took over much of the work formerly done at home, lessening the housewife's burdens. Industrialization also created job opportunities which caused widespread movement from farm to city and attracted large numbers of foreign immigrants. These developments, in turn, furnished a source of cheap and abundant domestic help. This combination of circumstances provided urban middle-class women with greater leisure to carry on reform activities; on the other hand, it also left them with a diminished usefulness which grated on the consciences of many who had been trained, like their brothers, in the work ethic. The wife's status became more ornamental, more often derived from her husband's worth than from her own—a situation which was anathema to independent-minded women. Both opportunity and

1

discontent, therefore, contributed to the making of the nineteenth-century "new woman" who created new directions for herself, including feminism. The question of woman's proper sphere became debatable only in the nineteenth century because then, for the first time, many women found it possible to engage in work that was unrelated to family needs.[1]

If the boundaries of woman's sphere constituted the first important issue to be raised publicly, the question of her legal rights followed close behind. The issue of citizens' rights in the new republic was an important one, and debate on this question led to significant gains for white men. This situation contributed to an atmosphere of rising expectations, while at the same time calling attention to the widening gap between the rights of women and men. The women's rights movement was, among other things, a response to the reality of the married woman's "legal death." The single woman had few civil rights, but the married woman had virtually none. She was a *femme couverte,* giving up her legal identity in marriage, as well as abandoning any claim to property or guardianship of her children in case of divorce or her husband's death. Even her wages automatically belonged to her husband. Nowhere could she obtain a divorce on the grounds of her spouse's drunkenness, a widespread condition. This was the slavery of sex in its most concrete and visible form.

The religious revivalism that flourished in the 1820's and 1830's was a crucial element in the general antebellum agitation for reform. Particularly relevant to the growth of feminism was the ultraist vision which led to religious and secular perfectionism, a radical offshoot of evangelicalism. This philosophy governed the Garrisonian abolitionists and was an important influence on the early women's rights leaders. The passion for self-improvement and the perfection of society had special meaning for women who were seeking to develop themselves to the fullest in order to play an equal role with men in all aspects of society.

More subtle forces involved the moral and religious ambiance of the period.[2] The idea of woman as moral guardian, which became a central theme in feminist ideology, grew out of the climate of religious revivalism and romanticism. The content of literature and thought, as well as religion, became increasingly moralistic. Special emphasis was placed on the spirituality of woman's character and on her innocence and purity. This elevation of woman to a moral pedestal, symbolized by the "cult of true womanhood," entailed new obligations and duties for the middle-class lady.[3] While her husband competed fiercely in the money-grubbing world outside the home, the woman's job was to preserve the old values and transmit them to her children. Perhaps this was unconscious compensation for her loss of function, or an effort to create a moral bastion in a society growing more materialistic and complex.

With increased differentiation of sex roles came greater polarization in the popular view of sex differences: women were seen as delicate, sensitive, and altruistic; men were aggressive, uncouth, and hopelessly susceptible to the lower passions. This view was accepted by feminists as well as antifeminists. Elizabeth Cady Stanton, one of the more radical and irreverent thinkers of the movement, praised her father by describing him as embodying not only the best virtues of manhood but also "the tenderness, purity, and refinement of a pure woman."[4]

Although the cult of true womanhood confined women in a narrow, private sphere, it also provided the opportunity for limited escape into the public arena. Women's moral superiority conferred on them an obligation to exert their beneficent influence outside the home, as well as on their families. Spurred on by the prevailing climate of religious enthusiasm, women in evangelical Protestant sects became active in church-related philanthropic and missionary efforts. Several historians have seen this activity as the precursor of the women's rights movement. One study of these "ladies bountiful" concluded that the expansion of woman's sphere to include charitable organizations involved a significant change in the status of women, giving them a "half-taste" of freedom and power which encouraged discontent, leading them to antislavery work and, ultimately, to organized feminism.[5] Another study, dealing with the changing image of woman between 1828 and 1848, concluded that the new view of woman as moral guardian enabled women to justify the expansion of their sphere to include teaching as well as charitable work.[6] Still another work investigated the female moral reform societies which sprang up in the 1830's and concluded that this activism was an effort to challenge the passive, home-oriented image of woman; indeed, that study further suggested that moral reform was an outlet for women who resented the limitations of their assigned roles but who were unable to protest openly.[7] The circumscribed sphere of women was particularly galling when contrasted with the opportunities and expectations of their male counterparts in Jacksonian America.

Moral and philanthropic work may have been an indication that some women needed a more active role, and perhaps it planted the seeds of discontent in others. Such work unquestionably provided some women with organizational and leadership experience, and in this sense "prepared" them for future activism. Those women were, however, in no way defying tradition or questioning male authority. The leap from moral reform to feminism was considerable, and most women could not and did not make it. Missionary and charitable work was well within the sphere assigned to women and was viewed as merely an extension of their major duty to preserve and extend religious values. That work was quite acceptable to men as long as the women maintained their proper subservience and did not challenge male prerogatives. Only in the 1830's, when abolitionist women demanded an equal role with men in antislavery work, was the feminist gauntlet thrown down. The consciousness of even the earliest feminist-abolitionist women was "woman-defined," not "male-defined";[8] and therein lay the crucial difference.

NOTES

1. See Janet Wilson James, "Changing Ideas about Women in the United States, 1776–1825" (Ph.D. dissertation, Radcliffe College, 1954), and Gerda Lerner, "The Lady and the Mill Girl: Changes in the Status of Women in the Age of Jackson," *Mid-Continent American Studies Journal* 10 (Spring 1969): 5–15.

2. See Keith Melder, "The Beginnings of the Women's Rights Movement in the United States, 1800–1840" (Ph.D. dissertation, Yale University, 1964).

3. See Barbara Welter, "The Cult of True Womanhood," *American Quarterly* 18 (Summer 1966): 151–75.

4. James Parton et al., *Eminent Women of the Age* (Hartford, Conn.: S. M. Betts, 1868), p. 334.

5. Melder, "Beginnings"; also his "Ladies Bountiful: Organized Women's Benevolence in Early 19c America," *New York History* 48 (July 1967): 231–54.

6. Glenda Lou Gates Riley, "From Chattel to Challenger, the Changing Image of the American Woman, 1828–1848" (Ph.D. dissertation, Ohio State University, 1967).

7. Carroll Smith-Rosenberg, "Beauty, the Beast and the Militant Woman: A

Case Study in Sex Roles and Social Stress in Jacksonian America," *American Quarterly* 23 (Oct. 1971): 562–84.

8. I am indebted to Gerda Lerner for this terminology; see her "Placing Women in History: Definitions and Challenges," *Feminist Studies* 3, nos. 3/4 (Fall 1975): 5–14.

1

Abolitionist Beginnings

ABBY KELLEY FOSTER, writing her reminiscences in 1886, described the work of the early antislavery women. No other women did so much, she said; "they 'scorned delights and lived laborious days.'" No burden was too heavy and no work too revolting, "yet we were standing against the whole world on the woman question."[2]

These women who "stood against the whole world" in the 1830's were not only abolitionists, but also the first feminists. Motivated to work against slavery by the same moral indignation as men, they found themselves outside woman's traditional sphere and were faced with cries of "unsexed women." Though their primary commitment was to abolitionism, they moved surely and inevitably toward the realization that human enslavement took many forms. As deeply religious people, they felt that divine will placed them in a position to fight for the emancipation of women as well as of slaves, and they responded to what they considered a sacred obligation. The resulting controversy, which divided the antislavery movement, produced the first public discussion of women's rights.

The actions of Abby Kelley Foster and other abolitionist women constituted the vital link between abolitionism and feminism. Their efforts to gain support from other antislavery women in the 1830's was essentially a "pre-movement" which led directly to the first attempts to organize for women's rights in the 1840's and 1850's. The arguments the female reformers used to defend their unpopular position as public antislavery agents would become the basis for a feminist ideology. Though at this early date they could not anticipate the full-fledged women's movement, they were remarkably prescient in articulating the issues around which it would be organized.

The abolitionist women prepared the way for the feminist movement in another equally significant but more subtle way. By venturing into the male domain of antislavery work, they set precedents for future feminists and became the cutting edge for the creation of new social roles for women. In defending woman's domestic role but demanding that she have equal access to a broader sphere, they foreshadowed the basic spirit of nineteenth-century feminism. By expanding their own spheres to include the dual roles of wife-mother and reformer, they provided models for other women eager to free themselves from old patterns in order to exert an influence on the world around them. In ideology, personality, and lifestyle, they were prototypes for a whole generaton of women's rights leaders. In a broader sense, they set the example for a new type of nineteenth-century woman who was both a private and a public person.

Though the "woman question" did not burst into public view until William Lloyd Garrison launched his radical crusade for immediate emancipation in the 1830's, intimations of the issue appeared earlier, in the writings of Elizabeth Chandler. A little-known reformer whose extraordinary career was cut short by her early death, Chandler was a serious and scholarly writer; she was raised in Philadelphia by her Quaker grandmother and began her antislavery work in 1826, at nineteen, by sending contributions to Benjamin Lundy's weekly, *The Genius of Universal Emancipation.* Lundy, an antislavery advocate who favored gradual or compensated emancipation and colonization of emancipated slaves,[3] was an important precursor of radical abolitionism, just as Chandler was a harbinger of feminist abolitionism. Lundy described Chandler as gifted with "a talent of high order, a genius versatile, a mind expansive." He was so impressed with her ability that he placed her in charge of the "Ladies Repository" section of the paper when she was only twenty-two.[4]

Though Chandler migrated to Michigan territory with a Quaker group in 1830, she continued her work with Lundy and also contributed to Garrison's newly founded *Liberator.* After her death in 1834 she was hailed as the foremost female worker for the cause; she was revered as a saint by abolitionists, who made pilgrimages to her grave. Her poems were sung as hymns at meetings of female antislavery societies and were quoted by antislavery lecturers, especially this stanza:

> Shall we behold, unheeding
> Life's holiest feelings crushed;
> When woman's heart is bleeding
> Shall woman's voice be hushed?[5]

Elizabeth Chandler, so modest that she left her articles unsigned, had nevertheless assumed a daring role for a woman. Though she was not consciously a feminist, Chandler's writings suggested many of the themes that would become important in the antebellum women's movement. She saw her main function as agitator, with her goal the arousal of American women to their special moral duty, as women, to oppose slavery. In her first column, "An Appeal to the Ladies of the United States," she exhorted: "By all the holy charities of life is *woman* called upon to lend her sympathy and her aid. . . . Will Christian sisters and wives and mothers stand coldly inert, while those of their own sex are daily exposed, not only to the threats and revilings, but to the very *lash* of a stern unfeeling taskmaster?"[6]

Here were two themes that would appear regularly in the rhetoric of the feminist-abolitionists: women, as the more sensitive and sympathetic sex, were the natural foes of slavery; furthermore, they had a special obligation because members of their own sex were in bondage. Chandler appealed to the consciences of her female readers by contrasting their own privileged lives with the insecurity and degradation suffered by their enslaved sisters:

> Pity the negro, lady! her's is not
> Like thine, a blessed and most happy lot
> She is thy sister, woman! shall her cry
> Uncared for, and unheeded, pass thee by?[7]

Chandler's emphasis on the plight of slave women was a useful rhetorical device, but it also reflected the abolitionists' belief that women were especially victimized by slavery because of their delicate nature and their vulnerability to sexual abuse.

Chandler became the first antislavery woman called upon to defend her right, as a woman, to speak out against slavery. Shortly after she became an editor for the *Genius,* she was rebuked by a New England woman who questioned the propriety of females becoming public advocates of emancipation, taking over a "man's work."

Chandler denied that she was acting improperly: "To plead for the miserable . . . can never be unfeminine or unbefitting the delicacy of woman." She was not advocating emancipation for political (i.e., "male") reasons, but because slavery was "an outrage against *humanity* and *morality and religion* . . . and because a great number of *her own sex* are among its victims." Woman was not seeking to share a political role with man; rather, she was only pleading that he "lift the iron foot of despotism from the neck of her sisterhood." This work, she argued, was "not only quite within the sphere of her privileges, but also of her positive duties."[8]

In this defense, Chandler also related the cause of slave women to that of all women: "It is a restitution of *our own* rights for which we ask:—their cause is our cause—they are one with us in sex and nature."[9] Here she came very close to an idea that would be expressed a few years later and that became a mainstay of feminist-abolitionist rhetoric: women, like slaves, were in bondage. Even this earliest antislavery argument contained the unspoken, and perhaps unconscious, assumption that slaveholding was a male institution; southern white women were seen as victims, not perpetrators, of the system. Later abolitionist women made more specific an argument that Chandler only hinted at: both slave and free women suffered from the oppression of dominant males.

Elizabeth Chandler's female critic assailed her with that classic tenet of antifeminism: women are privileged by having their duties confined to the domestic sphere, and ought to be properly grateful. To this Chandler replied: "It is because we highly prize . . . the domestic privileges of our sex, that we would have them extended to those who are less fortunate than ourselves." Like all feminist-abolitionists, Chandler shared the nineteenth-century belief in woman's special moral and domestic attributes and used these very distinctions to justify expanding woman's sphere: antislavery was a natural activity for woman, calling on her tenderness, pity, and devotion to philanthropic causes. At the same time that Chandler defended women's domestic and philanthropic work, she expressed a feminist objection to limiting women to these activities. Woman, she argued, should be free to share equally with man the world of the mind: "She with him shall knowledge's pages scan/ And be the partner not the toy of man."

Unlike the women who followed her, Chandler's vision never

extended to men and women sharing power. ("It is not hers to guide the storm of war, to rule the state, or thunder at the bar . . . these things are not for her. . . ."[10]) Her voice was nevertheless prophetic, a portent of feminist awareness to come.

The controversy over the "woman question," only hinted at in Chandler's experience, came to a head in the late 1830's. Although these events have been detailed in antislavery studies, they need to be reexamined here from a new perspective. For the abolitionist movement, the internal dispute over women's role was a serious, divisive blow. However, this same controversy sparked an increased feminist consciousness and the beginnings of an important and continuing debate over women's rights. It also led to an expanded role for women in the radical wing of the movement.

William Lloyd Garrison was the catalyst who changed the nature of the antislavery movement and helped to transform women's role in it. In the first issue of his *Liberator,* published in Boston in 1831, Garrison renounced all gradualist solutions to the problem of slavery. Declaring that there could be no compromise with sin, he called for immediate and unconditional emancipation. By focusing dramatically on the moral issue and hammering away at it week after week, he launched a religious crusade which drew the hostility of most of New England and eventually of the nation. He also attracted a small band of dedicated followers, most of whom had been raised with a Puritan sense of moral duty and took this obligation seriously. A large number of these followers were women. They were incensed by the injustice of slavery, as Chandler had been; similarly, they had talent and energy to contribute to the cause. Many also enjoyed the benefits of education, leisure, and money by virtue of their positions in the middle and upper classes.

Garrison made a special effort to appeal to women and to arouse their indignation and sympathy for the cause. His early issues contained a "Ladies Department" headed by a picture of a kneeling slave woman in chains and captioned with the entreaty "Am I Not a Woman and a Sister?" He implored his female readers to take note of the one million enslaved women "exposed to all the violence of lust and passion—and treated with more indelicacy and cruelty than cattle," and he urged them to work for immediate emancipation. He continued to pound away at this theme in articles, speeches, and letters: "Women of New England . . . if my heart bleeds over the degraded and insufferable condition of a large portion of your sex, how ought you, whose sensibility is more susceptible than the windharp, to weep, and speak, and act, in their behalf?"[11]

The majority of New England women, like their male counterparts, were indifferent or hostile to Garrison's appeal. A few unusual Boston women, however, responded enthusiastically and became his staunch supporters. The abolitionist cause changed their lives drastically, moving them from positions of status and respectability to places among the outcasts and the martyrs of their society. They, in turn, transformed the traditional auxiliary role of women in antislavery into a more active, independent force in the next decade.

Maria Weston Chapman was one of the first to respond to Garrison's appeal; she became so important in his campaign that she was known as "Garrison's chief lieutenant." Born to one of the first families of Boston and educated in England, Chapman was a strong-minded and elegant young matron; her friend Harriet Martineau, the English writer and reformer, called her the most beautiful woman in Boston.[12] Self-confident, with a strong consciousness of class as well as pride in her sex, she was a controversial, heroic type worshiped by friends and vilified by enemies. Her domineering manner earned her the furtive title "Captain Chapman" even among admiring co-workers. Her grandson, the critic and writer John Jay Chapman, recalled her as an imposing figure who looked like a cameo but was a "doughty swordswoman" in conversation. Antislavery memoirs frequently include an account of her dramatic stand at an 1835 meeting (which ended with a mob dragging Garrison through the streets at the end of a rope). Confronted by a hostile mayor who tried to disperse the group, Chapman resisted with the true fervor of the revolutionary: "If this is the last bulwark of freedom, we may as well die here as anywhere."[13]

In 1832, Maria Weston Chapman and three of her sisters organized the Boston Female Anti-Slavery Society to serve as an auxiliary to Garrison's newly formed New England Anti-Slavery Society, an all-male group. They were supported in their work by Maria's husband, Henry Chapman, a wealthy merchant, and by the entire Weston and Chapman families. As the moving force of the female society, Maria Chapman concentrated initially on fundraising, which became the main task of all the women's groups. She organized yearly antislavery fairs which became models for fairs in other cities, and she edited the *Liberty Bell,* a gift book containing articles and poems by well-known abolitionists.

From this relatively conventional start, Maria Chapman subsequently moved to the more "male" role of propagandist and agitator, initiating petition campaigns and publishing the annual report of the Society as a propaganda vehicle. Increasingly she took on aspects of Garrison's job, editing the *Liberator,* for example, when he was busy elsewhere. When the American Anti-Slavery Society was formed in 1833 as a national organization, she became, in effect, its general manager. In the next decade she applied her enormous talent and energy to a wider circle of activities and became an organizer and spokeswoman for many radical causes of the day.

Garrison's crusade for immediate emancipation changed the life of another well-known Boston woman, Lydia Maria Child, who met him following her marriage in 1828 to one of his disciples, David Lee Child. In the 1820's she was a popular author of romantic novels, the editor of the first periodical for children, *Juvenile Miscellany,* and a versatile writer. Her book *The Frugal Housewife,* published in 1829, was a cookbook which also gave abundant practical advice on living in a thrifty and industrious manner. It was so successful that it went through thirty-three editions.[14]

Child herself was a temperamental romantic who was more interesting and complex than most feminist-abolitionists. Portraits show her plain, square face as kindly but determined; however, her warm, motherly exterior hid a soul in conflict. She was torn throughout her life between her desire to retreat from the public sphere into the world of music and literature, and her strong sense of moral obligation to work in the broader world and help reform it. Her "savage love of freedom," she explained, compelled her to aid in the emancipation of slaves and women.[15] She was also a self-styled "free spirit" who felt oppressed by the "machinery" of societies and conventions.[16] Except for a brief stint as an antislavery editor, she solved this dilemma by contributing her name and her words to both causes, but withholding her person.

Lydia Maria Child's name and words proved to be formidable weapons. She later recalled how Garrison had gotten hold of the strings of her conscience and pulled her into reform: "It is of no use to imagine what might have been if I had never met him. Old dreams vanished, old associates departed, and all things became new." He inspired her to write *An Appeal on Behalf of That Class of Americans Called Africans* (1833), the first antislavery work to be published in book form in this country, and an influential tract that had a strong impact on distinguished Bostonians such as Charles Sumner, Wendell Phillips, and William Ellery Channing. Basically a call for immediate emancipation, it is also notable for its condemnation of racial prejudice in the North, an important Garrisonian theme. Child documented her attack by compiling facts on the treatment of free blacks in the schools, churches, and public accommodations, as well as on the illegality of interracial marriages. She concluded with the prediction that "public opinion is on the verge of a great change." She felt that antislavery reformers would be successful because "God and truth is on their side."[17]

The *Appeal* was a turning point in Child's career, antagonizing Boston's literary circles with its controversial and unwelcome subject, and bringing a sharp halt to her popularity with the general public. Anticipating this reaction, she had explained in the text that duty and conscience compelled her to write the tract, at the risk of displeasing all classes. Her courage in taking this step is especially noteworthy, since Child disliked controversy more than any of her contemporaries. When she had published her first novel in 1824, she had been warned that female writers were considered "unsexed," but at that time she had chosen not to take issue with her critics.[18] Now, too, she preferred to stay in the background and let her words speak. In spite of herself, she became a symbol of independent, defiant womanhood.

Though individual women were challenging the traditional female role, in the early 1830's the issue of women's rights was still far from the minds even of abolitionists. Events of the first national convention in 1833 confirmed this fact. In December, male antislavery workers from New England and New York joined their co-workers in Philadelphia for a three-day meeting at which the American Anti-Slavery Society was organized. On the second day, apparently as an afterthought, an invitation was sent to the Philadelphia antislavery women. Lucretia Mott, accompanied by her mother, her daughter, and two sisters, joined the group of about sixty men. All the women were Quakers—as were seventeen of the men—and were accustomed to speaking in mixed assemblages.[19]

Mrs. Mott, tiny but with a commanding presence, was a Friends' minister who, with her husband, James, had been involved with antislavery since the 1820's. Their home was a focal point of the Underground Railroad which helped fugitive slaves, and it became the Philadelphia outpost of Garrisonian abolitionism.

The other women who attended this first convention left no record, but Lucretia Mott's contribution was reported by the abolitionist J. Miller McKim. When the crucial first session of the day was delayed because two prominent men failed to appear, causing doubt and confusion, Mrs. Mott rallied the group by reminding them that "right principles are stronger than great names." She also helped in lesser ways. When a "Declaration of Sentiments and Purposes" was drafted, she suggested that it would sound better if its key sentences were transposed. Later she recalled "one of the younger members turning to see what woman there was there who knew what the word 'transpose' meant."[20]

Though Lucretia Mott helped to draft this historic document, it did not occur to her, or to any other member of the convention, that the women present should also sign it. Instead, they were rewarded with a resolution of thanks "to our female friends, for the deep interest they have manifested in the cause of antislavery." The fact that the women present were not invited to add their signatures, and did not expect to be so invited, reveals the state of feminist consciousness even among the more independent and outspoken women in 1833. Samuel J. May, a Unitarian minister and beloved elder statesman of the feminist-abolitionist group, wrote many years later that his pride in recalling this convention "will be forever associated [with] the mortifying fact, that we *men* were then so blind, so obtuse, that we did not recognize those women as members of our Convention. . . ."[21]

Following this convention, the women organized a meeting of female abolitionists. The group, which was biracial and consisted mostly of Friends, like the parent body, became the Philadelphia Female Anti-Slavery Society. (Even an experienced speaker like Lucretia Mott hesitated to take on the "male" role of chairing this meeting, and a black male friend was called upon for the job. Mrs. Mott later recalled the irony of the situation: "You know that at that time, even to the present day, Negroes, idiots and women were in legal documents classed together; so that we were very glad to get

one of our own class to come and aid in forming that Society."[22])
This group of Quaker women functioned as the core of an important
female network that offered support and a home base for feminist-
abolitionist women for the remainder of the century.

Lucretia Coffin Mott was the pivotal person among antislavery
women in Philadelphia, just as Maria Weston Chapman was in
Boston. However, Mrs. Mott's role in the development of a women's
movement was even greater; indeed, her stature and influence among
the feminist-abolitionists was unparalleled. In 1833 she was forty,
about ten years older than Chapman and Child; already she had
behind her a career as minister, reformer, and scholar, as well as
accomplished housewife and mother of five. She had been a precocious child, taking to serious literature and Bible study "as a cat laps
milk" (and also falling into the common error, her sister recalled, of
"judging other people's minds by her own"). She continued her
systematic and scholarly study of the Bible throughout her life, but
found in it "a wholly different construction of the text from that
which was forced upon our acceptance." Early in life she decided that
much of it belonged to "a past, barbarous age."[23]

An important part of Lucretia Mott's enormous influence among
the feminist-abolitionists involved moving them from orthodox
religious dogma to her special brand of intellectual liberalism, built
upon Quaker beliefs but extending beyond them. Extraordinarily
open and tolerant of nonconforming ideas, she carried on a lifetime
crusade for freedom of religion and liked to say of this effort, "Call
me a radical of the radicals." She prided herself on always placing
fidelity to conscience above external strictures and relied on her
favorite motto in speeches and sermons: "Truth for authority, not
authority for truth." The superiority of practical Christianity over
ceremonial religion was a favorite theme, and she was a steadfast
critic of narrow dogmatism and petty sectarianism. Garrison described Mott's influence precisely when he wrote that he felt indebted to her (and her husband) for helping his mind to burst the
bonds of theological dogmas and to interpret the Scriptures so that,
instead of being "killed by the letter," he had been "made alive by
the spirit."[24]

Lucretia Mott was an especially influential teacher and model for
the younger women in the antislavery movement. Elizabeth Cady
Stanton, her most important protégée, later recalled that Mrs. Mott

15

was the first woman she had ever met who was progressive in her religious beliefs as well as in her concept of woman's role. She described her friend as having a magnetic presence: "The amount of will force and intelligent power in her small body was enough to direct the universe."[25] To her younger admirers, Lucretia Mott was the ideal woman, both consummate reformer and perfect wife and mother. Her marriage to James Mott was the model union to which all aspired; her success in balancing family and reform work was an example which all tried to emulate.

This kind of leadership—by women who rejected traditional social roles as well as orthodox religious beliefs—inspired the small groups of abolitionist women in Boston and Philadelphia to organize in their separate female societies and later to think about challenging the accepted pattern of segregation and male dominance. (The women in antislavery circles in New York City, with close ties to evangelicalism, were not sympathetic to feminism.[26]) In the years following the 1833 national meeting, the women busied themselves with circulating petitions, raising funds, and organizing new groups. The movement was expanding in an exciting manner—in 1838, the Massachusetts society alone recorded 183 local chapters including 41 female and 13 juvenile auxiliaries, with memberships ranging from fewer than twenty to more than three hundred.[27] Though abolitionists were still a tiny minority, their success in this period undoubtedly raised some women's sights in the direction of greater participation.

By 1837 there were intimations that abolitionist women were feeling hampered in their auxiliary role. Their first attempt at national organization, the Anti-Slavery Convention of American Women, met in May, with about one hundred delegates from ten states attending the three-day meeting. Lucretia Mott, recalling the mood of the group, noted that one of their first resolutions proclaimed it time for "woman to act in the sphere which Providence had assigned her, and no longer to rest satisfied with the circumscribed limits in which corrupt custom and a perverted application of the Scriptures had encircled her." Mary S. Parker of Boston, president of the convention and sister of the Unitarian minister and reformer Theodore Parker, was authorized to send a circular to all female antislavery societies of the country. In it she urged action on current petitions and gave the women some feminist advice: they should

16

follow their own consciences, not the wills of their husbands
—women could be "very obstinate concerning a gay party, a projected journey, or a new service of china; but when great *principles*
were at stake, they very promptly sacrificed them to earn the
reputation of meek and submissive wives."[28]

The question of woman's proper role in the antislavery movement
was finally raised publicly later in 1837, and the women's rights
issue was never quiescent thereafter. The central figures in the first
stage of the controversy were Angelina and Sarah Grimké. Born
in South Carolina and reared in an aristocratic, slaveholding family, they were unlikely additions to the New England–dominated
movement. Angelina was thity-two; Sarah, her sister and god-
mother (Angelina called her "sister mother"), was forty-five. Both
were unmarried. As young women they had become alienated from
their proslavery environment, and in the 1820's they had moved to
Philadelphia. Looking for something that would give their lives
meaning, they found a sense of purpose first in Quakerism and, more
lastingly, in antislavery work. Caught up in the enthusiasm of
Garrison's crusade, the Grimkés became active in the Philadelphia
Female Anti-Slavery Society.

Like all abolitionists, the Grimkés felt they were doing God's
work in battling slavery; this sense of divine mission would enable
them to endure the even greater public censure and private criticism
heaped on them when they became active feminists. Angelina especially exhibited a self-assurance that came from feeling "called" to
the work of reform. Responding only to the demands of an inner
voice, she seemed naturally endowed with the kind of protective
shield that other reformers worked hard to acquire. She had displayed an awesome sense of duty at an early age—a sister recalled her
single-minded "devotion to an idea" as a girl. As a young woman of
twenty-three, preparing to leave South Carolina, she wrote in her
diary, "I feel that I am called with a high and heavy calling, and that
I ought to be peculiar, and cannot be too zealous." Wendell Phillips
described her as a woman "morally sufficient to herself" who reminded him of "the spotless dove in the tempest." Although this
image of innocence amid the storm of abuse and controversy would
fit others as well—they were shielded by righteousness and moral
certainty from knowledge of the complex realities that surrounded
the evils they opposed—it applies best to Angelina Grimké.[29]

In 1836 Angelina came to public attention by writing *An Appeal to the Christian Women of the South,* in which she urged her southern sisters to influence husbands and brothers to act against slavery. In explaining her bold action she wrote: "God has shown me what I can do . . . to speak to them in such tones that they *must* hear me, and through me, the voice of justice and humanity."[30] Her pamphlet was published by the American Anti-Slavery Society and circulated widely in the North. In the South it coincided with a swell of anti-abolitionist activity and was publicly burned by the postmaster in Charleston, making its author an outlaw in her home state.

Angelina followed this *Appeal* with an eloquent address to the convention of antislavery women in 1837, challenging the "Women of the Nominally Free States" to break their own bonds to aid those of their sex who were in slavery. Published as a seventy-page pamphlet by the convention, it served to enhance the reputation of both sisters among the abolitionists. Following this convention, they were invited by Maria Weston Chapman to address the Boston Female Anti-Slavery Society. The Grimkés were especially desirable as speakers because of their unique experience with slavery. They went on from Boston to speak to other women's groups in the area. Prim and plain in their Quaker bonnets, they impressed their audiences with their intense devotion to their cause. In addition, Angelina was becoming known as an eloquent orator. For all of these reasons, churches and meeting halls were filled to overflowing when the Grimkés lectured. They found themselves addressing mixed audiences, a situation which abolitionist women had not faced before. Even staunch antislavery people doubted the wisdom of defying convention to this extent. The Reverend Samuel J. May, for example, was hesitant about allowing Angelina to speak from his pulpit before a mixed congregation, but he was won over completely by the force of her address and became her ardent supporter.[31]

The Grimkés' speaking tour lasted about six months and included over sixty New England towns. They addressed an estimated 40,500 people and may have been influential in the formation of six new societies during this period.[32] Though they successfully gained attention for their cause, they also brought down upon themselves the wrath of the orthodox clergy of Massachusetts. This body was already hostile to the Garrisonians, who constantly attacked the church for its complicity with slavery. The action of the Grimkés in defying much-hallowed custom, in addition to preaching radical abolitionism, was more than the clerics could tolerate. The General Association of Congregationalist Ministers issued an edict to all its member churches, in effect condemning the Grimkés (without specifically mentioning them) for the unfeminine act of addressing "promiscuous" or mixed audiences.

The pastoral letter attacking the Grimkés triggered the first extended public controversy over women's rights because it spoke directly to the question of woman's proper sphere, an issue that would dominate the nineteenth-century movement. Its language clearly revealed the boundaries of acceptable female behavior in 1837. Citing the New Testament as its authority, the letter emphasized that woman's power lay in her dependence. Likening her to a vine "whose strength and beauty is to lean upon the trellis-work," it warned that the vine which "thinks to assume the independence and the overshadowing nature of the elm" not only would cease to bear fruit, but also would "fall in shame and dishonor into the dust." The character of the woman who "assumes the place and tone of man as a public reformer . . . becomes unnatural." The action of the sisters, according to the clergy, presented dangers which threatened the female character with "permanent injury" and opened the way for "degeneracy and ruin."[33]

This harsh public attack on the Grimkés served as a warning to other women who might dare to venture outside their prescribed sphere. To withstand such statements the sisters could rely on their own piety, an important weapon in the battle as well as a source of strength for them personally. Frances Wright, a Scottish radical reformer, had lectured on women's rights in 1828–29 but, as a "notorious" advocate of free love, she was not taken seriously. The Grimkés were so obviously pious and respectable that their defiance of social custom forced many people to rethink the question of woman's proper sphere.

Their own state of mind is revealed in the large correspondence which the Grimkés carried on during the ensuing controversy, each letter closing with "Thy sister in the bonds of woman and the slave." To Henry C. Wright, their most loyal supporter, Sarah wrote that Angelina was troubled about the clerical uproar, "but the Lord knows that we did not come to forward our own interests but in simple obedience to his commands." In another letter she reiterated their determination to resist intimidation: "If in calling us thus publicly to advocate the cause of the downtrodden slave, God has unexpectedly placed us in the forefront of the battle which is to be waged against the rights and duties and responsibilities of woman, it would ill become us to shrink from such a contest."[34]

Though their critics initiated the controversy, the abolitionist women were not entirely unprepared for it. At the start of their New England tour the Grimkés had spent a social evening at the Chapman home and discussed their situation with "the brethren" (a term they, like their contemporaries, used to denote sisters as well as brothers). Angelina's comments on this meeting, written in a letter to a friend, are significant: "I had a long talk with the brethren on the rights of women, and found a very general sentiment prevailing that it is time our fetters were broken. L. M. Child and Maria Chapman strongly supported this view; indeed, very many seem to think a new order of things is very desirable in this respect . . . I feel it is not only the cause of the slave we plead but the cause of woman as a moral, responsible being. . . ."[35]

The most immediate issue for the women was the right to continue their public antislavery work. The question of women's equal participation in the work of the American Anti-Slavery Society was not made explicit at this point, but emerged naturally from the initial debate. Other basic grievances were also brought to mind by the controversy: the denial of legal rights to married women, the lack of opportunity for higher education and dignified employment, and a host of other inequalities and indignities. The cause of the slave opened a Pandora's box of grievances and demands on behalf of women.

Many abolitionist women were not ready for the Grimkés' "new order of things." Instead, they felt comfortable in their separate female auxiliaries and useful in their work of gathering petitions and holding fund-raising affairs. Sharing the prevalent view of woman's sphere, they were content to allow their men to represent them in public and make the decisions for the national organization. Although radical in their defense of the slave, they had not made the connection, as the Grimkés had, between the rights of slaves and the rights of women. The controversy over the sisters' public speaking forced them to become involved in this "woman question."

Anne Warren Weston, sister of Maria Weston Chapman, was one

of those who attempted to gain support for the Grimkés' right to speak. Addressing the Boston Female Anti-Slavery Society, she used many of the principal arguments of the feminist-abolitionist cause. The very theologians who had used the Scriptures to justify slavery were now "perverting the same sainted oracles" to sanction woman's inferiority and subordination. "Will you," she demanded, "allow those men who have been for years unmindful of their own most solemn duties to prescribe you yours?" Those who considered women as goods and chattels were not fit judges of the sphere woman should occupy; they had not objected that the slave woman in the rice fields was "out of her sphere," nor the southern woman who held her fellow creature as property. Weston concluded that the Grimkés, working for the slave, were "in the very sphere to which God has appointed every Christian."[36]

The Grimkés also stood firm in their own defense, claiming that men and women had the same moral right and duty to oppose slavery. They were clearly sensitive to the broader implications of the controversy and made a conscious decision to speak for all women, calling on the broad doctrine of human rights, rather than merely claiming rights for themselves. At stake was the right of women not merely to an equal role in antislavery, but to an equal position in all areas of society. The sisters were defending not only their right to speak publicly, but also the right of all women to be as free as men to develop their talents and to enjoy lives of usefulness, respect, and independence. The arguments they had used to defend slave women merged easily and logically with their own defense to become an ideology espousing equality for all women.

A high degree of feminist consciousness was revealed in their correspondence in this period. "The whole land seems aroused to discussion on the province of woman," Angelina noted defiantly in 1837, "and I am glad of it. We are willing to bear the brunt of the storm, if we can only be the means of making a break in that wall of public opinion which lies right in the way of woman's rights, true dignity, honor and usefulness." She had a strong sense of the importance of their role and understood that the question, once raised, could not be suppressed. To Anne Warren Weston she confided, "It is causing deep searchings of heart and revealing the secrets of the soul." She also displayed a keen insight into the basic nature of the opposition. In a letter written during her speaking tour, she admitted to scolding "most terribly" while lecturing on slavery, and noted that many of the men in the audience "look at me in utter amazement." "I am not at all surprized," she wrote, "they are afraid lest such a woman should usurp authority over the men." Sarah later revealed a similarly sophisticated understanding of the power struggle between the sexes.[37]

Because Angelina was more in demand as a speaker, Sarah Grimké took on the job of publicly defending their position in a series of "Letters on the Province of Woman" which ran in the *New England Spectator* beginning in July, 1837. The publication of these letters caused the sisters difficulty with friends who had not opposed their speaking but who feared that a public defense would stir unnecessary controversy and injure the antislavery cause. John Greenleaf Whittier, the noted poet and abolitionist, asked whether their aggressiveness was really necessary: "Is it not forgetting the great and dreadful wrongs of the slave in a selfish crusade against some paltry grievance of our own?"[38] Theodore Weld, their close co-worker who was to become Angelina's husband, took their cause more seriously and, in fact, was a solid "woman's rights man." But even he, for purely tactical reasons, opposed "agitating the question" and advised them to go on with their lecturing "without making any ado about 'attacks' and 'invasions' and 'oppositions' "; their example alone would be the most convincing argument for women's rights and duties.[39]

To the sisters, the issue of women's rights was not "a paltry grievance." As Angelina explained in a letter to Whittier and Weld, *"We must establish this right* for if we do not, it will be impossible for *us* to go *on with the work of Emancipation."* She pleaded with them: "Can you not see that woman *could* do, and *would* do a hundred times more for the slave if she were not fettered?" Responding to the charge that the time was not right, she wrote to Weld: "I think this must be the Lord's time and therefore the *best* time, for it seems to have been brought about by a concatenation of circumstances over which we had no control." After much debate, a compromise was effected: Sarah's letters were continued in the press, but the subject was not discussed in their talks. Angelina gave up her idea of a series of lectures on women's rights.[40]

Sarah's letters, published in 1838 as *Letters on the Equality of the Sexes, and the Condition of Woman,* constituted the first serious discussion of women's rights by an American woman, preceding Margaret Fuller's *Woman in the Nineteenth Century* by seven years. Lucretia Mott called it "the best work after Mary Wollstonecraft's *Vindication of the Rights of Woman*"—no small praise from a feminist who kept the earlier revolutionary work on the center table in her home for forty years, lending it "when she could find readers."[41]

In her *Letters,* Sarah Grimké made an important contribution to the development of a nineteenth-century feminist ideology by basing her defense of woman on the Scriptures, thus challenging her critics on their own ground. Starting from her belief that the Bible had been falsely translated by men, she developed her thesis that men and women had been created in perfect equality, subject only to God; as human beings, they had the same responsibilities and the same rights. Adam and Eve fell from innocence, *but not from equality,* since their guilt was shared. This argument remained at the heart of much of the debate over women in the next decades.[42]

The controversy that followed the pastoral letter served to heighten all abolitionist women's awareness of the obstacles they faced because of their sex. It also intensified the feminist sensitivities of some not yet in the movement. Lucy Stone, who in the 1840's became the first abolitionist to lecture solely on women's rights, heard the pastoral letter read in the Congregationalist Church in North Brookfield, where she was teaching. Only nineteen years old, she was already sensitive to her inferior position as a woman. Her church had refused to permit her to vote or join in its discussions, and her father adamantly objected to her plea to follow her brothers to college. The low pay she received as a teacher, compared with male salaries, undoubtedly added to her mortification. All these resentments were intensified as she heard the condemnation of the Grimkés. She later described her feeling of rebelliousness: "If I had felt bound to silence before by interpretation of Scriptures, or believed that equal rights did not belong to woman, that 'pastoral letter' broke my bonds."[43] The orthodox church became anathema to Lucy Stone, as to most feminist-abolitionists, because of its proslavery stance as well as its antifeminism.

More significant even than the pastoral letter was the condemnation of "women out of their sphere" by clergymen *within* the anti-slavery movement. What began in 1837 as a confrontation with forces which were anti-abolitionist as well as antifeminist, became an internecine conflict which lasted from 1838 to 1840 and eventually contributed to the division of the entire abolitionist movement. The focal point of this controversy was the right of women to vote and participate in the business of the "male" antislavery societies. The final division in the movement came in 1840, when Abby Kelley was appointed to a committee of the American Anti-Slavery Society—Whittier called her "the bomb-shell that *exploded* the society."[44] Garrison and his supporters defended her, while their opponents in the organization demanded her resignation. Kelley refused to resign and, like the Grimkés, defended her position on the ground that men and women had the same moral rights and duties. The impasse over her appointment split the national society. The group of New York abolitionists who opposed her—the Garrisonians called them "New Organization men"—seceded to form a second organization.

Abby Kelley was the appropriate person to stand firmly at the center of the explosion over the woman question. An intense young Quaker whose attractive features were set against a severe hairdo and plain dress, she was among the most radical and uncompromising Garrisonians. While the Grimkés' role in the limelight was brief, Abby Kelley's public stand in 1840 was only the beginning of her long and arduous service in defense of the rights of slaves and women. When the sisters retired to the sidelines after Angelina's marriage to Theodore Weld in 1838, the role they had created as female antislavery lecturers was taken over by the younger Abby Kelley.

Like the Grimkés, Kelley was driven by a desire to rid the world of evil, a religious perfectionism that was shared by all the Garrisonians. As a young teacher in Massachusetts, she had circulated petitions and solicited funds for her local antislavery society. She saw her father's death in 1836 as a sign of God's will and threw herself even further into reform work, contributing her small inheritance to the cause and selling some of her clothing to obtain additional funds. A family letter written the following year reveals her ingenuous optimism: " 'Tis a great joy to see the world grow better in anything—Indeed I think endeavors to improve mankind is the only object worth living for."[45]

Abby Kelley gave her first public speech at the second Anti-Slavery Convention of American Women in May, 1838, a meeting which coincided with the Grimké-Weld wedding. This convention was a traumatic one for all concerned, and a dramatic beginning to Kelley's career. The abolitionists were attacked by a stone-throwing mob on the first day and saw their newly built Pennsylvania Hall burned to the ground on the second. Maria Weston Chapman became so distraught that she suffered a temporary mental breakdown.[46]

In spite of the threatening crowd outside, Abby Kelley's speech had been so eloquent that Theodore Weld assured her that God meant her to take up the antislavery mission: "Abby, if you don't, God will smite you." She spent the next year in intense soul-searching, confessing in a letter to the Weld-Grimké family that she was praying most earnestly "that this cup might pass from me." They responded that the Lord was trying her faith and advised her "to wait for *him* to make a way where there seems now to be no way." In 1839 she decided to go ahead, after seeing divine confirmation for her "call" in this scriptural passage: "But God hath chosen the foolish things of the world to confound the wise. . . ." She gave up her teaching job to become an antislavery agent. A year later she was at the center of the culminating controversy over women in the movement.[47]

The "woman question" was the more explosive of the two issues dividing the abolitionists in 1840. The other conflict, more tactical and less ideological, was over the value of political action. The radical Boston group, which defended women's equal participation, chose to continue using moral suasion as their chief antislavery tactic. These Garrisonians were "come-outers" who opposed any association with institutions tainted by slavery, which included the government as well as the established churches. The New York group, led by Lewis Tappan, James G. Birney, Henry B. Stanton, and others, favored broadening the base of the movement by political activity and coalition tactics, and many of them went on to form the Liberty party. They accused the Garrisonians of dragging in "extraneous questions," like the women's rights issue, which they feared would antagonize possible supporters and hurt the antislavery cause. They sensed that women's rights was an even more controversial issue than abolition.[48]

While some "New Organization" men wished to suppress the women's rights issue purely for tactical reasons, their leaders included a core of evangelical clergymen who, like their proslavery counterparts, saw the "woman question" as a social threat. One of this group expressed "grief and astonishment" that this issue was forced upon the antislavery cause. Women's rights principles, if carried out, "would strike a death blow at the purest and *loveliest* social condition of man" and tear up the "foundations of human virtue and *happiness*."[49] This group was already antagonistic to Garrison because of his head-on assault on the churches, as well as his espousal of nonresistance and other ultraist causes. The Garrisonians' defense of women's rights was the final insult.

The Garrisonians accused their opponents of sectarianism and argued that women's rights, like antislavery, constituted only one aspect of the broad struggle for human rights. James Mott commented in a letter to Anne Weston: "Verily some of our northern gentlemen are as jealous of any interference in rights they have long considered as belonging to them exclusively as the southern slaveholder is in the right of holding his slaves—both are to be broken up, *human* rights alone recognized." Maria Weston Chapman viewed the women's rights controversy as an inevitable development of the antislavery struggle. She summed it up tersely: "Freedom begets freedom." Lydia Maria Child accused the New Organization men of harboring the "pro-slavery spirit in new disguise," although she acknowledged that many were sincere abolitionists who were "frightened at new and bold views." Summing up the Garrisonian philosophy, she wrote to Lucretia Mott: "It requires great faith to trust truth to take care of itself in all encounters."[50] Though the Garrisonians exhibited the righteousness of true believers by claiming a monopoly on the truth, in practice their philosophy often meant that they were open to new ideas and supported a variety of reforms, like women's rights, believing "all good causes help one another."

The women received some support from political abolitionists who were not antifeminists. Joseph C. Hathaway, antislavery agent in western New York, could not remain silent while the rights of women were "rudely trampled upon by a corrupt clergy" who thought that "woman was made for the slave of man, instead of a *helpmeet* for him." "What earthly objection can there be to her standing on the same platform with us," he asked. "Are we afraid that the overflowing exuberance of her sympathizing heart will eclipse *us*?"[51]

Regardless of their stand on political action, virtually all of the antislavery women who were feminists remained with the Garrisonians; only there were they accepted on an equal basis with men. Many women were not sympathetic to the feminist cause, however, and chose to maintain their traditional role in male-dominated organizations. One of Maria Chapman's associates described a New Organization meeting where the women dutifully left when the men got down to business. She deeply regretted "that they can find any 'sisters' who will allow themselves to be dismissed for I feel that if Woman would not consent to her own degradation her Emancipation would be sure."[52]

Maria Weston Chapman and her sisters themselves resisted an attempt by anti-Garrisonian women to dissolve the Boston Female Anti-Slavery Society. Chapman was a fierce protagonist in the controversy, condemning her opponents as traitors and tools of the clergy and citing their "hypocrisy as abolitionists" and "want of integrity as women." When her opponents withdrew from the organization to form the Massachusetts Female Emancipation Society, Chapman wrote a friend that the group would continue without the defectors and with "more vigour than ever." She only regretted not being able to change the name to one she far preferred: "Anti-Slavery Society of Boston Women."[53] ("Woman" had a rebellious connotation; "female" was the more proper term.) This unwillingness of many women to be "emancipated" would remain, of course, one of the major obstacles in the women's movement.

Following the fight over the woman question in this country, the Garrisonians shortly faced a similar challenge at the World's Anti-Slavery Convention in London in 1840. This meeting became another direct link between abolitionism and feminism. The controversy at home had been so traumatic and so destructive of antislavery unity that even the most dedicated feminist-abolitionists felt ambivalence about further harming the movement. Sarah Grimké wrote to a friend that she hoped women would not present themselves as delegates in London. Ironically, in claiming that such action would "divert the attention of the meeting from the great subject of human liberty," she was using the same argument that had been used against her in 1837.[54]

Lucretia Mott and the other women delegates from the United States did, however, stand on principle and demand to be seated in spite of intense opposition. (Though the Motts' liberal Quaker views were also anathema to the orthodox Friends who organized the convention, it was Mrs. Mott's sex that was crucial; James Mott had no difficulty being seated.[55]) In a heated debate reminiscent of the exchange between the Grimkés and the Massachusetts clergy, members of the English clergy cited the Scriptures as the authority for relegating women to their "God-ordained" sphere. To give the vote to females, they argued, was to act in opposition to the word of God. They also called upon the powerful source of custom which prevented them from subjecting the "shrinking nature of woman" to the indelicacies involved in a discussion of slavery.[56]

The ultimate decision was to adhere to custom. The women were compelled to view the proceedings from a screened-off area; they were accompanied there by Garrison and a few other male supporters. Among the women was Elizabeth Cady Stanton, then a young bride who had chosen to accompany her husband to this meeting as a honeymoon trip. Henry Brewster Stanton, a delegate and leader of the New Organization faction, voted with the women. Though undoubtedly antagonizing most of his co-workers, fresh from the same battle at home, he got his marriage off to a good start.

The rejection of the women delegates was an important feminist experience for Elizabeth Cady Stanton, who would become the major thinker and propagandist of nineteenth-century feminism. Her long talks with Lucretia Mott made an even more lasting impression on her. Hearing Mrs. Mott deliver a sermon in a Unitarian church in London was to her "like the realization of an oft-repeated, happy dream."[57] Out of the meeting of these two came the idea to organize women to take action in their own defense. The Seneca Falls meeting would be the logical fruition of the "woman question" controversy.

In the period following the split in the movement and the London meeting, the Garrisonian women merged their societies with the male groups which remained in the American Anti-Slavery Society. They were now able to work with greater freedom and to expand their activities. Child, Chapman, and Mott served on the executive committee of the national society; Child became editor of their newspaper, the *National Anti-Slavery Standard;* Abby Kelley lectured and organized in the West. Maria Chapman insisted that they were stronger for the defection because women "who were not easily discouraged" were more valuable to the cause than men "whose dignity forbade them to be fellow-laborers with women."[58] This rhetoric notwithstanding, the movement as a whole was weakened by the division and never again achieved the strength and unity which it had possessed in the 1830's. The New Organization abolitionists moved into the broader stream of political antislavery, while the Garrisonians continued their "no-government" moral crusade. However, the decade had been a productive one for radical reform. Not only had the question of the immediate emancipation of the slaves been raised, but the possibility of the future emancipation of women had also been initiated.

The Garrisonian women—the Grimkés, Mott, Chapman, Child, Kelley, and their supporters—were actually playing two kinds of roles on two separate but overlapping stages. The more visible drama revolved about their part in antislavery. On the larger stage, a more subtle kind of action was occurring: a new dialogue for women was being shaped, and new images were being created that would endure long after antislavery action ended. Although the women were propelled into this dual action by circumstances they had not controlled, they were fully aware of the implications for the future.

Angelina Grimké, spectacularly capping her brief public career by appearing before a committee of the Massachusetts legislature in 1838, typified this new image and feminist awareness. Accompanied by Chapman, Child, and other friends, she presented antislavery petitions on behalf of 20,000 women. Child later recalled Grimké's pale face and trembling, frail frame as she faced her audience: "The feminine shrinking was soon overcome by her sense of the duty before her, and her words flowed forth free, forcible, and well-arranged." Arguing for the right of women to have an equal voice in political decisions, and clearly anticipating the later demand for suffrage, Grimké declared: "Are we aliens, because we are women? Are we bereft of citizenship because we are mothers, wives and daughters of a mighty people?" Excited by her triumph, she wrote to a friend: "We Abolition Women are turning the world upside down. . . ."[59]

While "turning the world upside down" was more hyperbole than fact, Grimké and others were setting important precedents and helping to raise the feminist consciousnesses of future leaders. Mary Livermore, who would become a leading suffragist, ran away from school for the day to hear Angelina Grimké address the legislature.

She later recalled that the experience forever fixed in her mind the conviction that women ought to be free to do whatever their powers enabled them to do well.[60]

The early feminist-abolitionists were not only sources of inspiration for the later movement; they were also role models for a new type of woman. They served this purpose by challenging their society's view of woman's proper sphere and expanding their own roles to include public work as well as private duties. With the support of their feminist-abolitionist husbands, they became antislavery agents, lecturers, editors, agitators—a blasphemous violation of their society's code of behavior for well-bred ladies. Not incidentally, they also created precedents for a radically new kind of marriage involving shared responsibility and shared public work, a partnership in which the woman was viewed as an equal and autonomous member.

In the process of expanding and reshaping female roles, the abolitionist women also set precedents for different styles of feminist leadership. Maria Weston Chapman and Abby Kelley were boldly aggressive, willing to take on "male" roles and choosing agitation and direct confrontation as their tactics. They were archetypal leaders of the radical, uncompromising sort whose positions move the mainstream into action, albeit reluctantly, and force public discussion of issues which other more moderate types could then negotiate and attempt to resolve.

Lydia Maria Child preferred a softer, more private way, using her pen rather than her voice and putting a high value on setting an example for others. When criticized for not being more zealous in defense of the Grimkés, she explained her position in the *Liberator:* "It is best not to *talk* about our rights, but simply go forward and *do* whatsoever we deem a duty. In toiling for the freedom of others, we shall find our own."[61] Through her writings she exerted her greatest influence in the women's movement. Her *History of the Condition of Women,* written in 1835 as a pioneer effort to uncover the origins of women's inequality, was an important source for Sarah Grimké's *Letters* as well as for later feminists. An early novel, *The Rebels* (1825), embodied a protest against the position of women in eighteenth-century society. *Good Wives,* written between 1832 and 1835, was a collection of biographies of women (significantly, wives) who had achieved fame in earlier times.

Lydia Maria Child departed from her preferred style only once when she agreed, in 1841, to take on a "male" role as editor of the new *National Anti-Slavery Standard,* despite her aversion to controversy and organizations. Her first editorial revealed her cautious ambivalence. She wrote of the woman question: "A budding conscience must struggle for human rights," but added that she herself preferred "quietly and unobtrusively to take her freedom without disputing it." Her attempt to follow a middle course on antislavery as well as on the woman question caused her difficulty with her more radical co-workers; she left after three years, determined "never to work in harness again." Wendell Phillips criticized the mildness of her editorial tone in the *Standard,* declaring the paper was "but a holiday banner compared with the real black pirate flag of Abby Kelley." Much later, however, he praised her for her gentle, "feminine" manner and eulogized her as "the kind of woman one would choose to represent woman's entrance into broader life."[62]

Probably the most effective style of leadership was displayed by Lucretia Mott, whom historian Mary Beard perceptively described as "a genuine radical with balance." Her practical brand of idealism enabled her to work with, and be accepted by, all of the factions in abolitionism and feminism, and to act as a bridge between the two movements. While Kelley and others were rigid and uncompromising in their perfectionism, Mott was able to combine her radical vision of the future with a realistic assessment of what was possible in the here and now. Though she appreciated the importance of a few women leading the way, for example, she understood that centuries of custom and indoctrination could not be swept aside overnight. During the storm over women speaking to mixed audiences, she encouraged those who wished to take this step to "act in accordance with the light they have." There was no better way of preparing the public for "Christian equality, without distinction of sex." Meanwhile, she suggested, other women might go on meeting by themselves "without compromise of the principle of equality" until they were ready for "more public and general exercise of their rights." Like Child, she put a high value on the creation of models and new female roles, but she was also unwilling to force women into those new roles until they were ready.[63]

All of the women were keenly aware of the responsibility, as well as the difficulties, of taking on "male" roles. Child, working as a "first" woman editor, had come to New York alone and left her husband to pursue his own antislavery activities in Massachusetts. To Maria Chapman she wrote: "You may well suppose that a woman is obliged to take more pains than a man would do. . . ." She also complained to friends that, in addition to the work which male editors had to perform, she was obliged to do her own washing and ironing, as well as cleaning and mending for her husband on her periodic trips home. Nevertheless, she managed both jobs successfully enough for Lucretia Mott to write to Ann Weston, "I rejoice with thee that L. M. Child is doing so much for the cause and for woman by acquitting herself so nobly in the editorial chair. It is one of the best things we have done."[64]

The double heresy of acting both as abolitionist and as public woman was committed by such leaders at immense personal cost. Maria Weston Chapman told friends of the total loss of social prestige and the personal indignities she suffered. She was afraid to walk on Boston streets alone, she wrote, because clerks came out of their shops to shout insults at her. Criticism of her "unfeminine" behavior came from antislavery people as well. Her private mail contained this typical rebuke: "For the sake of the honor of the sex to which you belong, strive to put on the garb of modesty, which you are at present so totally destitute of. . . ." This critic went on to condemn her for pursuing a course "which God and nature never intended" and advised her, if she must do something charitable, to help the poor in Massachusetts.[65]

As a counter to this kind of criticism, the women were sustained and comforted by their close-knit circle of sister abolitionists. They were also encouraged by the Garrisonian men, who functioned as family and support in the early years and continued to do so, both literally and in a broader sense, throughout the antebellum period. The sympathy and help of such husbands made it possible for their wives to defy convention and pursue unorthodox careers. At a time when women were legally subservient to their husbands, male approval was necessary and crucial. Henry Chapman, David Lee Child, James Mott, Theodore Weld, and Stephen Symonds Foster (who married Abby Kelley in 1845) all believed in the right of women to equality and to independence in marriage. This belief made them initiators of the early women's movement and models for later feminists.

As co-workers, the Garrisonians provided the feminists with the psychological and material resources that families customarily offer to fledglings. The feeling of being "kindred spirits" extended over the entire antislavery movement but was particularly strong among the feminist-abolitionists, who were carrying a double burden of unpopular causes. The parent body served a vital function as a reference group, providing the social approval and reinforcement of values that made it easier for the women to defy social mores. Abby Kelley received this kind of support from the Grimkés and from Theodore Weld; in turn, the sisters themselves had been bolstered by the encouragement of Garrison and his friend Henry C. Wright. Sarah Grimké wrote with great emotion, in 1838, of the blessings that would "come upon those of our brethren who have been willing to stand by us, notwithstanding the contumely and ridicule and reproach to which it has subjected them."[66]

As a group, the abolitionist women had other important strengths which helped them endure constant criticism and harassment. Brighter and better educated than average, they were also "strong-minded," with a sturdy consciousness of self and a keen sensitivity to all infringements on personal liberty. Most significant was the strength of their religious beliefs. Though they rejected the orthodox tenets and formal trappings of Protestantism, their personal perfectionism and sense of moral duty and "calling" sustained them through difficult trials. In all these ways, they were prototypes for future feminist leaders.

There was still another important link with the future: by defending their own right to speak publicly, the early women helped to establish the same right for those who followed. At Abby Kelley's death in 1887, Lucy Stone noted that Kelley's greatest service had been to earn "for us all the right of free speech." Mary Livermore similarly observed that "all the women of today" were in Kelley's debt. Kelley herself recognized her unique contribution in preparing the way for the acceptance of women as public lecturers and reformers. She addressed the first national women's rights convention in 1850 with these words: "Sisters, bloody feet have worn smooth the path by which you came up here."[67] Though she and the others played only a peripheral role in the postwar suffrage movement, they were its legendary heroines.

In the 1830's there was as yet no women's rights "movement"—it would begin in the next decade with lecturers, newspapers, political campaigns, and the first conventions. Significant beginnings had occurred during these early years, however, and the important bond between abolitionism and feminism had been forged. The two movements were linked in crucial ways: by the antislavery events and controversies, which proved to be feminist consciousness-raising experiences; by the feminist-abolitionist people, whose leadership spanned both movements; and by the belief in human rights, which provided the ideological underpinning for both causes.

The controversy over woman's role in antislavery had been the important catalyst, moving a few independent-minded abolitionist women to take action in defense of women's rights. Stirred to a realization of their own enslavement in "woman's sphere," feminism became for those women a necessary adjunct to abolitionism. Abby Kelley expressed this fact best when she noted, in 1838, that women had good cause to be grateful to the slave "for the benefit we have received to *ourselves* in working for *him.*" "In striving to strike his irons off," she continued, "we found most surely that *we* were manacled *ourselves*. . . ." In order to free the slaves, women were forced to free themselves.[68]

In this early period an important start was also made in laying the groundwork for a feminist ideology. Forced to justify their "unfeminine" behavior, the abolitionist women articulated arguments that were repeated through the entire movement: the equal moral rights and responsibilities of men and women as sanctioned by the Bible; the special obligation of women to aid their oppressed sisters; the need of women for independence, self-respect, and a serious purpose in life. Much of their rhetoric was patterned after antislavery language. The parallel between the status of woman and slave came naturally out of a common belief in human rights, expressed in both secular and religious form.

Abolitionism also bequeathed to feminism the basic philosophy which sustained all radical reform: the idea that all good causes are linked together. "Truth is like a strong cable," as Maria Weston Chapman expressed it. The belief in fundamental principles would lead inevitably to the emancipation of *all* people from bondage—not only slaves, but also "women from the subjugation of men," and people oppressed by poverty, religion, and government. In short, Chapman wrote of emancipation "of the whole earth from sin and suffering."[69] With this belief, the women who began their anti-slavery work with the plea "Am I Not a Woman and a Sister?" went on to speak in the name of a sisterhood which included not just slave women, but all women.

NOTES

1. Motto used on stationery of Boston Female Anti-Slavery Society and in antislavery literature.

2. Abby Kelley Foster to *Woman's Journal*, Jan. 23, 1886; her quotation is from Milton's *Lycidas*.

3. See Louis Filler, *The Crusade against Slavery, 1830–1860* (New York: Harper & Row, 1960).

4. Elizabeth Margaret Chandler, *Poetical Works, with a Memoir of Her Life and Character by Benjamin Lundy* (Philadelphia: L. Howell, 1836).

5. Ibid., p. 64.

6. *Liberator,* Feb. 13, 1852; Chandler, *Poetical Works,* p. 16.

7. Chandler, *Poetical Works,* p. 59.

8. Ibid., pp. 22–23; emphases hers.

9. Ibid., p. 23.

10. Ibid., pp. 24, 177; see also Chandler's "Female Character," in her *Essays, Philanthropic and Moral* (Philadelphia: L. Howell, 1836; reprinted, Philadelphia: T. E. Chapman, 1845), pp. 50–51.

11. *Liberator,* Jan. 7, 1832; *Letters of William Lloyd Garrison; Vol. 1: I Will Be Heard, 1822–1835,* ed. Walter M. Merrill (Cambridge: Belknap Press of Harvard University Press, 1971), p. 209.

12. Harriet Martineau, *Harriet Martineau's Autobiography,* ed. Maria Weston Chapman (Boston: J. R. Osgood, 1877), 1:349; see also Alma Lutz, *Crusade for Freedom: Women of the Antislavery Movement* (Boston: Beacon Press, 1968).

13. Julia Ward Howe, *Reminiscences, 1819–1899* (Boston: Houghton Mifflin, 1899), p. 154; John Jay Chapman, *Memories and Milestones* (New York: Moffat, Yard, 1915; reprinted, Freeport, N.Y.: Books for Libraries Press, 1971), pp. 209–22; W. P. and F. J. Garrison, *William Lloyd Garrison 1805–1879, the Story of His Life Told by His Children* (Boston: Houghton Mifflin, 1894), 1:15.

14. See Herbert Edwards, "Lydia Maria Child's 'The Frugal Housewife,' " *New England Quarterly* 26 (June 1953): 243–49.

15. Lydia Maria Child, *Letters of Lydia Maria Child* (Boston: Houghton Mifflin, 1883), pp. 67, 239, 248.

16. L. M. Child to Caroline Weston, Aug. 13, 1838, Lydia Maria Child and David Lee Child Papers, Boston Public Library.

17. Child, *Letters,* p. 255; Lydia Maria Child, *An Appeal on Behalf of That Class of Americans Called Africans* (New York: John S. Taylor, 1836), p. 146.

18. "Concerning Women" (n.d.), Lydia Maria Child Scrapbook, in Antislavery Papers, Cornell University.

19. Filler, *Crusade*, p. 66; Martha Coffin Wright to David Wright, Dec. 5, 1833, Wright Family Papers, in Garrison Family Papers, Smith College.

20. Anna Davis Hallowell, ed., *James and Lucretia Mott: Life and Letters* (Boston: Houghton Mifflin, 1884), p. 115.

21. *History of Woman Suffrage* (New York: Fowler & Wells, 1881), 1: 324.

22. Otelia Cromwell, *Lucretia Mott* (Cambridge: Harvard University Press, 1958), p. 131.

23. Ibid., p. 28; Hallowell, ed., *Mott*, pp. 91, 54.

24. Hallowell, ed., *Mott*, pp. 470, 296–97.

25. *History of Woman Suffrage*, 1:428.

26. Amy Swerdlow, "Abolition's Conservative Sisters: The Ladies' New York City Anti-Slavery Societies, 1834–1840" (paper given at Third Berkshire Conference on the History of Women, June 9–11, 1976).

27. Massachusetts Anti-Slavery Society, *Annual Report*, vol. 6 (Boston, 1838; reprinted, Westport, Conn.: Negro Universities Press, 1970), Appendix, p. xxxix.

28. Hallowell, ed., *Mott*, p. 233; see also Lutz, *Crusade*, pp. 101–5; circular to the Societies of Anti-Slavery Women in the United States from the Anti-Slavery Convention of American Women, 1837, Weston Family Papers, Boston Public Library.

29. *Woman's Journal*, Aug. 7, July 24, 1880; Gerda Lerner, *The Grimké Sisters from South Carolina* (Boston: Houghton Mifflin, 1967), p. 74.

30. Catherine H. Birney, *The Grimké Sisters, Sarah and Angelina Grimké* (Boston: Lee & Shepard, 1885; reprinted, Westport, Conn.: Greenwood Press, 1969), p. 138.

31. Samuel J. May, *Some Recollections of Our Antislavery Conflict* (Boston: Fields, Osgood, 1869), pp. 234–35.

32. Lerner, *Grimké Sisters*, p. 227.

33. Maria Weston Chapman, *Right and Wrong in Boston* (Boston: Annual Report of Boston Female Anti-Slavery Society, 1837), pp. 46–47; *History of Woman Suffrage*, 1:81–82.

34. S. Grimké to H. C. Wright, Aug. 27, 1837, Garrison Papers, Boston Public Library; S. Grimké to Amos A. Phelps, Aug. 3, 1837, Amos Phelps Papers, ibid.

35. Birney, *Grimké Sisters*, p. 178.

36. Anne Warren Weston, Address to Boston Female Anti-Slavery Society, Aug. 21, 1837, Weston Family Papers.

37. Lerner, *Grimké Sisters*, p. 183; A. G. Weld to A. W. Weston, July 15, 1838, Weston Family Papers; Weld et al., *Letters of Theodore Dwight Weld, Angelina Grimké Weld and Sarah Grimké, 1822–1844*, ed. Gilbert H. Barnes and Dwight L. Dumond (New York: D. Appleton-Century for the American Historical Association, 1934), 1:417.

38. Weld et al., *Letters*, 1:424.

39. Ibid., p. 433.

40. Ibid., pp. 429, 415.

41. L. Mott to E. C. Stanton, Mar. 16, 1855, Elizabeth Cady Stanton Papers, Library of Congress; Cromwell, *Mott*, p. 29.

42. Sarah Grimké, *Letters on the Equality of the Sexes, and the Condition of Woman* (Boston: Isaac Knapp, 1838; reprinted, New York: Source Book Press, 1970).

43. Address by Lucy Stone, "Workers for the Cause," ca. 1888, Blackwell Family Papers, Library of Congress.

44. John B. Pickard, "John Greenleaf Whittier and the Abolitionist Schism of 1840," *New England Quarterly* 37 (June 1964): 250–54.

45. Abby Kelley to Olive and Newbury Darling, Dec. 10, 1837, Kelley-Foster Papers, Worcester Historical Society.

46. William Lloyd Garrison, *Letters of William Lloyd Garrison; Vol. 2: 1836–1840,* ed. Louis Ruchames (Cambridge: Belknap Press of Harvard University Press, 1971), p. 366.

47. Garrison and Garrison, *Garrison,* 2:216; Weld et al., *Letters,* 2:747; Angelina and Theodore Weld to Abby Kelley, Feb. 24, 1839, Kelley-Foster Papers, WorHS; Abby Kelley Foster's Reminiscences, ibid.

48. See Aileen S. Kraditor, *Means and Ends in American Abolitionism* (New York: Pantheon Books, 1969).

49. Rev. Rufus A. Putnam to Rev. Amos A. Phelps and Rev. Orange Scott, Mar. 27, 1839, Amos Phelps Papers.

50. James Mott to A. W. Weston, June 7, 1838, Weston Family Papers; *National Anti-Slavery Standard,* Mar. 20, 1845; L. M. Child to Louisa Loring, June 28, 1840, Loring Family Papers, Radcliffe College, and L. M. Child to Lucretia Mott, Mar. 5, 1839, in Hallowell, ed., *Mott,* p. 137.

51. J. C. Hathaway to James C. Jackson, Aug. 12, 1839, Garrison Papers, BPL.

52. Charlotte Austin to M. W. Chapman, Oct., 1839, Weston Family Papers.

53. M. W. Chapman to Elizabeth Please, Apr. 20, 1840, Garrison Papers, BPL.

54. Sarah Grimké to Elizabeth Pease, May, 1840, ibid.

55. See Lucretia Coffin Mott, *Slavery and "The Woman Question," Lucretia Mott's Diary of Her Visit to Great Britain to Attend the World's Antislavery Convention of 1840,* ed. Frederick B. Tolles (Haverford, Pa.: Friends Historical Association, 1952).

56. *History of Woman Suffrage,* 1:58–59, 60.

57. Hallowell, ed., *Mott,* p. 187.

58. Maria Weston Chapman, *Right and Wrong in Massachusetts* (Boston: Dow & Jackson's Anti-Slavery Press, 1839; reprinted, New York: Negro Universities Press, 1969), p. 12.

59. Child, *Letters,* p. 259; Angelina Grimké to Sarah Douglass, Feb. 25, 1838, in Weld et al., *Letters,* 2:574.

60. *Woman's Journal,* July 23, 1870.

61. *Liberator,* Sept. 6, 1839.

62. *National Anti-Slavery Standard,* May 13, 1841; L. M. Child to Samuel

May, Jan., 1862, Alma Lutz Collection, Radcliffe College; E. Lewis, ed., "Letters of Wendell Phillips to Lydia Maria Child," *New England Magazine* 5 (Feb. 1892): 730–34; Child, *Letters,* Appendix, p. 268.

63. Mary Beard, "Lucretia Mott," *American Scholar* 2 (Jan. 1933): 4–12; Lucretia Mott to Abby Kelley, Mar. 18, 1839, Kelley-Foster Papers, American Antiquarian Society.

64. L. M. Child to Maria Weston Chapman, Apr. 26, 1841?, Child Papers, BPL; L. M. Child to James Miller McKim, Nov. 24, 1841, Child Papers, CU; Lucretia Mott to Anne Warren Weston, July 8, 1841, Weston Family Papers.

65. Lillie Buffum Chace Wyman and Arthur Crawford Wyman, *Elizabeth Buffum Chace, 1806–1899, Her Life and Its Environment* (Boston: W. B. Clarke, 1914), 1:57; letter from Calvin Allen, Jan. 5, 1840, Weston Family Papers.

66. S. Grimké to H. C. Wright, Nov. 19, 1838, Garrison Papers, BPL.

67. *Woman's Journal,* Jan. 22, 1887; M. A. Livermore to W. L. Garrison, Jr., Jan. 18, 1887, Alma Lutz Collection; Kelley is quoted in Lucy Stone's speech, "Workers for the Cause," Blackwell Family Papers, LC.

68. 1838 Album, Western Anti-Slavery Society Papers, Library of Congress.

69. Maria Weston Chapman, *Ten Years of Experience: Ninth Annual Report of Boston Female Anti-Slavery Society* (Boston: Oliver Johnson, 1842), p. 15.

2

The Antebellum Women's Movement

THE EMERGENCE OF FEMINISM from abolitionism was a drama that began with self-discovery and excited defiance, later became a chronicle of high idealism, small successes, and enormous tensions, and ultimately ended with conflict, frustration, and postponement. The cast of characters included the leaders of the small band of abolitionists associated with William Lloyd Garrison. The major development was the transformation of feminist-abolitionism into a women's movement. Feminism appeared in the 1830's as an offshoot of abolitionism, focusing on the right of women to play an equal role in antislavery; it developed a life of its own in the 1840's, with the proliferation of new demands essentially unrelated to antislavery, though voiced by abolitionists; by 1850 it was well on its way to becoming a movement independent of abolitionism. The conflict between the needs and priorities of the two movements, set against the growing national debate over the expansion of slavery, constituted a major theme in the developing drama and provided the primary tension. The urgency of the slavery issue in the 1850's finally forced the temporary submergence of the women's campaign, and the Civil War ended the first stage of the feminist movement.

Angelina Grimké, appearing before the Massachusetts legislature in 1838 to present female antislavery petitions and proclaim women's equal rights as citizens, epitomized the early excitement. ("We Abolition Women are turning the world upside down!") Abby Kelley spread the message of antislavery and women's rights throughout the rapidly growing nation in the next decade and gained new recruits for both causes. The most important of these new workers, Lucy Stone, came to personify the tensions inherent in espousing feminist-abolitionism. Eloquent and projecting a child-like intensity, she lectured as a Garrisonian agent in the West in the late 1840's and became so aroused by the similarities between women's grievances and those of slaves that she introduced this theme into most of her speeches. When admonished for distracting her audience from the main cause, she replied: "I was a woman before I was an abolitionist. I must speak for the women."[2]

In the 1830's a few abolitionist women fought for the right to expand their sphere of action so that they could be free to work against slavery. In the 1840's a slightly larger group moved to the next logical step, viewing female emancipation as an end in itself. Where earlier the image of woman as slave had been used primarily to arouse female audiences to antislavery action, now it also served as a focus for the campaign on behalf of the women themselves. Advancing from their earlier roles as models for the future feminist movement, abolitionist women now began to serve as organizers and innovators, initiating new demands and setting new directions.

The broadening of feminist activity in the 1840's, still too sparse and diffuse to be called a full-fledged movement, was given impetus by the expansion and ferment in the nation as a whole. The mass uprooting caused by the great movement west, the unflagging religious revivalism, the widespread social and spiritual experimentation, the growth of political antislavery, and the conflict over the western expansion of slavery—these phenomena composed the backdrop against which the agitation for women's rights was carried on. Other reforms, especially the temperance crusade, also bolstered the new movement. The campaign against liquor underwent a revival in this period and became inextricably linked to new feminist demands, especially the right of women to divorce drunken husbands. All of these crusaders—abolitionists, feminists, and temperance advocates, as well as health crusaders, educational reformers, phrenologists, communitarians, and millennialists—were part of the mid-nineteenth-century American impulse to perfect society and fulfill the promise of the nation.

The tone of the early crusade for women's rights, reflecting this cultural milieu, was clearly evangelical. Later the movement would assume a more secular bent and would focus on the pragmatic reform of social and political institutions, in keeping with the changed atmosphere of the nation. In the antebellum period, however, the earliest and strongest thrust was the missionary one, involving the conversion of sinners and the spreading of the gospel of human rights. This was the perfectionism of Garrisonian abolitionism, an unorthodox version of the prevailing evangelicalism. An intense and eclectic religious world-view, it drew on the beliefs of Puritanism and its radical offshoots, as well as on the Enlightenment ideology of the American Revolutionary era. The feminist-abolitionists fervently sought to reshape their society to conform to the ideals of Christianity and republicanism.

The spread of feminist ideas in the 1840's and 1850's was achieved largely through the efforts of female antislavery agents who acted as propagandists and agitators for both causes, and who served as missionaries to the burgeoning western areas. In an age when public lecturers were a major form of entertainment and families traveled long distances to attend them, the influence of antislavery orators cannot be overestimated.

The Grimké sisters had been among the first of these public orators, and the debate over their public speaking in the late 1830's had caused the initial stirring of interest in women's rights. Their letters published during the controversy not only influenced future leaders like Lucy Stone, but also affected countless women, most of whom left no record. One who did was Elizabeth Robinson, a young Quaker woman from Mount Pleasant, Ohio, who wrote to a friend that the controversy over the woman question was a "cause for rejoicing." She was delighted with Angelina's eloquent response to Catharine Beecher, who had declared that public speaking by women was unfeminine and contrary to divine law. Angelina's letters "contained so many truths," Robinson exulted, and "exposed [the] many inconsistencies" by which woman, "like the person of color," was treated as an inferior and came to view herself in that light and to act accordingly.[3]

Other young women responded to the first stirrings of feminist-abolitionism with equal enthusiasm. In Bradford, New Hampshire, Elisabeth Tappan confided to a close friend in 1840 that she found the new talk of abolitionism and women's rights "exciting." A year later she was writing her letters on stationery that bore the heading "Am I Not a Woman and a Sister?" and describing her "Anti-Slavery sewing circle." The group had only twelve regular members but, she said, "we believe our cause and our motives, to be good. . . ." Tappan had attended many talks by Stephen Foster, despite the warnings of the local Congregationalist minister, and she liked him better each time, believing him to be "a good Christian." Her father and sister were abolitionists as well. She had also given a great deal of thought to the woman question and felt strongly that she would like to be considered "more than a cypher" at church meetings. Her indignation continued to grow, and the following year she was giving serious consideration to remaining an "old maid" because "most married women are not better than slaves." (Married people could avoid this "tyranny," she noted thoughtfully, "if both would do right.") Subsequent letters reveal her enthusiasm also for temperance, phrenology, physiology lectures, and all the "isms" of the day. In short, a typical feminist-abolitionist had quietly been born.[4]

The crusade that began with the Grimkés continued in the 1840's and 1850's with Abby Kelley as its most dedicated apostle. As an agent of the American Anti-Slavery Society, she traveled through New England, western New York, and Ohio—lecturing, raising funds, organizing new societies, and enlisting workers for the cause. Convinced very early in her career that the rights of women and slaves were inseparable, she made converts to both causes wherever she went, holding the attention of her audiences for as long as three hours at a time by her eloquence and earnest pleading. An Ohio woman wrote to an abolitionist paper that a female antislavery group had been formed in her town after Abby Kelley spoke there, and described the effect of her oratory: "When Abby was here, I felt convinced that God was in his providence sending her through the country to proclaim the truth of his word, against the sin of slavery, and I said, don't let us oppose her lest we be found opposing God."[5]

Unfortunately, Abby Kelley's zeal also had an emotional impact on those who opposed abolitionism and feminism. In her travels she faced such continuous and merciless persecution that she earned the title "our Joan of Arc" among her co-workers. Lucy Stone later described Kelley's career as "long, unrelieved, moral torture." The Grimkés, in their 1837 speaking tour, had been supported by the presence of friends and had lectured only on invitation; in contrast, Kelley made long trips through remote rural areas, speaking wherever she could find a schoolhouse or, less often, a church available to her. Sometimes arrangements were made for her, but often she made her own contacts, writing ahead to Friends or antislavery people who she thought might give her shelter and hire a hall. In the beginning she was unsalaried, accepting only traveling expenses, and she relied on the contributions of friends when she desperately needed clothing. After her marriage in 1845 she reluctantly agreed to accept the small salary that agents received.[6]

More than any of the other abolitionist women, Kelley lived perpetually with abuse, slander, and the threat of physical harm. Because she often traveled alone, or (worse) with male agents, she was vilified as a "bad" woman. Wendell Phillips wrote to a friend of "the indecent innuendos and dastardly sarcasm flung at her, in her presence." A New York paper referred to her as "that monstrosity, a public speaking woman." In one Connecticut town, the minister preached his weekly sermon from the text "thou sufferest that woman Jezebel to teach and to seduce my servants." He referred to Kelley in her presence as a "vile character" and "a servant of Satan in the garb of an angel of light" who violated the divine command: "Let your women keep silence in the churches." This in spite of her intense, single-minded devotion to high moral standards and Christian principles.[7]

Abby Kelley's marriage in 1845 did not put a stop either to her career or to the slander against her. Both she and her husband, Stephen Symonds Foster, were denounced as "low, degraded, licentious vagabonds." She was further reviled when she continued to appear in public while pregnant. Deeply wounded by these charges, she protected herself by repressing the memory of violence and abuse; she wrote to a friend that she could barely recall the previous six weeks. Friends often found her cold and even abrasive. She consciously developed this stance in her work: "I always get most when I am most severe." She explained to her husband the cause of her "lawlessness" and "outlandish" manners: "It consists in the fact of my feeling that I am as much unobserved as if I were entirely alone. I don't feel the presence of the multitude, even when I am crowding among them."[8] This shield of toughness enabled her to survive. Her husband, one of the boldest of the abolitionists, seemed to relish the challenges and even thrive on them, but there is no evidence that she enjoyed her martyrdom.[9]

Though Abby Kelley's appeal to women was primarily to work

against slavery, her example inevitably stirred feminist feelings and inspired feminist pride. Esther Moore, one of the Philadelphia group of antislavery workers, heard Kelley speaking in 1840; she later wrote to Garrison that women "have little need to call upon men to address them while they can employ so much talent and unborrowed eloquence." She hoped "those noble women of Boston" would continue to fight valiantly in the holy cause of "the emancipation of woman from her degraded state . . . one of the imperative demands of the age." This letter reveals the high level of feminist consciousness that had been aroused among antislavery women as a result of the "woman question."[10]

Few of the abolitionist women whom Abby Kelley met in her travels were ready to become antislavery lecturers—still an unpopular choice for women, even within the movement. With Abby's example and encouragement, several women took the plunge. Sallie Holley, daughter of a prominent New York abolitionist, made this decision on Kelley's advice and lectured in the West for ten years. Abby, hearing her speak, thanked God that "when I am so worn, weary, and feeble, He has raised one up who can and will speak so nobly. . . ." Sallie, for her part, felt "richly rewarded" by the work and wrote close friends that she had at last found her "sphere." Betsy Cowles, who would later preside over the first Ohio women's rights convention, also became an antislavery agent and a feminist through Abby Kelley's influence.[11] And so went the westward expansion of the female network that began in the 1830's in Boston and Philadelphia, and later served as the organizational framework of the women's movement.

Lucretia Mott, Abby Kelley's older friend and adviser, also extended her area of activity in the 1840's. In the 1830's she had stayed close to home because her children were still young, but later she began traveling, preaching "in truth's service" to groups of Friends around the country. Wherever she went, she proselytized for the cause of woman as well as the slave, speaking eloquently and without notes, following the Quaker style of preaching. In all her speeches and sermons she argued for elevating women and enlarging their sphere. Woman's role in society, she lamented in a speech in Boston in 1841, was merely as "plaything of man and a frivolous appendage of society"; women, who had a solemn responsibility as mothers of future generations, had only a trivial concept of domestic duty. The

"Ladies Departments" in newspapers made her blush for her sex, "for the low sphere of action they are content with." She beseeched her sisters to exercise their highest powers of mind in order to lead useful lives and exert a beneficent influence on their families and society.[12]

Lucretia Mott's argument, that woman's moral and spiritual influence was needed by society, continued to be used as one of the prime justifications for broadening woman's limited sphere. Her appeal to female audiences to exert this influence as broadly as possible grew naturally and logically from the abolitionists' call to act against slavery, and in fact was merely an extension of that call. Though the precise influence of Mott, Kelley, and other female antislavery orators is difficult to measure, there is no doubt that they raised strong voices for woman's emancipation in this period.

Lecturers were one important medium for transmitting the feminist message in the antebellum period; newspapers, a popular means of communication, were another. Antislavery papers like Garrison's *Liberator* and the *National Anti-Slavery Standard* published the texts of speeches given by abolitionist women at meetings and on the lecture circuit. In the 1840's temperance papers also became vehicles for feminist propaganda. In the late 1840's and 1850's the first papers devoted to women's rights were published by feminist-abolitionist women. The circulation of all of these reform publications was limited, but they provided an important means of combatting the antifeminism of the regular press, as well as gaining new supporters for the cause.

An important new outlet for feminist protest in the West was the *Anti-Slavery Bugle,* edited by Jane Elisabeth Hitchcock Jones and her husband, Benjamin. Jane Elisabeth Hitchcock, from a wealthy New England family which had migrated to western New York, heard Abby Kelley speak in the early 1840's and was persuaded to become an antislavery agent. Like most people who made this difficult and unpopular decision, she explained that she thought it better for her friends to be displeased, "than that I should fail to do what appeared to me, very plainly, to be my duty to do."[13]

In 1845, Hitchcock joined a group of antislavery people who were establishing a base in Salem, Ohio, already a nucleus of radical abolitionism in the West. Abby Kelley helped to organize the Ohio (later Western) Anti-Slavery Society there as a branch of Garrison's national organization in 1842; three years later, the *Bugle* was established as the organ of this society. Hitchcock and Jones, a Quaker artisan from Philadelphia whom she married that year, became the editors. They continued this job until 1849, following a bone-wearying schedule of lectures in addition to their work on the newspaper. They often spoke at as many as fifteen meetings a month, each lasting one or two days.[14] Like the Fosters, to whom they were close, they lived a simple, frugal existence. Elisabeth supplemented her husband's meager salary as an antislavery agent with income from the sale of her writings, including *The Young Abolitionists,* a children's book about slavery. (There is no evidence that she received a salary, though the couple shared the work.)

Like Abby Kelley, Elisabeth Jones was subjected to insults and harassment by her audiences and by the press. Even a somewhat less hostile editor commented that "Abby and Elisabeth could spend their time more profitably at home, knitting stockings." In addition, the conflict between her duties at home and at work served as a constant reminder of the difficulties involved in leaving "woman's sphere." Perhaps for these reasons, Elisabeth Jones filled many columns of the *Bugle* with feminist articles, in addition to the regular appeals for women to work against slavery. She exhorted women to expand their horizons and applauded those who did. She noted a public temperance address by a woman with typical enthusiasm: "We rejoice to find those whose ideas of woman's duty and destiny extend beyond the making of bread and the darning of stockings." She extended a welcome to "all laborers in the moral vineyard," but added that those "who bring with them a woman's heart and a woman's sympathy" were "thrice welcome." The regeneration of the world would come about only when "woman is man's equal; his partner, his co-laborer; not his toy and drudge." Again the familiar themes emerge: woman's domestic chores were a sacred duty, but she could do more; by entering reform work, she would bring qualities especially needed for elevating mankind.[15]

Like many antislavery women in this period, Elisabeth Jones served as an important model of a woman in a new role. Though working primarily for antislavery, she was performing an important function for feminism. She was fully aware of the value of women placing themselves "in the position they ought to occupy"; in a letter to Lucy Stone she predicted that women would "hug their chains awhile," but that "at length they will begin to covet the freedom that we enjoy." Not only did she take on "male" roles as *Bugle* editor and antislavery agent; in addition, she traveled in the 1850's as a popular "science lecturer," speaking to women about health and hygiene. She was in the vanguard of an important nineteenth-century feminist movement to help women care for themselves and avoid reliance on the questionable practices of male doctors.[16] She also played an active role in the women's rights conventions of the 1850's and later served as "general agent" of the first Ohio women's rights association in the 1860's, managing a successful petition campaign for a married woman's property law. The general pattern of her reform career was duplicated by most feminist-abolitionist women.

The circulation of the *Bugle* and other radical antislavery papers was small, but such publications offered a vital outlet for feminist propaganda. The popular press was hostile to the cause, and conventional magazines like the *Ladies Repository,* the major women's periodical in the West, were also unsympathetic to radical reform. There were occasional exceptions to this rule. In the 1850's, the *Ohio Cultivator* was a semimonthly farm paper published in Columbus; Josephine C. Bateham, wife of the editor, was an Oberlin graduate who was in charge of the Ladies' Department and ran articles on women's rights.[17] Such instances notwithstanding, the feminists had a desperate need for newspapers supportive of their cause.

This void was at least partly filled by Amelia Bloomer's *Lily,* a newspaper she established in 1849 in Seneca Falls with the help of her husband, Dexter Bloomer, a lawyer, Whig editor, and Quaker antislavery advocate. Mrs. Bloomer had served a journalistic apprenticeship as co-editor of her husband's paper and had been encouraged by him to start her own. By the time she sold the *Lily* in 1856, after the Bloomers had moved first to Ohio and then to Iowa, it had achieved a national circulation of over 6,000 and was reaching into more homes than any other paper propagandizing for the women's cause. She gave up the paper reluctantly because of poor rail connections and lack of printing facilities. Subsequently she became a lecturer on women's rights and, after the war, the president of the first Iowa suffrage society. The Bloomer home in Council

Bluffs (where Dexter Bloomer developed a prosperous land business and became mayor) became the western outpost of the women's movement.[18]

The *Lily* and the career of Amelia Bloomer illustrate the close relationship between abolitionism, feminism, and temperance in this period. The rhetoric of all three movements shared a common theme, the emancipation of woman from man's brutality and oppression. The arguments for the three causes often meshed so closely as to be practically indistinguishable. The radical social reformers of the day viewed all three crusades as part of the broader effort to elevate all of humanity. Though many women temperance workers were not feminists (just as many women in antislavery societies were content to remain in traditional roles), every feminist-abolitionist felt that temperance was essential to the emancipation of woman and the reform of society.[19]

The *Lily* began in 1849 as a monthly "Devoted to Temperance and Literature" and "Edited and Published by Ladies." The first editorial announced, "It is Woman that speaks through the *Lily* . . . upon an important subject. . . . Intemperance is the great foe to her peace and happiness . . . surely she has the right to wield the pen for its suppression." Succeeding editorials concentrated on the evils of intemperance and discussed "woman's rights" in terms of the right of a wife to protect herself against a drunken husband, and the government's obligation to protect her by withholding liquor licenses. Within a year, however, articles began to appear by Elizabeth Cady Stanton, under the pseudonym "Sunflower," which were more feminist in tone. By 1850, Bloomer herself was writing articles demanding equal education and greater employment opportunities for women. (Her move from temperance to feminism was reflected in the masthead, which in 1852 was changed to read "A monthly journal devoted to the Emancipation of Woman from Intemperance, Injustice, Prejudice, and Bigotry.") In an "Address to the Women of New York," she argued that mothers ought to provide the same education for their daughters as for their sons. She also urged them to train both sexes in the same standards of purity, delicacy, and refinement. She beseeched mothers, "as they value their own personality and that of their daughters, to impress indelibly upon the minds of their children the idea of the perfect equality of the sexes." Here again was the familiar juxtaposition of piety, purity, and equality found in the rhetoric of all the feminist-abolitionists.[20]

Amelia Bloomer's ideas, publicized in the *Lily* in the early 1850's, were representative of antebellum feminist thought, which put a high value on the education of women to be better mothers as well as to play a greater role in the elevation of society. In a typical address, Bloomer outlined what would become the classic argument for broadening woman's sphere. The most important fact about woman, she said, was her motherhood of the human race. Future generations would be "blessed or cursed by her influence," depending on how qualified she was for that motherhood. Only her full mental and physical development, without restraints on her activities, would produce a generation of perfect offspring. Later in the 1850's Bloomer became convinced that suffrage was also essential to achieve liquor control and all other reforms necessary to perfect society.[21]

In the early 1850's Amelia Bloomer also took a position in support of the right of women to be divorced from drunken husbands. One consideration that moved her and her co-workers, all of whom came to support divorce or some type of separation in cases of intemperance, was the belief that such unions would produce imbeciles and criminals. In a typical temperance address, Bloomer warned that unless women were allowed to escape from such marriages, they would produce children who would grow up "criminal and vicious," endangering the morals of society and filling the prisons, poorhouses, and lunatic asylums. While she believed that laws abolishing liquor would produce a permanent cure, divorce laws were needed in the interim.[22]

Bloomer's style of activism was close to the mainstream of her generation of feminists. Her motivation was religious and her tone moralistic, but she was less fervently evangelical than more radical feminist-abolitionists like Abby Kelley Foster. Her emphasis in temperance speeches, for example, was less on drunkenness as an individual sin requiring personal salvation and more on intemperance as a social evil amenable to reform by society. She had faith that laws forbidding the liquor traffic would eliminate drunkenness and wife abuse, and would reduce crime and the evils associated with poverty. In this sense, Bloomer and her co-workers represented a transitional stage between the millennialist zeal of early antislavery days and the pragmatism of postwar reform. They were also in the mainstream of feminist-abolitionism in the 1850's because they looked for political solutions to the slavery question, while the most zealous of the Garrisonians still remained with their moral crusade. The perfection of society was still the common goal, but the means to achieve this end were undergoing a transformation.

Amelia Bloomer typified nineteenth-century feminists in suggesting radical means (full entrance of women into all avenues of education, employment, and government) for essentially conservative ends (more competent motherhood and the moral redemption of society). This was a useful strategy because it did not openly challenge social values, but it was more than a strategy. This approach reflected the feminists' view of woman as moral guardian of society, and their commitment to home and family. Even divorce was acceptable only as an expedient, until intemperance could be legislated out of existence. (The feminist concept of marriage, however, was a nontraditional one, emphasizing equality and sharing rather than submissiveness.)

Bloomer, though radical for her society, was criticized as timid and overly cautious by Elizabeth Cady Stanton, who remained among the bolder and more adventurous thinkers and strategists of the women's movement. On one occasion, Stanton complained that Bloomer did not have "the spirit of the true reformer" because she had not spoken out in the *Lily* against the fugitive slave law or against her church's equivocal stand on temperance.[23]

Compared with Stanton, and with the even more radical Abby Kelley Foster, Bloomer was indeed moderate. She firmly opposed both slavery and intemperance, however, and was closer to the spirit of the grass roots women's movement than either Stanton or Foster. She also stood firmly on the positions she did take. During her stay in Ohio, for example, she hired a woman typesetter for the *Lily*, an action which precipitated a strike of the men who worked on her husband's paper in the same office. Since the Bloomers refused to fire the woman, a new staff was hired for his paper, composed of four women and three men who were willing to work with them. Lucy Stone, visiting them during this crisis, found Mrs. Bloomer determined to "vindicate the principle involved."[24] The right of women to useful work and equal pay was a demand on which all of the feminists could agree.

Amelia Bloomer was in the avant-garde of the antebellum movement in wearing and publicizing the "short dress," a costume consisting of a knee-length or calf-length dress worn over pantaloons. This reform was originated by Elizabeth Smith Miller in the early 1850's to free women from the burdensome and unhealthful female costume of the day. To the feminists, it became an important symbol of woman's emancipation from the narrow social and intellectual sphere in which she had been imprisoned by a male-dominated society. The ridicule which greeted the new dress was so intense that many feminists, including Elizabeth Cady Stanton, quickly decided that it would do more harm than good for the cause. Bloomer wore the short dress for several years, even in the face of criticism from feminists who called it "immodest." She denied that wearing it made her less womanly: "I feel no more like a man now than I did in long skirts, unless it be that enjoying more freedom and cutting off the fetters is to be like a man." Continuing this idea, she added, "I suppose in that respect we are more mannish, for we know that in dress, as in all things else, we have been and are slaves, while man in dress and all things else is free." The total failure of this reform indicates how radical were the demands of even "moderate" and mainstream feminists like Amelia Bloomer.[25]

While antislavery and temperance women continued to proselytize for the feminist cause, others were following new directions. Moving away from a prime reliance on moral suasion, some women challenged the social and legal institutions of their society more directly. Even before the first conventions were organized to publicize women's grievances, a few feminist-abolitionists were acting, individually or in groups, to pursue new feminist demands.

The long battle against the exclusion of women from higher education and the professions began in this period. This concern reflected, in part, the upper-middle-class background of the feminist-abolitionist women, whose fathers and brothers were often doctors, lawyers, and respected community leaders. On this level, women were asking only to share the opportunities that were becoming increasingly available to their male counterparts in mid-nineteenth-century America. Their demands also derived from the feminist argument that women should be allowed to develop their talents to the fullest, and were part of the feminist-abolitionists' romantic vision of creating the perfect society. Elizabeth Blackwell's expressed goals in entering medicine were typical: "The true

51

ennoblement of woman, the full harmonious development of her unknown nature, and the consequent redemption of the whole human race."[26]

Elizabeth Blackwell, who in 1849 became the first American woman to receive a degree from a medical college (Geneva College in western New York) and to practice as a fully licensed doctor, is the best known of this group but one of the least typical. Most of the early woman doctors studied with husbands or other relatives because of a strong interest in medicine, and combined late careers as doctors with active interest in the women's movement. In contrast, Blackwell approached medicine with a sense of duty, rather than with personal enthusiasm; it was for her a means to avoid marriage as well as to serve humanity. She opposed agitation for women's rights and insisted that women would be accepted as equals when they had proved themselves deserving of equality. When her brother Henry married Lucy Stone in the mid-1850's, she found his protest against the marriage laws foolish and in bad taste. She considered her sister-in-law too radical, and the conventions she helped to organize "a waste of time." In spite of this reluctance (and this was one of the ironies of the women's movement), Elizabeth Blackwell became a feminist heroine, an example of what women could become.[27]

Antoinette Brown, who also became a Blackwell by marrying Elizabeth's brother Sam, has been neglected by historians but was an important feminist and more representative than Elizabeth of the antebellum women's movement. The first American woman to be ordained in an orthodox church, she also played a key role in the women's rights conventions of the 1850's and was active in the postwar period as a writer and scholar. The only one of her generation who lived to see women granted the vote, she would cast a ballot in 1920 at the age of ninety-five, a year before her death. Her life spanned the entire women's movement.

Brought up in western New York, Antoinette Brown was an extremely precocious child who made a public confession of faith at the age of nine and was accepted as a full member of her Congregationalist church. She recalled later that she expected from earliest childhood to have "a definite life work"; however, her goals in the early years were set within the framework of "the accepted Woman's Sphere." Her intellectual curiosity and natural ability and self-confidence led her to question these goals and to choose a career totally outside that sphere. With her family's encouragement, she entered Oberlin College and graduated in 1847. Proceeding entirely on her own from there, with typical determination in the face of opposition even from family and close friends, she entered Oberlin's theological program. She recalled later that people reacted with laughter, horror, and amazement. The college itself was initially ambivalent, later resistant. The administration permitted her to enroll but refused to grant her a student's license to preach. When she completed the course in 1850, she was not permitted to graduate. Many years later, Oberlin recanted and granted her an honorary A.M. (1878) and D.D. (1908).[28]

After spending several years lecturing on women's rights, anti-slavery, and temperance, Brown was finally ordained in her own pulpit in South Butler, New York, in 1853. Ironically, this event was followed by a period of religious crisis which ended with her resignation. Like virtually all of the feminists brought up with orthodoxy, she moved to more liberal beliefs and ultimately became a Unitarian minister, although she never occupied a permanent pulpit.[29]

The opposition to Brown's career, strongest among her clerical colleagues, was typical of the antifeminism which confronted the women's movement. The orthodox clergymen who led the attack on the Grimkés in the 1830's set the pattern for the next decades. The Scriptures continued to be used as the prime authority for keeping woman in an inferior position and limited sphere. For a woman to occupy the pulpit appeared to many as the ultimate defiance of God's law as well as of man's wishes. Antoinette Brown was occasionally invited to deliver guest sermons at the churches of sympathetic Unitarian friends, but even there she was often requested to stand in front of the pulpit, presumably to avoid defiling it by her sex.[30]

Brown's experience with hostile critics served to further fuel her feminism and to reinforce her consciousness of her responsibility as model and prototype for the budding women's movement. Typically she accepted an invitation to address a lyceum group by reminding her correspondent that her terms, "from principle," were never less than "the best prices received by the gentlemen of the particular association where I speak." Her manner, though firm, was soft-spoken and ladylike. Her good friend Susan B. Anthony pointed to her in speeches to illustrate that a woman could take her place in the pulpit and still remain "lovely, modest and womanly." Brown's political stance, though highly principled, was moderate in tone and open to compromise in strategy. Like her idol, Lucretia Mott, she achieved a reputation for personal integrity and calm independence that enabled her to remain above the movement's petty battles and to retain the respect of all sides.[31]

While Antoinette Brown and others were confronting the educational and theological establishments, other feminist-abolitionists were challenging the institutions of government and law. Especially important in the antebellum period were the state-by-state campaigns to gain legal rights for married women. While state laws discriminated against all women, married women were the hardest hit and were considered non-persons in most legal areas. The main focus of these campaigns was on the right of married women to retain legal possession of their property, a concern which again reflected the middle-class nature of the feminist movement. The campaigns' goals extended beyond this, though, to include the right of working women to keep their earnings, and the right of all married women to gain custody of their children in the event of separation, divorce, or the husband's death. None of these rights were granted by state laws when the challenges began in the 1830's.

New York had one of the earliest and best-organized campaigns for married women's property rights. A combination of factors contributed to the passage of the first law in 1848. Unusually talented and energetic feminists were involved—Ernestine Rose, Elizabeth Cady Stanton, and Paulina Wright Davis. They also received support from an important non-feminist source, the aristocratic New York families of Dutch descent who were anxious to keep the family money from falling into the hands of predatory young men. Ironically, the first successful efforts to liberalize state laws had been for similarly conservative reasons: in the 1830's and 1840's seven southern states had made changes in their laws to prevent confiscation of property for the husband's debts. In those states the wife still could not control the property, but it was safe from creditors.[32]

Ernestine Rose presented the first petition to the New York legislature in 1836, twelve years before the Seneca Falls meeting demanded the right of married women to own property. Rose came from a background highly atypical in this first generation of reformers, although she shared other traits with her New England co-workers. Born in Poland in 1810, she was the daughter of a rabbi and was a gifted, precocious child. At the age of sixteen she successfully sued in a Polish court to overturn the marriage contract her father had made for her, and to regain the property she had inherited from her mother. She spent her next years in a series of adventurous pursuits, ending in England in 1829. Here she became a disciple of the reformer Robert Owen; she married another Owenite, William Rose, and came with him to the United States in 1836. Without children and with the total support of her husband, Ernestine Rose turned her full energies to the reform cause, working for antislavery, temperance, and in the movement for free thought and religious liberty, as well as for women's rights. Her first effort to circulate a petition for a married women's property law took five months and yielded only five signatures. She persevered for twelve years, gaining the help of other feminist-abolitionists and addressing the legislature five times in this period.[33]

Some progress was made in other states as well. The successful campaign in Vermont was led by Clarina Howard Nichols, a feminist-abolitionist who edited the *Windham County Democrat,* the newspaper her husband published. Her series of articles in 1847, followed by public speeches and an address to the legislature, resulted in passage of the state's first married women's property law that year. In Massachusetts the fight for the first law, ultimately passed in 1853, was led by Mary Upton Ferrin, who was not active in other reforms but apparently was motivated by personal grievances against a tyrannical husband. In Pennsylvania, Jane Grey Swisshelm was impelled both by a strong reform impulse and by experience in an unhappy marriage. One of the first women to publish her own newspaper, Swisshelm used her *Saturday Visiter* to express her views on antislavery and women's rights, and to campaign for a property rights law in Pennsylvania, passed in 1848.[34] All of these efforts were forerunners of the more publicized postwar campaigns to gain suffrage and complete legal rights.

The feminist-abolitionist women began to think of their cause as a full-fledged, independent movement with the first national women's rights conventions of the 1850's. These meetings were called by antislavery people and were held in conjunction with abolitionist meetings (many members simply returned to the same hall the next day with a new agenda), but they were organized and run by women, and they focused entirely on feminist demands. The women and their male supporters met in national convention each year between 1850 and 1860 except in 1857; the impact of the Supreme Court's *Dred Scott* decision that year undoubtedly made it difficult to muster support for debate on less urgent issues. State conventions also occurred on an irregular basis in New York, Ohio, Massachusetts, Pennsylvania, and Indiana.[35] The national conventions, as well as the local and state meetings that usually followed them, helped publicize the women's demands, consolidate new ideas, and develop new leadership.

The conventions of the 1850's represented the first attempts to extend the movement on a national scale, but the local meeting which took place on July 19 and 20, 1848, in Seneca Falls was the important prototype. Though customarily described as the "beginning" of the women's movement, Seneca Falls was, instead, a significant transition point. The earlier movement had been diffuse and embryonic, still closely tied to abolitionism; in the future it would become more focused and visible, with a leadership clearly speaking for women. The feminist-abolitionist women at the Seneca Falls meeting also represented the transition between the two movements: Lucretia Mott had been a leader in antislavery and would lead and inspire the women's movement; Elizabeth Cady Stanton would work for both causes in the 1850's but put her indelible mark on feminism. Others were absent from the 1848 gathering: Abby Kelley Foster was in her tenth year of lecturing on antislavery and women's rights; Lucy Stone, newly graduated from Oberlin, was also eloquently defending women on the lecture circuit. Both were traveling as agents of the American Anti-Slavery Society. Susan B. Anthony, working for temperance and antislavery, had not yet become involved with the women's cause. Maria Weston Chapman, who so forcefully represented the first phase of feminist-abolitionism, was leaving the country as the delegates assembled, symbolically closing one era as a new one began.[36]

The same combination of talents that had originated the idea of a women's convention at the World's Anti-Slavery Convention in London in 1840 now brought that idea to fruition. James and Lucretia Mott were attending a yearly meeting of Friends and visiting Lucretia's sister in the vicinity of Seneca Falls, where Elizabeth Cady Stanton was now a housewife with three children. Recalling their earlier plan, the two women decided to join with Lucretia's sister, Martha Coffin Wright, and other abolitionist women in the area to issue a convention call, which appeared in the local newspapers. Though the feminist-abolitionists would view Mrs. Mott as the moving spirit of this historic event, in a letter to Elizabeth Stanton in 1855 Lucretia Mott reminded her friend that the first meeting had originated with her (Stanton). In writing the history of the women's movement, the older woman advised, "thou must do thyself justice."[37]

The declaration drawn up in advance by his wife was so bold that Henry Stanton, known for his fiery abolitionist oratory, made plans to be away on the day of the meeting. James Mott was there, however, and presided at the request of the women. Their courage and self-confidence may not have been sufficient for this task, or perhaps Mrs. Mott persuaded Mrs. Stanton that her demands were radical enough without further antagonizing the community by allowing a woman to preside. In either case, this, too, was only a brief transitional phase. The second convention, held in Rochester two weeks later, was chaired by a Quaker woman, Abigail Bush, and all subsequent conventions were in female hands.[38]

Elizabeth Cady Stanton modeled her "Declaration of Sentiments" closely after the Declaration of Independence, drawing on the rhetoric of the Revolution (as she and others would continue to do for forty years). The choice was a logical one for a movement that would be led by New England women whose grandfathers had served in the War for Independence. The form was appropriate and extremely effective, merely requiring the substitution of one tryant for another and declaring that all men and women are created equal. The Declaration constituted a broad denunciation of man's oppression of woman and, among other things, condemned man for usurping "the prerogative of Jehovah himself, claiming it as his right to assign for her a sphere of action, when that belongs to her conscience and to her God." It was presented with appropriate resolutions designed to remedy the proclaimed grievances.[39]

This Declaration of Sentiments and its accompanying resolutions articulated almost all of the demands to be made in the nineteenth century. The demand for suffrage was so radical that even Lucretia

Mott agreed to it only reluctantly, worrying that "this claim is so distasteful to the age."[40] This was the only resolution not adopted unanimously; it passed, instead, by only a small majority. Other resolutions called for increased opportunity for women in education, business, and the professions, generally seeking women's right to participate in the same public sphere as men. Resolutions also dealt with the rights of married women to their property and wages, and to guardianship of their children.

Though changes in the law were called for, the chief thrust of the Declaration was even more radical—an attack on the oppressive force of attitude, custom, and religious prejudice which confined women to a narrow sphere. This thrust reflects the thinking of Elizabeth Cady Stanton, who, more than anyone, shaped the developing feminist ideology and influenced the rhetoric of the antebellum period. The key to female emancipation, in her view, was not suffrage or new laws, though these were needed. The solution, read the Declaration, was the enlightenment of women, "that they may no longer publish their degradation by declaring themselves satisfied with their present position, nor their ignorance, by asserting that they have all the rights they want." Woman had too long been satisfied with "the circumscribed limits which corrupt custom and a perverted application of the Scriptures have marked out for her," wrote Stanton, and it was time for her to move "in the enlarged sphere which her great Creator has assigned her." This appeal was directed less at the tyrants than at the women themselves, in that it urged them to declare their independence and to regain self-confidence and self-respect, without which they had been "willing to lead a dependent and abject life."

There were, predictably, diverse repercussions from Stanton's call for women to emancipate themselves. At least one local woman, Emily Collins, gained the courage to organize an Equal Suffrage Society, and probably others did as well. The press, in varying degrees, expressed its indignation and disgust at the public display of "women out of their sphere." The *Oneida Whig*, for example, called the gathering "the most shocking and unnatural incident ever recorded in the history of womanity."[41]

Elizabeth Cady Stanton undertook to respond to press criticism of both the Seneca Falls and the Rochester conventions in a *National Reformer* article. The object of the meetings, she wrote, was to discuss the rights, duties, and "true sphere" of women. It was not man's job to decide woman's calling—he had quite enough to find his own. There was "no such thing as a sphere for sex," she went on; "every man has a different sphere, and one in which he may shine, and it is the same with every woman; and the same woman may have a different sphere at different times." She cited Angelina Grimké and Lucretia Mott as examples of women whose spheres and duties had changed with time, and dared her readers to say that these gifted women were at any time "out of their sphere."[42] The battle with the press over woman's true sphere had just begun, however, and would grow as the movement became more national in scope.

Just as antislavery women had called the 1848 meeting, so the first national and state conventions also originated with abolitionists. Paulina Wright Davis, who had been an active Garrisonian, temperance worker, and health lecturer, was the prime mover behind the first two national conventions, both held in Worcester, Massachusetts, in 1850 and 1851. The wife of a wealthy Rhode Island manufacturer who was also a reformer, she was childless and had leisure as well as energy and a talent for organization. In 1853 she launched her own newspaper, the *Una,* one of the first to be devoted exclusively to women's issues. The monthly paper lasted three years and provided a forum for feminist ideas, as well as a means of publicizing the women's conventions.[43]

Abolitionist men continued to play an active role as supporters and participants in these conventions. The seventy-nine signatories of the 1850 call to convention included twenty couples.[44] Leading antislavery men like Garrison, Wendell Phillips, Samuel J. May, Frederick Douglass, and Thomas Wentworth Higginson attended frequently and served as officers and speakers at the conventions. In the early 1850's, at least, the commitment of abolitionist men to the women's cause seemed firm. As the English feminist Harriet Taylor noted, speaking of the 1850 convention, "It was fitting that the men whose names will remain associated with the extirpation, from the democratic soil of America, of the aristocracy of colour, should be among the originators . . . of the first collective protest against the aristocracy of sex."[45]

The feminist-abolitionists had two main purposes in organizing the conventions of the 1850's: to call attention to women's enslavement, and to arouse women to indignation and protest. The first call to convention in Indiana (1851), for example, justified the action because women were "oppressed and degraded by the laws and customs of our country, and are in but little better condition than chattel slaves." The main address at the first Ohio convention (1850), probably written by Jane Elisabeth Jones, spoke of the "marks of inferiority branded upon our persons." In Pennsylvania, delegates to the first convention (1852) heard that "woman at length is awaking from the slumber of ages."[46]

These messages were directed primarily to the antislavery women who attended these meetings. Although there may have been early feminists who were not antislavery advocates, they left no record. Both the rhetoric and the style of these first meetings bore the imprint of radical abolitionism. Like their Garrisonian "parents," the women relied principally on the power of persuasion. Though not opposed to political action—many were involved in Free Soil campaigns as well as in petitioning for married women's property laws—they nevertheless retained their faith in the power of individual conversion. Even the idea of a permanent national organization was rejected in this period, in favor of a loosely formed steering committee to plan conventions. Many leaders felt that organizations would hamper the movement: Ernestine Rose compared them to "Chinese bandages," and Lucy Stone said she "had enough of thumb-screws ever to wish to be placed under them again."[47] Not until the postwar period, when crisis and conflict within the movement had dampened their optimism, did the women turn to more practical and long-range tactics and goals.

The third national convention, held in 1852 in Syracuse, was typical of all the larger meetings in format, rhetoric, and style. The state and local meetings drew mostly on nearby reformers, but the planners of the national conventions attempted, through the few antislavery and women's rights papers, to reach all parts of the country. The leading feminist-abolitionists usually traveled long distances, as they did for this particular convention. It was attended by an estimated two thousand persons and was presided over by Lucretia Mott. The convention call had been written by Elizabeth Cady Stanton and was signed by a long roster of prominent women and men. The call set the tone for the demands that would be presented by using Revolutionary rhetoric (the time had come for women to obtain the rights "for which our fathers fought, bled, and died"), by citing the abolitionist argument for human rights, and by declaring the need to apply women's greater "moral susceptibilities" to the elevation of humanity and the redemption of the race.[48]

At the convention itself, these arguments were spelled out in detail. Lucy Stone declared that the rights to vote, to keep one's own earnings, and to obtain equality under the law were "the Gibraltar of our cause." Clarina Howard Nichols called for legal rights for married women "in behalf of our sons, the future men of the Republic, as well as our daughters, its future mothers." Speaker after speaker demanded the broadening of woman's sphere to permit her to exercise her equal, divinely ordained rights and responsibilities. As always, the demand for emancipation was made within the conceptual framework of a traditional family, but modified by the presence of an enlightened mother who would be free to work for the betterment of society—directly, by her own efforts; and indirectly, by rearing superior children.[49]

The effectiveness of the national conventions is difficult to measure precisely, but they did provide support and encouragement for local groups as well as inspiration and concrete arguments to be used in gaining new recruits. Susan Anthony, for example, attended her first national convention in 1852 and moved rapidly after that to become more actively involved. Such conventions also raised the expectations of countless women. The *Liberator* carried a letter from an abolitionist woman who wrote to her "Sisters of Indiana" that these gatherings would produce "a golden era" where women, and men, too, would enjoy new freedom and equality. Lucy Stone was more specific when, in 1854, she defended the achievements of the conventions, citing "the action of several legislative bodies; the widened sphere of woman; the discussions through the public journals." She also noted the formation of societies in Ohio and New York and the appointment of standing committees for petitioning. Conventions, she insisted, were needed to prepare the way for individual action.[50]

There is evidence that even hostile listeners were occasionally converted by feminist rhetoric. The Reverend Henry Bellows, the editor of a Unitarian paper in New York, had condemned the women in 1850 for their loss of modesty and virtue in coming before the public. A year later he had second thoughts: "We confess our surprise at the weight of reasoning brought forward by the recent convention, and shall endeavor henceforth to keep our masculine mind—full doubtless of conventional prejudices—open to the light which is shed upon the theme."[51]

More typically, however, the press and clergy continued hostile, and in fact stepped up their opposition as the movement gained strength and the women were taken more seriously. Lucy Stone's optimism was premature when she declared at the 1852 national convention that, as the result of the perseverance of the Grimkés, Abby Kelley, and others, "now we meet in quietness, and our right to speak in public is not questioned." Ironically, this was the first of many stormy meetings at which speakers were subjected to shouting and hissing from the floor. The women attempted to hold a convention in New York City in 1853, to coincide with an antislavery meeting and a World's Temperance Convention. Unfortunately, they were forced to adjourn because of mob disturbances. Women were also excluded from speaking at this temperance meeting, which had been organized principally by clergymen, and Antoinette Brown's efforts to be heard were shouted down.[52]

Though the press took the women seriously enough to report their efforts in the news section, it proceeded for the most part to lash out at them in the editorials. After the New York rioting, only Horace Greeley in the *Tribune* and William Cullen Bryant in the *Evening Post* condemned the mobs who hounded the women at each convention. *Herald* editors described the "assemblage of rampant women" as a "phase in the comic history" of the century and declared themselves appalled that such "unsexed women" would appear in a public hall in broad daylight. The result of their stepping out of their sphere would be "neglect of those duties which both human and divine law have assigned them." James Watson Webb, the Free Soil editor of the *Courier,* deplored the "antiquated and very homely females" who "made themselves ridiculous by parading the streets in company with hen-pecked husbands, attenuated vegetarians, intemperate Abolitionists and sucking clergymen, who are afraid to say 'no' to a strong-minded woman for fear of infringing upon her rights."[53]

The feminist-abolitionists themselves reacted with typical optimism. Antoinette Brown noted in 1855 that the hostility she had encountered made it all the easier for her to identify with the slave's oppression, but she remained hopeful that the "seeds of liberty are taking root." Two years earlier Thomas Wentworth Higginson had observed that the women's efforts had moved "from the sphere of contempt into the sphere of hostility and persecution," but he added that "it is a step forward, none the less."[54]

The antebellum women's movement was characterized by unity and close cooperation between women and men, and between feminists and abolitionists. The members of the feminist-abolitionist "family" relied on each other in innumerable ways, and the men were frequently praised for their support of the women's cause. Lydia Maria Child responded to criticism of her close friend Thomas Wentworth Higginson by defending him and his co-workers as "the chosen sons and brothers of my soul."[55]

Still, behind the apparent unanimity of purpose there lurked intimations that the interests of men and women, and of abolitionists and feminists, would not always coincide. An incident suggestive of one type of difference occurred in 1852 at the first women's rights convention held in Pennsylvania. A male delegate spoke on the legal disabilities of married women and urged men to circumvent the law by drawing up wills leaving their property to their wives; he referred to the will of Martin Luther as an example. Lucretia Mott responded by pointing out that Luther's will, while giving evidence that he appreciated his wife's services, "still only proves the degrading relation she bore to her husband." The will, she went on, gave no recognition of her equal right to their joint earnings; since it obliged her to accept as a gift that which should have belonged to her, it left her still dependent.[56] Later, a few feminists would point to this kind of difference in perspective between women and men to argue that only women could understand the problems of their sex.

Another facet of this potential conflict can be seen in the relationship of two of the most brilliant and articulate feminist-abolitionists, Elizabeth Cady Stanton and Wendell Phillips. Phillips had defended the women delegates at the London meeting in 1840, but after the vote, according to Stanton's recollection, he assured the convention that the women would sit behind the bar with as much interest as if they had been accorded delegates' seats. This, said Stanton, represented a disastrous failure to understand women's feelings. In what subsequently became a familiar theme of hers, she questioned whether he would have been so insensitive had black men been refused seats.[57] Phillips's support of the women's cause derived from his belief in human rights and was bolstered by the feminism of his wife, Ann Greene Phillips. Abolitionism, however, was of greater urgency in his eyes and a cause closer to his heart. In addition, the paternalism that was part of his aloof, aristocratic personality irked independent women like Stanton. A patrician in her own right, she was an ardent abolitionist; nevertheless, her feminism was a strong emotional, as well as intellectual, part of her and clearly took precedence over other causes. These two gifted and strong-willed people were friends who respected each other, but their differences symbolized a basic tension among the feminist-abolitionists. This feeling erupted into conflict when they were faced with hard choices between the rights of black men and those of all women. Like many families, the feminist-abolitionist group would endure the trauma of internal struggle, alienation, and separation.

The last antebellum women's rights convention, held in New York City in 1860, represented the culmination of the feminist-abolitionists' work but also foreshadowed the end of their unity and combined strength. At this point the tensions and strains were visible, as were the differences in priorities and approaches which would separate the feminists from the abolitionists, the women from the men, those more radical from their more cautious and conservative colleagues.

The issue of divorce, and the broader "marriage question" of which it was a part, served as the wedge which forced the first major public break. The divorce problem had been simmering for some time, particularly at temperance meetings, where the need for some means of escape and protection for married women had been advocated by most feminists but was resisted by their antifeminist co-workers, male and female. Among the feminist-abolitionists, two separate but related issues were in contention: one of ideology, the other of strategy. The first involved the morality of divorce and the sanctity of the marriage bond. The second concerned the expediency and appropriateness of introducing such a controversial subject into the movement for women's rights.

In 1840 the abolitionists also had split over both the substantive issue of women's rights and the tactical question of introducing "extraneous" causes. In 1860 the feminist-abolitionists were divided less on ideological grounds, but more in areas involving differences in strategy and priorities. They were in accord on the importance of marriage as the central spiritual and social institution of society, and on the need for equality within marriage. All agreed that when women and men had been allowed to develop to their highest moral, intellectual, and physical capabilities, divorce would be undesirable and unnecessary. Given a still imperfect race, however, they were forced to weigh the effect of dissolving sacred bonds against the reality that, for many women, marriage was a permanent and not too holy prison.

Also involved was the desirability of airing such delicate questions publicly. Drunkenness and rights to property and children were not the only issues involved; indeed, these were the least controversial questions among feminists. The central abuse in marriage was sexual: the most fundamental demand made by the bolder feminists was "the right of a woman to her own body." There was little argument about the grievance, but timidity and prudishness made it difficult to discuss even privately, and feminists expressed widespread anxiety that it would frighten away potential supporters who could accept less controversial but much-needed reforms.

The course of Lucy Stone's thought on the subject in the 1850's mirrored many of the tensions and ambivalences that existed even among the women in the movement. In 1850 she wrote to Elizabeth Cady Stanton, in connection with a forthcoming convention, asserting that the marriage question, while just as imperative as women's rights, should be taken up at a separate convention. They do not belong together, "just as temperance is not part of our distinct movement." Stone agreed that drunkenness should be grounds for divorce, and declared at the 1853 temperance convention that women had a right and duty to withdraw from all unholy relations. On the broader question of sexual abuse in marriage, she agreed privately with Stanton that "the truth lies there," but she also argued that discussion was "premature" and "will frighten them away." Stone admitted that "the abuse in question is perfectly appalling" and related the case of a "noble woman" she knew who had fled to the Shakers because "her husband gave her no peace either during menstruation, pregnancy, or nursing." She knew of many similar cases, she wrote, and added: "Shall we keep silence . . . ?" They were in agreement on "all except the *time* to strike," she concluded.[58]

Two years later, Lucy Stone was still agonizing over the issue. Noting that Paulina Davis wished to bring up the marriage question at the next national convention, she wrote: "It seems to me that we are not ready for it. . . . No two of us think alike about it," she continued, "and yet it is clear to me, that question underlies the whole movement, and all our little skirmishing for better laws, and the right to vote, will yet be swallowed up in the real question, viz: Has woman a right to herself? It is very little to me to have the right to vote, to own property, etc., if I may not keep my body, and its uses, in my absolute right. Not one wife in a thousand can do that now. . . ." Still, it seemed to her "untimely" to bring it up yet. She was not afraid of censure, but "not sure what is *right*." She was certain, she added, that when it was brought up, Mrs. Stanton was the one to do it. Her admiration for Elizabeth Stanton at this time was wholehearted, and she described her as "the bravest woman I know." Ironically, Stanton's very boldness later contributed to the rift between them.[59]

Though the question was frequently touched on, it was not fully debated. In planning a convention in 1857, Susan B. Anthony told Lucy Stone that they had "played on the surface of things" quite long enough. "Lucy," she wrote, "I want this convention to strike deeper . . . getting the right to hold property, to vote, to wear what dress we please, etc. etc., are all good—but Social Freedom, after all, lies at the bottom of all—and until woman gets that, she must continue the slave of man in all other things." Lucy responded indignantly that the legal and political reforms they were working for were hardly "surface" changes but "work most terribly in earnest, and lying so deep that it will take years after we are all dead to bring it to light." As for the marriage question, she had decided that it was a concern not only for women but for men as well. She would be glad when it could be raised but did not see how it could be done at that time. To this Anthony replied that they had always claimed their movement was *Human Rights*—not woman's only—therefore we need not confine ourselves to the evils that woman suffers alone —but enlarge our borders, as the truth shall be revealed." Anthony's willingness to enlarge the scope of their movement, and Stone's ambivalence on this issue, went to the heart of their postwar break. Ironically, Anthony later moved from her broader position closer to that of Lucy Stone and the mainstream of the suffrage movement, leaving Elizabeth Cady Stanton and her continued interest in marriage and divorce on the sidelines.[60]

In 1860, when Lucy Stone had temporarily given up speaking for motherhood, the marriage question was finally brought into public debate. Elizabeth Cady Stanton dropped the bombshell into the national convention by introducing ten resolutions favoring divorce; her immediate goal was to gain support for a divorce bill pending in the New York legislature. With the support of Anthony, Ernestine Rose, and a few of the bolder women, she argued that the sacred rights of the individual as well as the future development of the race were at stake. The institution of the family, "that great conservator of national virtue and strength," could not survive amid the "violence, debauchery, and excess" which often existed in marriage, especially in the presence of intemperance. Such conditions were degrading to women and produced the greatest harm in children, causing all forms of moral and physical deformity. In such a setting, she concluded, the greater morality lay with divorce.[61]

The other side was forcefully represented by Wendell Phillips, who spoke for some of the women and probably most of the men. He declared that the convention was "no marriage convention," and that therefore all of Stanton's resolutions were out of order. The questions of marriage and divorce concerned men as well as women and were "extraneous issues" which had nothing to do with the main order of business: "to discuss the laws which rest unequally upon women." The marriage issue was so complex and would so easily become involved with "free love" theories that it would unnecessarily burden the cause. His motion was rejected by the convention, which allowed Stanton's resolutions to stand on the record without formal adoption.[62]

The marriage question continued to disturb Elizabeth Cady Stanton, but it was never again a critical issue for most feminists. The war first interrupted the progress of the movement and then shifted the weight of concern back to the question of legal rights, where, in the conservative atmosphere of the postwar period, it stayed for the remainder of the century.

The war brought a halt to direct efforts to gain rights for women, but its liberating effect gave an indirect impetus to the movement. Women were compelled to expand their sphere of activity and become more self-reliant. Thousands enlisted as volunteer nurses and sanitary commission workers; many thousands more organized to supply needed funds and war materials, and took over field and factory jobs that men had performed before the war. Even when their service was compatible with the traditional image of woman as healer and comforter, they nevertheless gained new experience outside the home and new confidence to compete in a man's world.[63]

Most feminist-abolitionist women joined the war effort, and many rose to positions of leadership, first with the sanitary commission and other relief groups, later in the movement to aid the freedmen. They themselves saw the war period as a watershed in the expansion of woman's sphere. Elizabeth Cady Stanton wrote in 1864: "This revolution has thrown on woman new responsibilities, and awakened in her new powers and aspirations. . . ." Mary Livermore declared in an 1869 speech that women had grown "to the stature of men" and would continue in new roles because "we cannot go back and be the women we were before."[64] Many, like Livermore, had not felt the need of suffrage before, but now gained a new vision of what women could accomplish if they had a voice in government. Others who had long been suffragists, like Stanton and Anthony, now believed that women had unquestionably earned the right to vote because of their war efforts and sacrifices, and fully expected them to be so rewarded.

The war also put an end to feminist-abolitionist unity by forcing the group into a classic political dilemma. They could insist that Negro rights be linked to women's rights and risk failure to gain either, or they could accept "half a loaf" and hope that suffrage for black men would pave the way for woman suffrage later. This debate divided the Women's National Loyal League, organized by Stanton and Anthony in 1863 to encourage women to support the war actively and to pressure Lincoln into making it a war for emancipation. The same battle engulfed the American Equal Rights Association after the war. Organized in 1866 by feminist-abolitionists who wanted the body to work for the rights of both freedmen and women, it was quickly caught up in the debate over the Fourteenth Amendment. The pending amendment shocked feminists by specifically granting the vote to "male citizens" and introducing the word "male" into the Constitution, which had previously held no reference to sex and had not specifically barred female suffrage.

The large majority of feminist-abolitionist women strongly favored petitioning Congress to delete the word "male" from the amendment; however, most of the men, and a few women, were unwilling to jeopardize Negro male suffrage by pushing the women's cause. The arguments for postponing female suffrage centered on the greater urgency of blacks' oppression. Opponents of such arguments insisted that black women especially needed the vote for protection, since they were doubly oppressed. Sojourner Truth, one of the few black abolitionists to take part in the women's movement and virtually the only one to hold out for the broader position, spoke eloquently at the 1867 Equal Rights Convention. She argued that, if black men got their rights and black women did not, the "men will be masters over the women, and it will be just as bad as it was before."[65]

A long, poignant letter written in 1867 by Lucy Stone to Abby Kelley Foster, who supported the men on the Fourteenth Amendment, reveals the hurt and despair she felt at the abolitionists' desertion of the feminist cause. With disbelief Stone recalled the sentiments of the men at the last equal rights meeting, where they had expressed the feeling that this was "the Negro's hour," and that all their work should be for him. A few deepened the wound by adding that women were represented well enough by their husbands. Only Robert Purvis, a black abolitionist, said he would be ashamed to ask for suffrage for himself and not for the women who had worked for emancipation. All the brave workers, like Abby herself, and Garrison and Phillips, "who for thirty years have said, 'Let justice be done, if the heavens fall,' [are] now smitten by a strange blindness. . . ." Accepting "the poor half-loaf," Lucy pleaded, was against the principle of universal justice, the only thing that could save the nation in its hour of peril. Like the post-Revolutionary leaders who put union first and backed away from meddling with slavery, the antislavery people were making a terrible mistake—"the path of justice is the *only* path of peace and safety." Moving to the argument used so frequently in the antebellum women's movement, she continued: "There is no other name given, by which this country can be saved, but that of *woman*." More anguished than angry, Lucy Stone closed with these words: "Here is a kiss for the hem of your garment, and all good wishes for you and yours, but the tears are in my eyes, and a nail goes through my heart akin to that which I should feel if I saw my little daughter drowning before my eyes, with no power to help her."[66]

In 1867 Lucy Stone clearly felt that she was a woman before she was an abolitionist. This sentiment she shared with Stanton and Anthony, although it was a more painful decision for her to make. Others who would join Stone as leaders of the "moderate" wing, including Mary Livermore, were able to accept the compromise with less difficulty. Several bold actions taken by Stanton and Anthony in the next few years completely polarized the feminist-abolitionist group and pushed Lucy Stone to the side of the antislavery men: the two women's brief association with the eccentric George Train (and, later, their even briefer support of the notorious Victoria Woodhull); the belligerent tone of their newspaper, *The Revolution;* Anthony's action in issuing the paper in the name of the Equal Rights Association without, according to Stone, proper consultation with all the members. By 1869, personal antagonism had become more important than issues. Lucy Stone, recalling the 1840 split, claimed it was "New Organization" tactics all over again. Stanton, however, shrewdly noted that "divisions are always the most bitter when there is the least to differ about."[67]

The final rift in feminist-abolitionist ranks came at the last convention of the Equal Rights Association in 1869. Delegates debated the merits of the Fifteenth Amendment, which prohibited race, but not sex, as a qualification for voting. Anthony argued to reject the amendment as it stood, taking a position not completely unreasonable in a period of anticipated radical reconstruction. Frederick Douglass, who voted with the majority to support the amendment, was more correct in his assessment that woman suffrage was politically impossible to achieve. Anthony, and Stanton, remained uncompromising. Lucy Stone, and probably most of the women who worked to include "sex" in the amendment, reluctantly supported it in its inadequate form.[68]

In the period immediately following the convention, Stanton and Anthony called a meeting of their supporters and organized the National Woman Suffrage Association (NWSA). Lucy Stone, indignant at her exclusion from this action, was by this time thoroughly alienated from the "New York" wing. She joined with Henry Blackwell, Mary Livermore, Julia Ward Howe, and others in the "Boston" group at a convention in Cleveland later in the year; there they formed the American Woman Suffrage Association (AWSA) and launched the *Woman's Journal* as its organ.[69] The *Journal* was more restrained in style and rhetoric than the *Revolution*; the former eschewed other controversial questions to concentrate on women's rights, and especially on suffrage. It proved to be in the mainstream of the postwar movement and lasted until 1917. The *Revolution*, fiery in tone and embracing a broad array of issues, such as the controversial marriage question, lasted only two years and spoke for a minority of feminists.

The feminist-abolitionists in the postwar years were reliving earlier antislavery quarrels, but with an ironic twist. In the 1830's, Sarah Grimké had been chastised by anti-Garrisonians because they feared her letters on the woman question would hurt the abolitionist cause. In the 1860's, it was the old Garrisonian group that viewed Elizabeth Stanton's agitation for women's rights as jeopardizing Negro suffrage. Their opposition was hardly lessened by her angry references to the blindness of women like Lydia Maria Child, who were willing to stand aside while "two million ignorant men" went to the polls to legislate in her interest. Stanton herself compared her stand to that of the Garrisonians, who, in the 1830's, had uncompromisingly demanded immediate and universal emancipation and had actively opposed the extension of suffrage to all white men because they viewed it as added degradation for black men. She and her co-workers insisted that their *Revolution* was following in the footsteps of the *Liberator* by refusing to accept anything less than universal suffrage. Indeed, its militant rhetoric and broad scope of issues made the *Revolution* reminiscent of Garrison's paper, although Stanton's willingness to accept partial suffrage based on education, rather than on sex, tended to undercut her "human rights" argument.[70]

Another difference between the groups was also ironically reminiscent of antislavery days. Just as women found a more comfortable home with the more radical Garrisonians after the split among abolitionists in 1840, so now the men in the movement flocked to the more moderate faction because only there was male participation fully welcomed. Stanton and Anthony, disillusioned by the desertion of so many men in the controversy over the amendments, had concluded that not even the "best and most unselfish of men" could understand the feelings of "subjected womanhood." Only "woman's head and heart" could be relied on to guide the movement.[71]

Still a third type of irony should be noted in reflecting on the rivalry between the two groups: the smaller, more radical group, representing only a minority of feminists, wrote the history of the movement. In the 1870's Stanton and Anthony began to collect material for their *History of Woman Suffrage,* and they invited leaders of both groups to contribute. Lucy Stone, who never forgave her former friends for their rash acts and personal affronts, dissociated herself from this project and apparently influenced Mary Livermore, Julia Ward Howe, and others to boycott the work. The feud over the *History* brought out the most petty instincts on both sides and became a veritable farrago of traded insults and remembered wrongs—all carefully concealed in private communications, since both sides agreed that airing their grievances would hurt the cause. Pictures of the "other" group were obtained by much secret maneuvering, leading Anthony to ask gleefully: "How will *saints* Lucy, Julia and Mary A. feel to see themselves thus mixed up with ordinary sinners?" Stanton observed, with some justification, that Lucy "thinks it desecration of her immaculate being to be even mentioned by such profane lips as ours." "Hence," she concluded, "we had decided to say of her what History demanded and no more."[72] The end result was, of course, that the most valuable collection of documents and commentaries on the movement, an archive in itself, inevitably reflected the Stanton-Anthony view, although Stone, Blackwell, Livermore, Howe et al. were the more representative feminists. The *History*'s glorification of Seneca Falls as the beginning of the movement, for example, ignores the fact that Lucy Stone, Abby Kelley, and others had been speaking out for some time on women's rights, even including the right to vote.[73]

In spite of personal animosities that prevented them from reuniting for twenty years, both sides pursued similar goals through their national and local organizations. Greater educational and job opportunities for women were sought, and the primary goal remained suffrage. The questions of marriage and divorce were avoided even by the "radical" group after the demise of the *Revolution* in 1870. The two groups were united both in their radical desire for female equality, including equality in marriage, and in their conservative support of the family as the moral bulwark of society. Disagreements over tactics and priorities were always greater than ideological differences. Lucretia Mott, trying to unite the factions and stay above the battle, noted sadly in 1870 that both groups had met and separately advocated "the self-same measures."[74]

By the late 1880's even Lucy Stone admitted that the two groups had much in common. The NWSA was "doing very good work," she wrote her daughter in 1887, and she was willing to put personal feelings aside and talk about union for the sake of the cause. Stanton agreed that they "may as well combine for they have one mind and one purpose," but she felt alienated from both groups. The cause had become "too popular," the NWSA "had been growing polite and conservative for sometime," and neither Lucy nor Susan could see anything but suffrage. ("They do not see woman's religious and social bondage.") Stanton was still true to her main cause, but she was increasingly honored and ignored in the movement. With the help of Alice Stone Blackwell, the two groups were united in 1890; Elizabeth Cady Stanton played a brief and honorary role as the first president of the National American Woman Suffrage Association (NAWSA).[75]

The feminist-abolitionists were a remarkably long-lived group. Born during the presidencies of the founding fathers, a few still continued active into the twentieth century, although serious attrition by death began in the 1870's and 1880's. In this period there was much talk of holding one last reunion of the old Garrisonian abolitionists; the fiftieth anniversary of the American Anti-Slavery Society in 1883 provided one such occasion. Three years later, Mary Livermore assembled the group in her Unitarian Church in Melrose to hear William Lloyd Garrison II pay tribute to the late Maria Weston Chapman and to reminisce about their earlier struggles. The survivors continued to work for suffrage, temperance, and a variety of "good causes." Though their evangelical brand of optimism and faith was rooted in an earlier, simpler era, a surprising number were able to make the transition to the more complex and conservative postwar world. Others found themselves turning more and more to the past. Having seen their history repeat itself, having faced the same enemies and voiced the same arguments for so long, they longed for the fervor of the old antislavery days. In 1880, Lydia Maria Child wrote that the memory of the early days was sacred to her: "I look back lovingly upon them; and I find it very hard to realize that so much of it has passed into oblivion. . . ."[76]

The period from 1830 to 1860 had witnessed the emergence of a women's movement from feminist-abolitionism. Feminist activism arose initially out of necessity, the need of antislavery women to defend their right to speak publicly. It became quickly apparent, however, that the rhetoric of human rights applied also to them. Feminism was an almost inevitable outgrowth of a radical movement which had as its goal the emancipation of all enslaved humanity.

During the antebellum years the women's cause developed into an independent movement, gaining momentum by means of speakers, newspapers, conventions, and the formation of local and national organizations. Its constituents were those antislavery women whose experience, circumstances, and personal courage made it possible for them to understand and support feminism as well as abolitionism. This support emerged not from a vacuum, but from the religious motivation and ideological convictions that had already attracted them to the reform cause. The feminist-abolitionist women drew not only on their own individual strengths, but also on the heritage bequeathed them by family and culture: the Enlightenment ideas, especially the doctrine of human rights, valued by the Revolutionary generation of their parents and grandparents; the Quaker type of radical Puritanism which exalted the force of individual conscience over formal doctrine; the romanticism and optimism of an age that believed in the perfectibility of the human race. In addition, they had the crucial support of the Garrisonian men and especially of their own husbands, who encouraged them in their defiance of "woman's proper sphere."

Though the specific goals and tactics of antebellum feminism became distinct from those of abolitionism, the size and scope of the women's movement remained always smaller and less significant than antislavery in terms of national events and priorities. All of the approximately 6,000 subscribers to the *Lily* and the 2,000 persons who attended the 1852 women's rights convention were abolitionists, but the majority of Free Soilers and others who opposed the expansion of slavery were not feminists. Feminism was a low or nonexistent priority even among most of the abolitionists who opposed slavery itself out of religious conviction. Since feminism had such a tenuous hold outside the movement's dedicated core, even among reformers, it is easy to see how its momentum was destroyed by wartime events. With the passage of the war amendments, the major work of the abolitionists was essentially ended; in contrast, the principal thrust of feminism was still to come. The postwar movement had to be restructured on a foundation of limited goals within a framework of realistic possibilities, rather than visionary ideals.

The antebellum women's movement nevertheless made important gains, many of which could only have been accomplished in the fluid, optimistic mid-century years. Significant issues and demands were raised publicly and persistently for the first time: the right of women to equality in education, work, and government; the right of married women to equal protection of the laws and autonomy in the marriage relationship; the right of all women to government protection against the consequences of male intemperance. The widespread opposition which feminists encountered indicates that they were taken seriously and were viewed as a real threat to the status quo. Some inroads were made in opening the colleges and professions to women and in gaining married women's property laws. In addition, efforts were made to confront the ignorance and prejudices of women themselves, and to sensitize them to the existence of the slavery of sex, as well as the slavery of race.

Perhaps most important, precedents were set and models created which feminists would emulate long after the death of this first generation. Postwar suffragism also benefited from the training gained by its leaders in the prewar period. All future women's movements would look to the earlier era for inspiration, for statements of ideology, and for examples of emancipated womanhood.

NOTES

1. Lucy Stone to Samuel J. May, ca. 1847, in Alice Stone Blackwell, *Lucy Stone, Pioneer of Woman's Rights* (Boston: Little, Brown, 1930), p. 90.

2. Weld et al., *Letters,* 2:574; Blackwell, *Stone,* p. 90.

3. Elizabeth Robinson to Lucy M. Wright, Jan. 1, 1838, quoted in Melder, "Beginnings," p. 244.

4. Elisabeth Tappan to Elisabeth Douglass, Sept. 18, 1840, Mar. 23, 1841, July 10, 1842, Apr. 5, 1844, in James Douglass Adams, ed., *A Collection of*

Letters of Ephraim and Elisabeth Douglass Adams (Berkeley, Calif.: By the Author, 1973), 1:46, 47, 60, 85.

5. Letter from "Friend of the Cause," *Anti-Slavery Bugle,* Dec. 5, 1845.

6. Lucy Stone speech, "Workers for the Cause," ca. 1888, Blackwell Family Papers, LC; see also Stone's eulogy, *Woman's Journal,* Jan. 22, 1887; reminiscences of Abby Kelley Foster, Jan. 26, 1885, Kelley-Foster Papers, WorHS.

7. Wendell Phillips to Elizabeth Pease, Oct., 1844, Garrison Papers, BPL; Alla Foster's Reminiscences, in Julia Ward Howe, ed., *Representative Women of New England* (Boston: New England Historical Publishing, 1904), pp. 24–25.

8. *Anti-Slavery Bugle,* Nov. 14, 1845, Oct. 9, 1846; Jane H. Pease, "The Freshness of Fanaticism; Abby Kelley Foster: An Essay in Reform" (Ph.D. dissertation, University of Rochester, 1969), p. 256; Abby Kelley Foster to Stephen S. Foster, Apr. 3, 1848, Kelley-Foster Papers, AAS.

9. See Daniel MacGilvray, "Stephen Symonds Foster," typescript in Kelley-Foster Papers, WorHS; also Parker Pillsbury, "Stephen Symonds Foster," *Granite Monthly* 5 (1882):369–75.

10. Esther Moore to W. L. Garrison, Nov. 15, 1840, Garrison Papers, BPL.

11. For Holley, see Lutz, *Crusade for Freedom,* pp. 244–45, and Sallie Holley, *A Life for Liberty; Antislavery and Other Letters of Sallie Holley,* ed. John W. Chadwick (New York: G. P. Putnam's Sons, 1899), pp. 80–81. For Cowles, see Melder, "Beginnings"; see also A. K. Foster to Maria Weston Chapman, Feb. 16, 1846, Weston Family Papers.

12. Cromwell, *Mott,* p. 29; *Liberator,* Oct. 15, 1841.

13. Jane Elisabeth Hitchcock to Stephen Foster, July 23, 1844, as a postscript to a letter from Abby, Kelley-Foster Papers, AAS; see also A. K. Foster to M. W. Chapman, Jan. 14, 1846, Weston Family Papers.

14. Their schedule was listed in the *Bugle.*

15. *Anti-Slavery Bugle,* Oct. 24, 1845, Mar. 6, 1846, July 14, 1848.

16. J. E. Jones to Lucy Stone, July 1, 1848, Blackwell Family Papers, LC; see also *History of Woman Suffrage,* 1:37–38.

17. See Eugene H. Roseboom, *The Civil War Era: 1850–1873,* History of the State of Ohio Series, vol. 4, ed. Carl Wittke (Columbus: Ohio State Archaeological and Historical Society, 1944).

18. See D. C. Bloomer, ed., *Life and Writings of Amelia Bloomer* (Boston: Arena Publishing, 1895; reprinted, New York: Schocken Books, 1975).

19. See ch. 5 for a more detailed discussion of temperance.

20. *Lily,* Jan. 1, 1849; the address is in Bloomer, ed., *Life and Writings,* pp. 60–61; *Lily,* Oct., 1850.

21. *Lily,* Aug., 1851; Aug., 1852.

22. Bloomer speech to 1852 New York state temperance convention, *History of Woman Suffrage,* 1:484; see also Bloomer, *Life and Writings,* p. 112.

23. Elizabeth Cady Stanton, *Elizabeth Cady Stanton as Revealed in Her Letters, Diary and Reminiscences,* ed. Theodore Stanton and Harriot Stanton Blatch (New York: Harper & Brothers, 1922; reprinted, New York: Arno Press, 1969), 2:39.

24. The strike is described in Bloomer, *Life and Writings;* Lucy Stone to Henry Blackwell, Apr. 23, 1854, Blackwell Family Papers, LC.

25. Bloomer is quoted in Ida Husted Harper, *Life and Work of Susan B. Anthony* (Indianapolis: Bowen-Merrill, 1898–1908), 1:114.

26. *History of Woman Suffrage,* 1:90–91.

27. Elizabeth Blackwell to Henry B. Blackwell, Dec. 27, 1854, and Feb. 22, 1855, and to Lucy Stone, June 1, 1854; Lucy Stone's reply, June 10, 1854, all in Blackwell Family Papers, LC.

28. "Antoinette Brown Blackwell, the First Woman Minister," ed. Claude U. Gilson, typescript in Blackwell Family Papers, RC. (Written by Blackwell in 1896; hereafter cited as A. B. Blackwell Autobiography.)

29. Ibid. See ch. 4 for a more detailed discussion of the religious beliefs of the group.

30. A. B. Blackwell Autobiography, Blackwell Family Papers, RC.

31. A. L. Brown to C. H. Plummer, Dec. 15, 1854, Alma Lutz Collection; Anthony speech on Woman's Rights, 1854, Susan B. Anthony Papers, Radcliffe College.

32. Elizabeth B. Warbasse, "The Changing Legal Rights of Married Women, 1800–1861" (Ph.D. dissertation, Radcliffe College, 1960).

33. Sketch of Ernestine Rose, *History of Woman Suffrage,* 1:95–99; see also Yuri Suhl, *Ernestine L. Rose and the Battle for Human Rights* (New York: Reynal, 1959); *Revolution,* Sept. 16, 1869; Elizabeth Cady Stanton, *Eighty Years and More: Reminiscences, 1815–1897* (European Publishing, 1898; reprinted, New York: Schocken Books, 1971).

34. Clarina Howard Nichols Reminiscences, *History of Woman Suffrage,* 1:171–200; *Notable American Women, 1607–1950: A Biographical Dictionary,* ed. Edward T. James, Janet Wilson James, and Paul S. Boyer (Cambridge: Belknap Press of Harvard University Press, 1971), 2:625. For Ferrin, see *History of Woman Suffrage,* 1:211–12, *Notable American Women,* 1:611; Jane Grey Swisshelm, *Half a Century,* 2nd ed. (Chicago: Jansen, McClurg, 1880). Spelling of "Visiter" is hers.

35. *History of Woman Suffrage*; Harriet H. Robinson, *Massachusetts in the Woman Suffrage Movement,* 2nd ed. (Boston: Roberts Brothers, 1883), pp. 20–41.

36. Chapman, whose husband died in 1842, moved to Paris in 1848 to give her children a European education; she returned in 1855 and resumed her antislavery activities.

37. L. Mott to E. C. Stanton, Mar. 16, 1855, also July 16, 1848, for discussion of plans for the convention. Both in Elizabeth Cady Stanton Papers.

38. *Proceedings of the Woman's Rights Conventions Held at Seneca Falls and Rochester, N.Y., July and August, 1848* (New York: Robert J. Johnston, 1870; reprinted, New York: Arno Press, 1969).

39. Ibid.; see also *History of Woman Suffrage,* 1:70–77.

40. Hallowell, ed., *Mott,* p. 500.

41. *History of Woman Suffrage,* 1:88, 92–93; Elizabeth Cady Stanton Scrapbook on 1848 Convention, Elizabeth Cady Stanton Papers.

42. *History of Woman Suffrage,* 1:806.

43. See ibid., pp. 283–89, and her letters in Weston Family Papers.

44. *History of Woman Suffrage,* 1:821–22.

45. Alice S. Rossi, ed., *Essays on Sex Equality by John Stuart Mill and Harriet*

Taylor Mill (Chicago: University of Chicago Press, 1970), p. 96.

46. *History of Woman Suffrage,* 1:306, 108–10, 352.

47. Eleanor Flexner, *Century of Struggle; The Woman's Rights Movement in the United States* (New York: Atheneum, 1970), p. 348, n. 10.

48. *History of Woman Suffrage,* 1:522, 518–19.

49. Ibid., pp. 522–36.

50. Ibid., p. 310; Lucy Stone to Elizabeth Blackwell, June 10, 1854, Blackwell Family Papers, LC.

51. Suhl, *Ernestine L. Rose,* p. 123.

52. The Stone statement is in *History of Woman Suffrage,* 1:531; the 1853 conventions are described ibid., pp. 120, 152–58, 506–7, 555.

53. *Herald* editorial, ibid., p. 556; others appear in Harper, *Anthony,* 1:103, 90–91.

54. Antoinette Brown speech to American Anti-Slavery Society, May 9, 1855, Blackwell Family Papers, RC; *History of Woman Suffrage,* 1:132.

55. L. M. Child to Marianne Silsbee, Feb. 1, 1857, Lydia Maria Child Papers, American Antiquarian Society.

56. *History of Woman Suffrage,* 1:357–59.

57. Stanton, *Stanton,* 2:41; see also *History of Woman Suffrage,* 1:60.

58. Lucy Stone to E. C. Stanton, Sept. 17, 1850, Aug. 14, 1853, Elizabeth Cady Stanton Papers. The 1853 statement is in *History of Woman Suffrage,* 1:498.

59. Lucy Stone to Antoinette Brown, July 11, 1855, and to S. B. Anthony, Sept. 11, 1856, Blackwell Family Papers, LC; Stone to E. C. Stanton, Oct. 22, 1855, Elizabeth Cady Stanton Papers.

60. S. B. Anthony to L. Stone, June 16, July 18, 1857; L. Stone to S. B. Anthony, July 4, 1857, all in Blackwell Family Papers, LC.

61. *History of Woman Suffrage,* 1:716–22.

62. Ibid., pp. 732ff.

63. See Mary Elizabeth Massey, *Bonnet Brigades* (New York: Alfred A. Knopf, 1966), and Ann Douglas Wood, "The War within a War: Women Nurses in the Union Army," *Civil War History* 18 (Sept. 1972):197–212.

64. E. C. Stanton to W. L. Garrison, Apr. 22, 1864, Garrison Papers, BPL; *National Anti-Slavery Standard,* Dec. 25, 1869.

65. *History of Woman Suffrage,* 2:193–94.

66. Lucy Stone to A. K. Foster, Jan. 24, 1867, Blackwell Family Papers, LC.

67. L. Stone to W. L. Garrison, Mar. 6, 1868, Garrison Papers, BPL; E. C. Stanton to T. W. Higginson, May 22, 1868, Elizabeth Cady Stanton Papers.

68. *History of Woman Suffrage,* 2:382–83.

69. For views on the split from both sides, see *Revolution,* May 26, 1870, and *Woman's Journal,* Apr. 9, 1870.

70. E. C. Stanton to Olympia Brown, n.d. but written during the Fifteenth Amendment debate, Olympia Brown Papers, Radcliffe College; *Revolution,* May 20, 1869, Mar. 24, 1870.

71. S. B. Anthony to Harriet Robinson, May 12, 1881, Harriet Hanson Robinson Papers, Radcliffe College.

72. Lucy Stone to Harriet H. Robinson, Mar. 4, 1879, Blackwell Family

Papers, LC. See also Stone to E. C. Stanton, Aug. 3, 30, 1876, ibid.; Stone to Harriet Robinson, May 3, 1882, Harriet Hanson Robinson Papers; S. B. Anthony to H. Robinson, Apr. 4, 1882, and E. C. Stanton to H. Robinson, n.d., both in Harriet Hanson Robinson Papers.

73. Lucy Stone noted this grievance in a letter to Antoinette Blackwell, dated only "1887–1888," Blackwell Family Papers, LC.

74. L. Mott to Richard D. Webb, Jan. 22, 1870, Garrison Papers, BPL.

75. Lucy Stone to Alice Stone Blackwell, Apr. 12, 1887, Blackwell Family Papers, LC; E. C. Stanton to Olympia Brown, May 8, 1888, Olympia Brown Papers.

76. S. H. Pierce to A. B. Blackwell, Dec. 1, 1883, Blackwell Family Papers, RC; M. A. Livermore to W. L. Garrison II, Apr. 8, 1886, Garrison Family Papers, SC; Lucy Stone to Emma Blackwell, July 2, 1886, Blackwell Family Papers, LC; Child, *Letters,* p. 258.

3

A Trio of Feminist Leaders

THE THREE MAJOR LEADERS of the nineteenth-century women's movement—Lucy Stone, Elizabeth Cady Stanton, and Susan B. Anthony—belonged to that first generation of feminists whose roots were in the antebellum era of religious fervor and radical reform, and especially in the antislavery movement. These feminist-abolitionists, whose earliest leaders included Lucretia Mott, Abby Kelley, and the Grimké sisters, initiated the antebellum women's movement and continued active in postwar suffragism. In the prewar period they experienced the continuing tension between the demands of the antislavery cause and those of the nascent feminist movement. Many chose abolitionism as their first priority and continued to work primarily for the freedmen and freedwomen after emancipation. Others, like Stanton and Anthony, were "new women" among the feminist-abolitionists, making a commitment to female emancipation their primary goal. Lucy Stone personified the dilemma of those faced with this difficult choice, but ultimately she, too, made the cause of women her lifework.

A detailed look at the careers of these three women is useful in several ways. It reveals the common origin of both the abolitionist and feminist movements, and the logical transition from one cause to the next. The development of their commitment to feminism reflects the influence of abolitionist ideology, as well as the cultural milieu in which the abolitionists were raised. The personal histories of the three also tell us a great deal about the kind of women who became feminists in nineteenth-century America. Faced by many of the same frustrations and limitations that burdened all women, they responded with creative energy and the determination to enlarge woman's sphere, rather than with the illnesses, hysteria, and resignation that so often characterized women's reactions in this period.

A study of the careers of these three women reveals the basic tone and thrust of nineteenth-century feminism. It also permits a comparison of three different personalities and styles of leadership, and offers insight into the reasons for the divergence in the movement in the 1860's. While the three leaders shared similar beliefs, their actions suggested the range of subtle differences that were found in the larger group of feminist-abolitionists. Similarly, their responses to social changes mirrored the spectrum of responses in the entire movement.

Stone, Stanton, and Anthony were also "new women" in a sociological sense. They were models for a new type of woman who, faced with options, chose to work outside her home. All three combined a belief in woman's special moral and domestic responsibilities with a vision of her obligations in the broader world, and they demanded that woman not be limited to the domestic sphere. Stone and Stanton especially prefigured the new woman who would balance both career and traditional duties to home and children. Both faced, in their daily lives, the dilemma of creating new female roles while fulfilling their idealization of old ones. Though neither resolved this difficult problem completely, both were partners in relatively egalitarian marriages which suggested patterns and solutions for the future.

Of the three, Lucy Stone is closest to the prototypical feminist-abolitionist in personality, lifestyle, and world-view. To know her is to understand a great deal about many of her co-workers in this first generation: Mary A. Livermore, Antoinette Brown Blackwell, Elizabeth Buffum Chace, and others. Elizabeth Cady Stanton, while sharing the cultural roots and basic values of the group, was nevertheless in a class by herself, an original. She contributed a rare irreverence and wit to this generally staid and puritanical generation of reformers. Her ideas were always a little too radical, her strategies a little too bold; but, by the exercise of charm and brilliance, she won fewer enemies than many who were more cautious.

Susan B. Anthony was the least typical of the three. Not only did she remain unmarried, unlike most of her co-workers, but in her practical, down-to-earth manner she also seemed less touched than they by the romanticism and evangelicalism of her era, and thus more able to make the transition to the next generation. Nevertheless, as a liberal Quaker brought up in an atmosphere in which women were relatively equal and independent, she represented an important segment of the feminist-abolitionist leadership. The Garrisonian group included a disproportionate number of Friends, whose religious outlook permeated radical abolitionism and carried over into the women's rights movement. As Anthony's life illustrates, Quakerism was a logical training-ground for feminism. Because she, as well as Stone and Stanton, played a crucial role in determining the direction of the women's movement, a more detailed look at their lives is imperative.

Lucy Stone was probably the most influential feminist leader to emerge in the 1840's. As the first abolitionist to lecture solely on women's rights, she carried her message to parts of the country that had never before heard a woman speak publicly, in any capacity. It is noteworthy, as a portent of the movement to come, that admirers praised her more because she was "womanly" and "chaste" than because of the content of her speeches; to use a modern idiom, the medium in her case *was* the message. Abby Kelley Foster had a similar mission and was likewise personally attractive and demure. However, because of her aggressive righteousness and uncompromising manner—it was said that she "made the guilty tremble"[2]—unsympathetic audiences were quick to reject her as "unsexed" and "immodest." Lucy Stone, whose round, solemn face was rather plain looking, was small and looked like a schoolgirl; she projected an attractive, childlike quality even in later years. She had an unusually eloquent and pleasing voice and spoke directly to her audiences, using no manuscript or notes. A minister in Bangor, Maine, praised her as "one of the most womanly women I ever knew." She convinced, he wrote, not so much by logic as by "her beautiful spirit and noble utterance"; her strength lay "in the depth of her affections, her chaste rhetoric, and the justice of her words." The order in which he placed these qualities is significant and explains much of her success as an orator.[3]

Even non-abolitionist papers occasionally had kind words for Lucy Stone because she appeared to conform to the popular ideal of true womanhood. A Massachusetts paper in 1849 described her manner

as "gentle, calm, dignified, earnest" and "free from offensive boldness"; her language was "chaste and beautiful." "She had not in any
degree compromised the modesty belonging to her sex," the re-
viewer concluded. A St. Louis paper in 1853 noted that she had
drawn the largest audience ever assembled there (1,500–2,000
persons), including many who had come from curiosity and stayed to
admire her eloquent, earnest pleading on behalf of woman. The
reporter himself was taken with her "soft, womanly voice" and
"plain, rather priestlike gown" which "suggested sermons rather
than the voluptuous vivacity some had expected."[4] This is not to
say that she was not also maligned and vilified at meetings and in
the press; still, her modest decorum served to make her radical oratory more appealing and less threatening than it might otherwise
have been.

Lucy Stone is significant in other ways. In her religious fervor,
her romantic optimism, and her humorless and almost obsessive
Calvinist sense of duty, she typified the spirit and tone of most
feminist-abolitionists. Her deathbed utterance to her daughter
could have been an epitaph for the whole group: "Make the world
better!" In her marriage to a "woman's rights man," she also
followed a pattern which was common in her generation of
feminists, an important and neglected aspect of the nineteenth-
century movement.

Although Lucy Stone resembled the earlier abolitionist women in
personality and background, the major thrust of her career came
later, in the women's cause rather than in antislavery. In this sense
she bridged both movements. She also personified the difficulties
confronting the group as a whole when it was forced to choose
priorities. Lecturing as an agent of the American Anti-Slavery
Society in the late 1840's, she was taken to task by her superiors for
introducing the subject of women's grievances into all of her talks.
An agreement was finally worked out whereby she divided her time
and lectured on women's rights on her own. She made her own
arrangements, put up her own handbills, and met her expenses by
passing a hat around after her lectures.[5] For Lucy Stone more than
anyone else, this conflict would cause continuing tension.

Lucy Stone was born in Massachusetts in 1818 and, like most of
her co-workers, could claim an ancestor who had come to New
England in its earliest years and a grandfather who was an officer in

the Revolution. Her father was a well-to-do farmer with an obedient wife, nine children, and orthodox views on women and religion. Lucy was bright, determined, and influenced at an early age by strong feelings about duty, morality, and justice. She resented the hard life her mother led and the unjust manner in which women were treated. Her father rejected her own plea for higher education but sent her less talented brothers to college. One of her most painful recollections was of raising her hand to vote on an antislavery issue in their Congregational church and hearing the minister give instructions not to count her. Women in the church, she said later, were "as hewers of wood and drawers of water." Like so many feminists, she turned against the orthodox church early because of its stand on slavery as well as on women. She was especially intent on going to college to learn Greek and Hebrew in order to read the Bible in its original form, so she could prove "that inspired truth shows God loves his daughters as well as He loves his sons." For a time Lucy rejected organized religion totally, but she later became a Unitarian. The orthodox church expelled her for her radical antislavery views.[6]

In a speech to the national women's rights convention in 1855, Lucy Stone explained how she became a feminist. Hers was a familiar story. From her earliest memories, she said, "I have been a disappointed woman." She was willing to go anywhere in the world for an education, but was told: "It isn't fit for you." All employments were closed to her except teacher, seamstress, and housekeeper. "In education, in marriage, in religion, in everything, disappointment is the lot of woman," she went on. "It shall be the business of my life to deepen this disappointment in every woman's heart until she bows down to it no longer." Every feminist had, in one form or another, a similar response to woman's situation, and a similar goal.[7]

Lucy Stone's girlhood experiences were not unusual, but she was growing up at a time when it seemed possible for an assertive woman to change her condition. Religious fervor was in the air, as was enthusiasm for individual salvation and the perfectibility of society. New sects that preached the goodness of man and the lovingness of God offered hope to potential reformers. Economic opportunities and the advantages of democracy were becoming more available to the common man, if not to the common woman. In addition, some women were already trying to bring about change, and Lucy Stone could look to them for her models. At sixteen, she had sat with the local sewing circle which was working to educate a theological student, and she listened to Mary Lyon, trying to raise funds for Mt. Holyoke Seminary, talk of how hard it was for girls to get an education. Lucy decided that she had better work for the advancement of her own sex. She left unfinished the shirt she was making, and hoped that no one would ever complete it.[8]

The earlier feminist-abolitionists made the deepest impression on Lucy Stone. As a twenty-year-old teacher she read Sarah Grimké's "Letters on the Province of Woman"; she wrote to her brother that they were "first rate" and "only help to confirm the resolutions I had made before, to call no man master." Abby Kelley had an even more personal impact on her. Stone first met her and was impressed by her courage and independence when Kelley gave an antislavery speech in West Brookfield, where Lucy was teaching. Abby and Stephen Foster later held a series of meetings at Oberlin College while Lucy was a student there. Faculty and other students denounced them as radicals and infidels, but Lucy Stone was deeply moved. Writing to them about their effect on her, she noted gratefully that they had "set a ball in motion."[9]

Lucy Stone also benefited by the fact that Oberlin College opened its doors to women—in 1833, the first college to do so. By teaching for nine years, she was able to save enough to enter in 1843, at the age of twenty-five. She continued to work there to pay her expenses. Ironically, both she and her best friend, Antoinette Brown, had very stormy careers at Oberlin because of their feminist views. The major aim of the college was to educate men; women were there to prepare themselves to be good wives and mothers, and because their presence was considered a good influence on the men. Both women were crushed to find their professors espousing woman's natural inferiority. One such session, Antoinette confided to Lucy, "put me into such agony as I never wish to feel again." In addition, Lucy wrote home that her academic schedule was interrupted on Mondays, when the female students did the laundry for the whole school. She was forced to practice debating in secret because women were not allowed to participate in the debating program. Most of the women were in the "literary" course, which had been made shorter and easier in keeping with their "inferior" abilities and lesser goals. Lucy was one of the first women to finish the "regular" course (and the first New England woman to do so, her admirers like to remind people).

She was asked to write an essay for commencement but refused to do so because she was not allowed to read it herself. Antoinette, in the "literary" program, was permitted to read her speech because the faculty and students present at the commencement were all women.[10]

At Oberlin, Lucy Stone decided not to marry but instead to become a lecturer and devote her life to usefulness and public service. This decision was made only after much inner torment. She felt that marriage was the natural state for both men and women, and confided to Nette: "My heart aches to love somebody that shall be all its own." She concluded, however, "though it is sad and desolate to live unmarried . . . nothing is so bad as to be made a *thing,* as every married woman now is, in the eye of the law." The most hopeful solution she could arrive at was a compromise: "Nette, let us get down these laws, and then marry if we can." This kind of tension, which arose from conflict and inner compulsion, probably caused the severe headaches and periods of depression which plagued her all her life.[11]

When her mother expressed disappointment at her decision to become a public speaker, Lucy wrote that conscience and duty demanded that she seek the difficult way; otherwise "I should have no right to think myself a Christian, and I should forever despise Lucy Stone." There would be no objections if she were a man, and "surely the moral character of the act is not changed because it is done by a woman." "I expect to plead not for the slave only," she went on, "but for suffering humanity everywhere. ESPECIALLY DO I MEAN TO LABOR FOR THE ELEVATION OF MY SEX."[12]

Lucy Stone gave her first lecture, on women's rights, from her brother's pulpit in 1847. A year later the Garrisonians enthusiastically welcomed her to their ranks. Through Abby Kelley Foster and Maria Weston Chapman she received invitations to lecture for the Western and the Massachusetts Anti-Slavery Societies. The women were especially delighted. As Lucretia Mott wrote her friends in Dublin, "Lucy Stone is an acquisition to our ranks. She is such a thorough woman's-rights woman too." Lucy, in turn, confided to Nette, "I love the Abolitionists better and better. It seems to me there is no class of people as free from selfishness. . . ." To Mrs. Mott she wrote in 1850 that she had "lectured a few times on Woman's Rights, with some success." Apparently the difficulties were greater than the rewards, for she went on: "But our cause is onward slowly. It will triumph, as all good causes will."[13]

In her antislavery lectures, Lucy Stone stressed the usual Garrisonian themes, making particular mention of the plight of slave women and the breaking up of families under slavery, as well as the guilt of the American churches. Over and over again she delivered to her audiences the same message that Sarah Grimké had made a *cause célèbre* ten years earlier: "God demands the same duties of women as of men." Women had yielded to "corrupt custom" for so long, she argued, that their moral vision had become blinded. All her speeches were permeated with this central concern, a basic theme of the whole women's movement: "As moral and responsible beings, God has given the same sphere of action to man and woman, and the same duties devolve on both." Like the Grimkés, she found it impossible to speak against slavery without defending her right and duty as a woman to do so.[14]

In all her lectures Lucy Stone exhibited a lifelong preoccupation with duty and a singleness of purpose which was characteristic of most feminist-abolitionists. She also displayed an innocence and otherworldliness that often betrayed a naivete about mundane problems—an extreme example of what was also a common characteristic of this middle-class, Puritan group. In an 1853 speech to the "colored people" of Cincinnati, at a time when the very survival of free blacks in the North was in question, especially in the border states, Lucy Stone lectured on the importance of useful knowledge and the need to establish literary societies and circulating libraries.[15] She later revealed a similar lack of understanding about the problems of working women and, failing to see the relevance of labor issues for women, opposed strikes while she worked for woman suffrage.

Like all the Garrisonians, Lucy Stone was imbued with a perfectionist fervor and an evangelical zeal for reform. She shared with them a millennialist faith in the elevation of woman and the consequent redemption of society. The women's rights movement was "the central reformatory movement of the age," she exclaimed in 1854, "and what infinite blessings it will bring to the race!" Like most of the group, she did not expect the millennium in her lifetime. "So the good seed is being sown," she wrote after a particularly successful women's rights convention, "it will grow and bear fruit when we are dead."[16] Her faith in the ultimate perfection of society blinded her to the urgency of many of the problems of the here and now.

As the foremost speaker for the women's cause in the 1850's, Lucy Stone offered her listeners several lectures, all variations on her central subject, "The Disabilities of Woman." On several occasions she also presented these views before committees of the Massachusetts legislature. She stressed, as her major themes, the removal of all obstacles to the highest development of woman, the opening to her of all avenues of useful knowledge, and the placing before her of "adequate motives" to the fullest execution of all her God-given faculties. Woman's sphere should be limited only by capacity, and would normally change during her lifetime as her responsibilities varied; her life goals should be usefulness and independence.[17]

Since Lucy Stone felt that the "unnatural dependence of woman" had distorted the marriage relation, "equal sovereignty in marriage" was a constant theme of hers. She deplored the situation in which women were forced to marry for financial security rather than for love, in which she had a highly romantic faith. Woman's lack of training made her unfit for motherhood, and her treatment as a "paltry toy" degraded her. "God gave woman her mission," Stone told her audiences, "he never meant her to sit down in utter idleness while others earn their bread." Despite this strong statement, she gave only abstract attention to the fact that many married women were forced to work outside the home. She also ignored the new factories, springing up in Lowell and elsewhere, which employed women workers. She included higher wages in her demands, but even this issue was typically clothed in moral uplift—when wages were too low, many women were driven to prostitution.[18]

A great number of women came to listen to Lucy Stone, and some spoke to her afterward about their own problems. She was constantly incorporating these tales of woe into her talks as fresh illustrations of her themes. She was responsive to the women as individuals and often was deeply moved. After one lecture tour she wrote: "I pity them and get sermons from them all . . . more than all, a deeper detestation of our social systems which seem contrived to crush all real nobility out of woman with a deadly and destructive certainty and perforce, to make her an empty nothing." On a trip to a frontier area of Illinois in 1856, she was profoundly disturbed by the plight of many of the women, who worked as hard as the men in spite of frequent child-bearing. In one family, she reported, the wife slept in an outhouse all winter, while her husband had his bed near the fire—his way of punishing her for giving birth to a girl. "If she will have gals, cold is good enough for her," he had said. This experience shook Lucy Stone's customary optimism. She wrote to her family: "I care less and less every day which triumphs, freedom or slavery. In either case, all the women of the land are yet subjects . . . my heart . . . breathes the prayer that slavery may yet crush every white man into the same condition in which the white men have placed women."[19] Ultimately, she would be forced to decide whether the situation of women was indeed more urgent than that of slaves.

With her strong aversion to marriage, Lucy Stone would certainly have remained single had not Henry Browne Blackwell matched her in persistence and dedication to female equality. Described by a friend as a "short, stout, pleasant-looking person," he was also kind, warm, and witty. Talented at both business and poetry, he was more outgoing and fun-loving than she, but just as romantic and intensely idealistic. An antislavery worker himself, though not a Garrisonian, Blackwell met Lucy Stone when she gave a series of lectures in his hometown, Cincinnati, and was immediately taken with her "spirit and individuality." His family was an extraordinary one, and his background helps to explain his choice of a wife. His father was an antislavery man, his mother a strong "woman's rights woman." His sisters Elizabeth and Emily were two of the earliest women doctors; two other sisters became known in art and literature. His brother Sam, also active in political antislavery, married Antoinette Brown in 1856, producing another successful egalitarian household.[20]

For two years Henry Blackwell courted Lucy Stone with grace and diligence, assuring her that marriage to him would help, rather than impede, her reform career. She would be "free to be at home when she pleases and to leave it when she thinks it best," and he would put all his resources at the command of her cause. There was no degradation in an harmonious marriage based on equality and mutual dependence, he declared; furthermore, the law would not affect them, because they would obey "a higher law." "Will you permit the injustices of the world to enforce upon you a life of celibacy?" he wrote. "I do not want you to *fetter* yourself *one particle* for my sake—

I do not want you to forego *one sentiment* of independence . . . I want only to help you, as best I can, in achieving a really noble and *symmetrical* life." This "symmetry" could be best achieved for her, he argued, by combining marriage with public service.[21]

Lucy was attracted to her suitor but feared losing the independence she had worked so hard to achieve. She was deterred, she wrote him, by "the horror of being a legal wife, and the suffocating sense of the want of absolute freedom which I now possess." She also confessed to having "revulsions of feeling" about marriage, which he attributed to the "unfortunate impressions" of her childhood. She was prudish and repressed about sexual matters, but probably not more than most of her generation. These attitudes were reinforced, though, by the thoughts of her mother's frequent childbirth and heavy burdens; such memories were surely discouraging, if not prohibiting. Blackwell tried to overcome this revulsion and to convince her that her concept of duty was mistaken, that any "philosophy which commands us to *suppress* our natural instincts is false and that a true life can never be one which is false to any portion of our human nature." His delicate references to sexuality could not be misconstrued as excessive interest in the "lower passions"; he assured her constantly that "we will live a pure and rational life." He also promised to take legal steps to guarantee her right to her own property and earnings and, upon their marriage, to make a public protest: "I wish, as a husband, to *renounce* all the privileges which the law confers upon me which are not strictly *mutual*." Such a marriage, he vowed, would not degrade her.[22]

In 1855, when she was thirty-seven and he thirty, he finally persuaded her that she could gain love and companionship without losing her independence. She confessed that "my heart *yearns* towards you *all the time*." "Dear Harry," she wrote, "we can and will help each other, and we will be *forever better* for our wedded love." In a series of impassioned letters they vowed that their life together would be dedicated to "noble aims" and "self-improvement." She introduced (or exacerbated) a conflict in his life by asserting that a truly honorable life was "free from all the meanness of trade"—a rather unrealistic goal, since he earned his living as a merchant. He promised to retire from business as soon as he could, and to devote all his energy to good causes.[23]

Lucy Stone and Henry Blackwell were married in May, 1855, by her friend and Unitarian minister Thomas Wentworth Higginson, whom Lucy called "one of the anointed." Higginson had expressed himself strongly on the need for independence and mutual respect in marriage, and now he had an opportunity to act on his principles. In a simple ceremony, the bride promised only to "love and honor" her husband, and the groom in turn read the protest, in which they declared their intention to disobey all laws which "refuse to recognize the wife as an independent, rational being, while they confer upon the husband an injurious and unnatural superiority."[24] This became an important model for their own time, as well as a blueprint for future egalitarian marriages.[25]

As a student at Oberlin, Lucy Stone had been impressed by a professor's observation that "women are more sunk by marriage than men" because their loss of name meant a loss of identity. She had decided then that married women should keep their own names.[26] Following her own dictum, she was known as "Mrs. Lucy Stone." She signed legal documents "Lucy Stone, wife of Henry Blackwell," and all of her letters, even to her husband, were signed "Lucy Stone," never "Lucy." By doing this she set an important precedent; future career women who followed her example were known as "Lucy Stoners." Though all feminists felt strongly about retaining their identities after marriage and viewed the loss of one's name as a symbol of slavery, most of them settled for adding their husbands' names to their own. Lucy Stone was passionately concerned with keeping both name and identity, and saw this as an important feminist issue. To Elizabeth Cady Stanton, who felt just as strongly on this question, she wrote: "It is not a trifle to claim and will be reluctantly yielded but a great deal *hangs by it*."[27] Stanton had taken her husband's name at her marriage fifteen years earlier; those intervening years saw the beginning of the women's movement and undoubtedly made a difference in Lucy's decision.

Lucy Stone never softened on this issue. When Susan Anthony inadvertently allowed "Blackwell" to be added to her name on a call to convention, Lucy felt "grieved and hurt" and suffered a "loss of faith." In 1879 women were permitted to vote in school elections in Massachusetts; however, Lucy Stone, after fighting for suffrage for over two decades, chose to have her voting registration annulled, rather than to register under her married name as the law required. She was equally adamant on other questions involving her personal independence, although she reluctantly allowed her earnings from property and investments owned before marriage to be kept in a joint bank account—because, she later explained to her husband, "you did so much for women."[28]

Henry Blackwell kept every one of his promises. He and Lucy Stone had a happy marriage for almost forty years and he, more than any other man, devoted much of his life to the women's movement, contributing time, money, and true devotion. He co-edited the *Woman's Journal* with Lucy and continued his association with it and with the movement until his death in 1909, sixteen years after Lucy's death. They had one daughter, Alice Stone Blackwell, who also became an important suffragist. The three were a close-knit family, a small island of pure-minded innocence and hope, devoting their energies to "making the world better."

The Stone-Blackwell marriage created a small furor in the press. Editors unfriendly to abolitionism and feminism gloated over Lucy Stone for "repudiating" her principles, and they ridiculed the protest. The *Washington Union,* recalling that Henry Blackwell had recently helped in the escape of a fugitive slave, noted with satisfaction that he had been justly punished. Lucy was defended by other feminists. Typically, Frances Gage wrote in the *Lily* that Lucy Stone had wisely married a man "pledged not to use the tyrant power which the law gives him." The couple's protest, she asserted, had already had the beneficial effect of stirring people up and making them think about the marriage laws. Out of this "clashing and discussing," she predicted, "truth will be evolved."[29]

Lucy Stone took great pains to assure her co-workers that her efforts would continue, and she became indignant at intimations to the contrary. Her legal position as a wife, she reminded Susan Anthony, gave her all the more reason to work for the cause. After her daughter was born in 1857, however, she went through a period of intense conflict and guilt about leaving the child with a nurse-maid, and she finally decided to give up lecturing temporarily. She told Susan in 1858 not to fret about it; God "knew what he was about when he made the mothers so cleave to their children." She assured Anthony that, when her child was older, she would be a "better world worker" than before. She supported the Women's Loyal League during the war and resumed her work for women's rights afterward.[30]

Like many nineteenth-century feminists, Lucy Stone was compulsive about being a devoted mother and a neat and efficient housekeeper. She smothered her daughter with constant attention and insisted on making her own yeast, bread, soap, and preserves. She obviously felt the need to prove that woman's emancipation would entail not the slightest neglect of her maternal and domestic duties, but she had so thoroughly internalized the importance of this dual role that her actions came naturally and were not merely a defensive tactic. Her philosophy was expressed in a speech to the 1853 national women's rights convention; she defended the value of the work women did at home, while also encouraging them to enter business and the professions. "I think that any woman who stands on the throne of her own house, dispensing there the virtues of love, charity, and peace, and sends out of it into the world good men, who may help to make the world better, occupies a higher position than any crowned head." "However," she continued, "woman could do more. . . ."[31]

Lucy Stone probably would have approved of the eulogy given at her funeral in 1893, for the words praised her for embodying "our highest conceptions as daughter, sister, wife, mother, friend, and citizen," in that order. Her wish to chart new paths for women continued until her death at seventy-five—she was the first person in New England to be cremated. Though her leadership in the movement has become dimmed, she was greatly acclaimed by reformers in her day. Her funeral, noted the presiding minister, was more like a coronation.[32]

Lucy Stone was in the mainstream of the first generation of feminists in her style, her values, and the nature of her marriage. Elizabeth Cady Stanton, who emerged in the late 1840's as the boldest thinker and the most prolific propagandist of the movement—the Sam Adams of the women's revolution—is not so easily categorized. Aileen Kraditor has dubbed her "the *enfant terrible*" of the movement; and indeed, Stanton thought of herself as "the first of the 'new women.'"[33]

Although Stanton was in the vanguard of the early feminists, she nevertheless belonged with them. Her roots, like theirs, were in the aristocratic soil of New England, and she too moved from Calvinist orthodoxy to an optimistic, socially oriented brand of religious liberalism. Like them, she worked in the abolition and temperance crusades before concentrating all her energies on women's rights. She shared the feminists' belief that the elevation of woman and the introduction of her greater moral and spiritual gifts into the broader stream of society would bring the redemption of the race. Like her contemporaries, she saw motherhood as woman's highest function but rebelled vehemently against her imprisonment in this role.

Even more than most of her generation, Elizabeth Cady Stanton was an elitist, albeit a radical one. Her New England brand of class consciousness blended with her feminism to produce a faith in the superiority of the "best women." Historians like Kraditor have emphasized the conservatism of the second generation of suffragists and have condemned their expedient alliances with racists and nativists. Though it is true that the earlier group was more endowed with romantic idealism, the differences between them have been exaggerated. Stanton's 1848 Declaration of Sentiments, for example, included the protest that man has withheld from woman "rights which are given to the most ignorant and degraded men—both native and foreigners." Like most feminists, she found it particularly galling that the "lowliest white man" (and later the most ignorant black man, whom Stanton contemptuously referred to as "Sambo") was given suffrage before the most educated woman. In the postwar period, disillusioned with the fact that civil rights had not been extended to women while they had been granted to freedmen, Stanton advocated suffrage limited by educational qualifications.

Though Elizabeth Cady Stanton was not always as democratic as her rhetoric would suggest, she brought to the movement a brilliant, questioning mind and an irreverent bent that made her a peerless gadfly. She saw her main task as getting women to think about their oppressed state—today it would be called "consciousness-raising." In speeches and in conversation she was witty and devastating in striking down arguments and opponents, although her attractive personality and perpetual good humor made the defeats somewhat more bearable. A friend admired her ability to "clothe her thoughts in words that burn." With customary immodesty, she described herself as "cool and self-possessed, and with wit and sarcasm quite equal to any" of her critics.[34] She was less inhibited and prudish than most nineteenth-century feminists, and

more sophisticated in her analysis of women's needs and her understanding of the causes of women's oppression. Stanton was never
deluded into thinking that either suffrage or the elimination of the
double standard would end inequality, though she firmly supported
both causes. The chief enemy, as she saw it, was the tyrannical force
of custom and attitude that underlay the social structure, especially
as reinforced by the church.

Elizabeth Cady Stanton was more vigorous and open than most
feminists of her generation in attacking marriage as it existed, and in
advocating easier divorce. Basically, though, she supported the
institutions of marriage and family and was conventional in her
opposition to "free love" doctrines. Like most feminists, her goal
was to make marriage more egalitarian and to protect women
from its abuses. It was, therefore, in style and strategy, rather than
in substance, that she differed most from her more conservative contemporaries.

This "cheerful and brilliant" woman was born in 1815 in western
New York, the daughter of Daniel Cady, a wealthy and prominent
lawyer and a judge of the state supreme court.[35] As a child she was
gifted, fun-loving, and constantly rebellious. Her father's influence
in shaping her life was crucial, even dramatic. (She herself expressed
the belief that "daughters take after their fathers, mentally."[36]) A
constant visitor to his law office, she overheard pitiful stories from
married women who came to her father for help, and learned at an
early age of the tragic "defect of sex" written into the laws. She
vowed to do something about this injustice, but faced her father's
lifelong opposition to her ambition. Grief-stricken when his only
son died in 1826, he told Elizabeth: "Oh, my daughter, I wish you
were a boy." All through his lifetime she tried to prove that a
daughter could be as good as a son but, in spite of her successes, he
never gave her the approval she wanted. Though she was precocious
and learned Latin, Greek, and mathematics via tutor, private
academy (where she was the only girl), and female seminary, he
refused to send her to her brother's college. He later opposed her
feminist activities so strenuously that he disinherited her for a time.
After one confrontation, when she was a mature woman, she confessed that the iron had entered her soul deeply. "I never felt
more keenly the degradation of my sex," she wrote to a friend; "to

think that all in me of which my father would have felt a proper pride had I been a man, is deeply mortifying to him because I am a woman."[37]

In spite of her failure to please her father, Elizabeth Cady Stanton was always, by her own description, "endowed with a good degree of self-esteem." (Her handwriting, which grew more magnificently illegible with each passing year, reflected her personality.) Her self-confidence may have been bolstered by her mother, whom she described as courageous and self-reliant. Mrs. Cady was a strong abolitionist and more sympathetic than her husband was to women activists; at least once, in 1852, she entertained Susan Anthony in her home and attended a temperance meeting that Susan organized. Her mother may have been more of an influence and a model than Elizabeth herself realized. Elizabeth's daughter, Harriot, later displayed more awareness of the early influence, on her, of her independent-minded grandmother.[38]

Elizabeth Cady was brought up with a stern brand of religion and the ever-threatening shadow of eternal damnation. She often felt tormented by anxiety and guilt, especially after her brother's death. Like most feminists, she later rebelled against this Calvinist preoccupation with sin. Like them, the fire of her feminism was fueled by her religious experience. After working with the Presbyterian girls' club to educate a student for the ministry, she was rewarded by hearing him preach a sermon against women. The pastoral letter denouncing the Grimkés in 1837 was an outrage for which she never forgave the orthodox clergy. She later liked to recall how, through her reading and the influence of her brother-in-law, she finally "found my way out of the darkness into the clear sunlight of Truth; my religious superstition gave place to rational ideas based on scientific facts." Her early hurt and indignation against the church never left her, and she frequently referred to it as "a terrible engine of oppression, especially as it concerns women." Although never an atheist, Elizabeth was likewise never a church-goer, and she encouraged young women to ride bicycles in the fresh air on Sundays, rather than "playing the role of miserable sinners" in church.[39]

Elizabeth Cady's move toward more liberal religious ideas was strengthened by the influence of her cousin Gerrit Smith, who also introduced her to antislavery and temperance. Through him she read the *Liberator* and became an abolitionist. In his home she met leading reformers, including Henry Brewster Stanton, who was one of the hardest working of the New York group of abolitionists. A handsome, dashing man who was described as one of the greatest orators of the age, Stanton swept Elizabeth Cady off her feet by his impassioned eloquence.[40] She was a vivacious and attractive young woman with good features and a bright, witty manner (although her short, plump figure became corpulent in later years). In 1840 she decided to marry Stanton in spite of her father's opposition to his radical antislavery views.

Their honeymoon trip to the World's Anti-Slavery Convention in London was an appropriate culmination of their courtship. The rejection of the women delegates was, for Elizabeth Cady Stanton, "fresh baptism into woman's degradation." Here she began her long and important association with Lucretia Mott. In their correspondence after returning home, they discussed religion as well as the position of women; the older woman encouraged the younger to divest herself of the "creeds and dogmas" that were encumbrances on "the simple and benign religion of Jesus."[41] Throughout her life, Elizabeth Stanton was close to Mott and the Garrisonians and considered herself one of them. This was not a source of conflict with her husband, who was a New Organization man but who stood with the Garrisonians on the woman question.[42]

Though Henry Stanton was a women's rights man, and the customary "obey" had been omitted in their wedding ceremony, their marriage was less harmonious than that of most feminist-abolitionists. Stanton respected his wife's right to equality in marriage but did not give her the support and encouragement that Abby Kelley Foster and Lucy Stone enjoyed. His career as a lawyer, journalist, and politician kept him busy and away from home much of the time—he was probably absent during the births of most of their seven children—and was the cause of some resentment on her part. Though he was a loving father, she apparently did most of the work in raising their five sons and two daughters. He, in turn, was annoyed with her increasing preoccupation with the women's movement; he complained that his letters were much more frequent than her replies, though his letters to her were generally warm and affectionate. He was not hostile to the women's rights cause as such and introduced his wife's petitions for woman suffrage into the New York legislature during his term there, despite the ridicule he received.[43] Both husband and wife had strong personalities and clashed frequently, though she was probably the more difficult to overrule. They pursued separate careers, both successfully, but without any noticeable help from each other. The published reminiscences of each contain virtually nothing about the other.

The Stantons spent their first years of marriage in Boston, where Elizabeth enjoyed the stimulating company of abolitionists and intellectuals. In 1847 they moved to Seneca Falls for Henry's health, and Elizabeth found herself chafing in the restricting company of three small children and two servants. She later spoke of the loneliness and "mental hunger" she suffered. Her discontent was not, as has been suggested, the prime cause for calling the 1848 meeting; rather, it was only the most recent of long-standing grievances.[44] The visit from Lucretia Mott in that year served as the spark to ignite an idea that had been simmering since 1840. Stanton was delighted with the publicity the convention received, convinced it "will start women thinking, and men too." In demanding the broadening of woman's sphere, Elizabeth Stanton was inspired by the competence with which Mrs. Mott had raised her large family and was now lecturing on behalf of slaves and women.[45]

While Lucretia Mott was able to execute her duties as mother and reformer in sequence, her friend Elizabeth had babies, speeches, petitions, and conventions all crowded into the same busy years. With a chronically absent husband, inefficient servants (her continual complaint about the "daughters of Erin"), and four more children born in the 1850's, she nevertheless managed to turn out an impressive stream of articles for the *Lily* and for Paulina Davis's *Una,* as well as speeches and resolutions for conventions which she usually could not attend. Motivated to excel in everything, her housekeeping and child-rearing were admirable by all accounts, and her propaganda was magnificent. She managed to travel to Albany in 1854, with children and nurses in tow, to make a major speech before the legislature on married women's property rights. Though she had a large share of the usual feminist conflicts and frustrations, she enjoyed her children tremendously and approached her challenges with enormous inner strength, abundant energy, good health, and a magnificent *joie de vivre*. Though she had moments of panic, she remained calm and cheerful most of the time.

Elizabeth Cady Stanton's meeting with Susan B. Anthony in

1850 supplied Stanton with the kind of steady support and prodding that she needed to keep up both with her children and with her cause. Their activities throughout most of their long, productive friendship revolved around the Stanton home—"the center of the rebellion," as Mrs. Stanton described it. Anthony, the more compulsive but less creative of the two, was relatively free of family duties and did the organizing, the fact-finding, and often the babysitting, while Stanton sat at her desk and turned out brilliant diatribes tailored to each occasion. This combination worked extremely well, although Stanton occasionally allowed her frustration to spill over. After rereading an account of the 1840 convention, she declared herself at the boiling point: "If I do not find some day the use of my tongue on this question, I shall die of an intellectual repression, a woman's rights convulsion!" On another occasion, she wrote Susan that she was pacing her chambers "like a caged lioness," longing to bring to a close her housekeeping cares. In a more typical mood, she urged Susan to rest and "let the world alone awhile; we cannot bring about a moral revolution in a day or a year." In the summer of 1859 she was full of energy and enthusiasm and planned to turn out "a half a dozen good tracts" but asked Susan to please "steer clear of statistics which I have no time to look up."[46]

Stanton's and Anthony's ventures were not confined to women. They made a brief foray into leadership of the women's temperance movement in New York, but Stanton's suggestion at the 1852 convention that drunkenness should be grounds for divorce resulted in a conservative takeover the following year. Stanton's involvement with antislavery was more enduring. She was much in demand at conventions for, as Stephen Foster put it, her wisdom even more than her eloquence. She attended when she could. On these occasions her speeches always tied antislavery to her broader goals: abolition was only part of the larger emancipation from the slavery of custom, creed, and sex which would lead to the elevation of the whole human family. More than anyone, Stanton found it impossible to separate the cause of the slave from that of woman.[47]

Elizabeth Cady Stanton was sympathetic to her husband's Free Soil politics until the *Dred Scott* decision, when she joined Anthony, Lucy Stone, and other Garrisonians who supported disunion as the only hope for emancipation. John Brown's death in 1859 caused her great trauma, especially as it was associated with the collapse of her cousin and good friend Gerrit Smith. (Stanton suffered the death of her father that year as well.) She was inspired by these crises to invest greater energy in the abolition cause. In late 1860 and early 1861, she and Anthony traveled the state on a lecture tour urging immediate emancipation, ignoring her husband's warning that it was too dangerous a venture. His prediction proved correct—they suffered constant harassment, and only police protection saved them. Stanton continued her participation in the American Anti-Slavery Society, and in 1865 voted (in opposition to Garrison) to extend the life of this organization. In later years she spoke proudly of her record "as one of the soldiers in that grand battle against slavery."[48]

Stanton reached new heights of eloquence in a powerful address to the New York State Anti-Slavery Convention in early 1861. Her subject, free speech, was chosen in response to several days of angry mobs. Slavery, she said, was no longer just a question of the black man's rights, but of the sacred liberties of all. Mob law moves "like a fearful iron horse with blind purpose." She had taught her five sons the purest principles of democracy, she said, but "we train them not for passing time alone but for the endless ages of eternity." Rather than see her sons false to freedom (like the young rioters), she would "consecrate them all to martyrdom, to die, if need be, bravely like a John Brown . . . boldly declaring that Jesus died to give to the nations of the earth a blood-bought liberty."[49]

It was not accidental that Stanton chose to speak as a mother on free speech. Her role as a woman dominated her thinking. Writer Grace Greenwood, describing Stanton's "rare talent for affairs, management, and mastership" exhibited at one convention, said she remained "in an eminent degree womanly, having an almost regal pride of sex." This pride in being a woman was displayed in endless ways: her use of a woman doctor (Caroline Cabot); her "great joy in finally having a girl" after five boys (the birth of a second daughter gave her "fresh strength to work"); her note to her newborn first granddaughter that she was "delighted you belong to the superior sex." She took pride in other women's accomplishments, "for whatever one woman does well, I feel that I have done it."[50] At least one of her sons, Theodore, seemed uninjured by her assertions of female superiority and also became involved in the women's movement.

Her strong sense of herself made Stanton all the more resentful of the freedom that was enjoyed by men but denied to her and to all women. Man's soul could never know the joy of motherhood, she wrote her cousin Elizabeth Smith Miller, but "we have purchased the ecstasy in deep sorrow and suffering." The crisis in the country, she wrote Susan in 1859, made her "regret more than ever my dwarfed womanhood. In times like these, everyone should do the work of a full-grown man." In future life, she joked with a heavy heart, she hoped to be "neither a negro or a woman" but would ask the angels to confer on her "the glory of white manhood" so she would finally enjoy "unlimited freedom." She envied her husband's job as an editor for the *New York Tribune* in the 1860's and dreamed of what she could do with such an opportunity.[51]

Stanton's iconoclasm was expressed both in her private life and in her public utterances. Her self-confidence enabled her to defy convention with a minimum of doubt and trepidation. She admitted to Susan that her ideas were so radical that many were afraid to stand with her, but "I am ready to stand alone. I never write to please anyone. . . ." To her son, who asked her not to visit him in school wearing the "short dress," she wrote: "You must learn not to care for what foolish people say." She herself was not immune to criticism and, like Lucy Stone, gave up this particular form of protest because of it, declaring with typically flamboyant rhetoric: "What is physical freedom compared with mental bondage?"[52]

Most of Stanton's ideas sprang from her intense feelings about the role of women. She revolted against the rigid sex roles of her society, and especially against the training of young girls to fulfill the current ideal of delicate, helpless womanhood. She argued again and again that girls should be brought up free and untrammeled, allowed to develop in mind and body as fully as boys, and trained in a trade or profession to be self-sufficient like their brothers. She treated her own children as much alike as possible, encouraging her daughters to engage in physical exercise and teaching her boys to sew and knit. (Martha Wright reported that one of them knitted a bag to hold his marbles.) When her daughter Margaret attended Vassar, she urged her to "fit yourself for a good teacher or professional so that you can have money of your own and not be obliged to depend on any man for every breath you draw." In 1898 she told an interviewer that she had made it her life's work to teach women to bring up their daughters with a definite purpose in life: "Self-development is a higher duty than self-sacrifice."[53]

Stanton used both pen and tongue to lash out at men as women's oppressors, and she regularly compared the relationship of husband and wife to that of master and slave. Her views on marriage aroused antagonism even among feminists who sympathized with her arguments but felt that her frankness would hurt the cause. Actually, her position was a logical extension of the views of most feminists. Women were degraded in marriage, she argued, tyrannized by men who acted according to their "lower" (i.e., sexual) natures. Only when woman's higher purity and moral standards governed marriage would there be hope for the future of mankind. "The right idea of marriage," wrote Stanton, "is at the foundation of all reforms." Her most radical demand in the antebellum period was the right of a wife "to her own person" and "the control of her own body," by which Stanton meant the right to refuse to have sexual intercourse with her husband.[54]

It is tempting to attribute these views on marriage to Elizabeth Stanton's personal frustrations and disappointments, but there are several difficulties with this analysis. She undoubtedly was influenced by her frequent pregnancies and obvious lack of contraceptive knowledge—on her sixty-fifth birthday she noted wistfully in her diary that she wished she had done more for her children, but "I then knew no better than to have seven children in quick succession."[55] She also suffered feminist frustrations and some difficulty in her marriage. But all of her children survived and were healthy, unusual good fortune for a nineteenth-century family. She herself was a self-satisfied woman who enjoyed life—her children, books, friends, music (she played piano and guitar)—and seemed to suffer far less than most feminist-abolitionists from the need for self-sacrifice and the pangs of Puritan guilt.

She probably also enjoyed sex. Even she was too proper to discuss this delicate question publicly, but two entries in her diary in later years reveal her private views on female sexuality. In one, she refers to "the great natural fact that a healthy woman has as much passion as a man." In the other, she concludes that "the first great work to be accomplished for woman is to revolutionize the dogma that sex is a crime, marriage a defilement and maternity a bane." Unless this was newly found knowledge, it reveals a private view somewhat inconsistent with her public rhetoric, which stressed woman's relative immunity to the "lower passions." Probably Stanton and other feminists believed that women were capable of greater control because of their higher moral standards.[56]

Stanton's beliefs cannot be attributed merely to her personality, because these views were shared in varying degrees by most feminists; however, she was ahead of her time in raising some of these issues publicly. Such concerns stemmed not only from feminists' desire for the improvement of the race, but also from the real need of women for independence in marriage and the freedom to dissolve the union if it proved burdensome. The "right of a wife to her own person" was of particular urgency in the absence of reliable information on birth control, and because of the prevalence of drunkenness, linked (at least in the feminists' view) to loss of control and sexual brutality. Stanton's grievances were universal ones.

Elizabeth Cady Stanton's burdens and frustrations were lessened in the postwar period. Freed of childbearing duties and with a competent housekeeper, she turned her enormous energies to the women's movement. In 1866 she ran for Congress as an independent candidate on a platform of "free speech, free press, free men and free trade" and received twenty-four votes. Her desire to test woman's constitutional right to stand for office was apparently frustrated.[57] In addition to leadership in the National Woman Suffrage Association, she lectured on the lyceum circuit for twelve years as one of the country's most popular speakers. Her most requested speech, "Our Girls," stressed the need to educate young women to independence. In her travels she also gave freely of her unorthodox but sound opinions on infant and child care. She saw herself, in effect, as a radical missionary. Stanton wrote to her daughter Margaret that she felt she was "doing an immense amount of good in rousing women to thought and inspiring them with new hope and self-respect" and "making the path smoother for you and Hattie and all the other dear girls." She was pleased with herself and her own accomplishments and wanted her daughters and other young women to know this satisfaction also.[58]

Elizabeth Cady Stanton continued vigorous and controversial in her later years; at seventy-five she was described in the press as "looking as if she should be the Lord Chief Justice, with her white hair puffed all over her head, and her amiable and intellectual face marked with the lines of wisdom." As the movement became more conservative and more narrowly focused on suffrage, she appeared even more radical and became even less acceptable. She complained to a friend: "I cannot sit on the door just like Poe's raven and sing suffrage evermore. I am deeply interested in all the live questions of the day . . . I cannot work in the old ruts any longer." She urged women to make a social revolution and "carry the war into their own homes" by diverting energies from husband and family to work for their own emancipation. These challenges and her continuing protests against racism were met with deafening silence. She persisted in arguing that bigotry and custom were the chief enemies. In the 1890's she produced her *Woman's Bible,* a feminist commentary on those portions of the Bible dealing with women, and a fitting summation to an unorthodox career. She was active until her death in 1902 at eighty-six. The eulogy delivered at her funeral by an old abolitionist friend was appropriate to her efforts to illuminate the dark corners of women's minds: "A lighthouse on the human coast is fallen."[59]

Susan Brownell Anthony came to feminism a little later than Lucy Stone and Elizabeth Cady Stanton, but she devoted herself to the cause more completely than any other leader of her generation. Because of this commitment, she appropriately became the symbol of the nineteenth-century movement, though she was far from the prototype of a feminist-abolitionist. Anthony was both atypical and misunderstood, even by many of her admirers, and her image (as well as her ego) suffered from comparison with her more brilliant and polished friend and co-worker, Elizabeth Cady Stanton. Anthony generated the stereotype of the suffragist as a gaunt spinster, embittered and aggressive, even though this image fit her only superficially and most of her colleagues not at all. She remained unmarried by choice. Although she was awkward and prosaic in style and angular in appearance, she was warm and loving in spirit and unusually broad and catholic in thought. Stern principles, strong character, and an optimistic faith in people were the sources of Anthony's strength; she was ruled by neither bitterness nor hatred. Her tendency to bossiness arose from impatience with less determined and efficient workers, but she was even harder on herself. Her intensity and doggedness made other reformers often seem almost casual, even dilettantish. Writer Eleanor Kirk described Anthony as always having her eye fixed on the distant point. While Mrs. Stanton was also an earnest worker, wrote Kirk, she sought her goal with calm and stately steps, often stopping to pluck a flower here and there by the roadside. For Susan there was no pause along the way.[60]

William Henry Channing, in a much-quoted encomium, called Anthony "the Napoleon of the women's right's movement" because of her great drive and organizational ability. Her leadership merited praise, but the military analogy—a common one—was inappropriate to this earnest Quaker lady. She was driven not by dreams of personal glory, but by an unselfish and consuming desire to see justice done to women. The image of Anthony as warrior also implied a lack of womanliness, as illustrated by a eulogy printed by the St. Louis *Globe Democrat* on her death in 1906:

> No ministering angel, she,
> To bind up wounds or cool the fevered brow
> With the soft hands of pity.
>   She was of that sterner stuff
> Whereof God makes his heroes.
>
> Hers was the warrior soul
> Locked in a woman's breast.
> Predestined to do battle. . . .

In an age which put a high value on true womanhood, this was faint praise, and undeserved. Though heroic, she was a "feminine" heroine, valuing highly the traits of tenderness, purity, and domesticity. Her natural warmth and directness of approach made her universally popular with children. Though childless, she embraced all women as her daughters—truly a mother figure despite her businesslike appearance and a straightforward manner which lacked the conventional coyness and modesty. Eleanor Kirk, defending Anthony against charges of being "unwomanly" and "aggressive," described this quality: "She has, as it were, adopted all womanhood as her child, and fights for it as naturally and unselfishly as the lioness fights for her young."[61]

Historians like Andrew Sinclair, who have glibly painted Anthony with a broad and unsubtle Freudian brush, have tried to diminish her genuine idealism.[62] Though all the feminist-abolitionists have suffered at the hands of interpreters, the few like Anthony who chose reform over marriage have aroused particular skepticism and endless quests for hidden motivations. Actually, it is not difficult to understand why an independent, reform-minded woman like Anthony, who had some private means and the ability and training to support herself by teaching, should prefer the freedom of spinsterhood to the undeniable limitations suffered by her married contemporaries. Unquestionably she found in the women's movement compensation for the family she never had, and she was nurtured and supported by her female co-workers; however, this was a natural and predictable consequence of the choices she made, not necessarily a neurotic sublimation of her natural desires. Like most feminist-abolitionists, Anthony's reform career was basically a humanitarian response to real injustice.

Susan Brownell Anthony, born in 1820 on a Massachusetts farm, grew up with idealism and reform. Unlike Lucy Stone, Elizabeth Cady Stanton, and other feminists who were forced to break away from orthodox, traditional families, Anthony's childhood was spent in a broad-minded Quaker atmosphere in which she was encouraged to develop her abilities and use them for reform work. Throughout her difficult and controversial career, her home was always what Stanton called a "safe harbor" to which she, and others, could return for comfort and support. After the death of her parents, sister Mary continued the family tradition of providing sustenance and a home base for the peripatetic Susan, who wrote toward the close of her life that Mary "has ever made it possible for me to go and do and be for our cause."[63]

Susan's father, Daniel Anthony, who moved the family to the Rochester area of western New York in 1826 and turned from farming to operating a cotton mill, was an important influence in Susan's life. He was a supporter of temperance and antislavery and had unusually advanced views on women's rights, going beyond the Quaker tenet that women were the spiritual equals of men. Believing that women should be trained for independence, he educated his daughters just as he did his sons. With eight children (Susan was the second and became used to responsibility at an early age), he set up a school in his own home. Susan was allowed to teach there at fifteen; she later attended a female seminary and taught in a nearby village during summers. Daniel Anthony gave her full support in her reform career, lent her money, and on one occasion even helped her hide a runaway wife, an action he found legally wrong but morally right.[64]

Susan's mother also offered total support and encouragement for her daughter's work. An aunt was a well-known Quaker preacher who undoubtedly provided the young Susan with an important model and served as still another source of inspiration. Given her intelligence and drive, Susan's decision to devote her life to reform seems a logical outgrowth of her family background and a strong reinforcement of the values she was brought up with.

Daniel Anthony was liberal and relaxed in his religion and, unlike many Quakers, allowed his daughters to wear pretty clothes and attend parties. He was chastised by people in his community for encouraging his daughters to teach, and the Friends disowned him for allowing the top floor of his house to be used for a dancing school. The family began attending the Unitarian Church in the 1840's, when their antislavery activities also provoked severe opposition among the Friends. Daniel Anthony became a close friend of Samuel J. May, and the Anthony home became a meeting house for Garrisonian abolitionists. The father's broad-minded and unorthodox approach to religion was transmitted to his daughter. Though she never renounced her Quakerism, she paid little attention to rituals and never adopted the plain speech or dress. Like Lucretia Mott, she vigorously opposed sectarianism and championed religious liberty. Characteristically, she defended Ernestine Rose's association with freethinkers against criticism by co-workers. She reviewed reform as practical Christianity, and indeed, her work became her religion; Stanton described her in later years as an agnostic to whom "work is worship." Anthony gave up belief in a personal deity and was fond of reminding people that God was not responsible for human ills, and that religion was an unreliable source of material aid. She depended ultimately on human goodness to triumph.[65]

Susan Anthony was an intelligent and intense young woman, interested in serious causes at an early age. At seventeen, her diary contained more references to slavery and intemperance than to social activities. She took an interest in the working conditions at the mills and in the girls who worked for her father, some of whom also boarded with him. On one occasion she was allowed to work with the mill girls for several weeks when a replacement was needed. When her father's business failed in the panic of 1837, she was determined to help him pay his debts and left home for a full-time teaching position.

Anthony had suitors in her youth, and also later, but she rejected them and expressed surprise that her friends were marrying just anyone for the sake of marriage. Her family obviously did not pressure her to take this route, although two of her sisters married. In 1849 Susan suffered a traumatic experience when she nursed a cousin through the last month of a difficult pregnancy and assisted at the birth, only to lose the patient shortly after. She expressed her anxiety in letters home: "It is rather tough business, is it not Mother?" She was twenty-nine at the time, though, and probably already set in her decision not to marry. Her diary in the 1840's and 1850's, written in clear but unimaginative prose, reveals her views of what woman's work should be: "What is most wanted, is to get the mind drawn off from the frivolous and centered upon the true and the right."[66]

Susan Anthony became sensitive to the injustices women suffered only after she left the benevolent environs of her home. As a teacher, she was acutely aware that it was common practice to pay women less than half as much as men received for the same work. Her interest in women's welfare led her at first to temperance, rather than to feminism. In 1848 she joined the Daughters of Temperance, seeing it as a means for women to help others of their sex who were victims of alcohol and poverty. She viewed her work as missionary labor, to combat heathenism and proclaim the truth. She canvassed the state, collecting signatures on petitions for a Maine (prohibition) law, organizing new temperance societies, and urging women to use their influence for the cause. Antoinette Brown described her in this period as "a typical school m'am, angular, witty, and dictatorial" who was "working for temperance tho opposed to suffrage." When Susan's parents and sister Mary attended the Seneca Falls meeting and enthusiastically supported the demand for suffrage, Susan "poked fun at the idea."[67]

Anthony gained a new respect for the women's rights cause when she attempted to speak at an 1852 convention of the Sons of Temperance. The chairman rebuffed her, explaining that "the sisters were not invited there to speak but to listen and to learn." She left indignantly and, with Elizabeth Stanton, organized a Woman's New York State Temperance Society. Her conversion to feminism was completed when she attended the state women's rights convention that year, and when she was refused recognition at the World's Temperance Convention in 1853. She also tried to participate in discussions at the convention of the New York State Teachers' Association, throwing that body into confusion. She continued to attend these annual teachers' conventions even after she was no longer a teacher, in order to fight for women's right to participate in the society and to receive equal pay for equal work. In this cause she apparently received little support, even among women teachers. Unlike the feminists, most teachers lived up to their image as docile and submissive helpmates, willing to take second place. These qualities undoubtedly endeared them to the administrators of the newly burgeoning public schools.[68]

Anthony gave up teaching in the early 1850's because she found the profession too narrow and limited; instead, she became a full-time antislavery and temperance worker. Her experiences had convinced her that women needed more power before their influence could be effective, so she began to work for women's rights as well. In 1853 she joined Amelia Bloomer and Antoinette Brown in a tour of the state, lecturing on temperance and women's rights, and she added her efforts to those of Stanton and Ernestine Rose in collecting petitions for a married women's property law in New York. As she traveled about the state, her contacts with women broadened her awareness of their problems and sharpened her indignation. Like that of her co-workers, her rhetoric reflected her abolitionist roots, as she compared women with slaves and condemned the sin of keeping women in sexual bondage. In the temperance speech which she gave many times during 1852, she argued that men "consider woman in her *proper sphere* only when she serves in the capacity of slave or administers to the pleasure of the opposite sex." "Woman," she declared, "will no longer submit to be the sufferer, that man may be the *sinner*."[69]

By the mid-1850's, the urgency of the slavery issue took precedence over other questions for the feminist-abolitionists. As early as 1851 Abby Kelley had urged Anthony to join her in working for antislavery. The latter was eager to comply but felt inadequate to the task, especially as a speaker. (Anthony spoke in what even a friendly critic could only describe as "an earnest, attractive monotone," although she improved over the years.) The Garrisonians, who were her friends, were also her heroes. She felt they had received "that higher, holier light," and her idealization of them made it difficult for her to believe she could join them at "the sublime height" where they stood. In 1856, however, she accepted their invitation to become the chief agent of the American Anti-Slavery Society in western New York, carrying out her job with her usual efficiency. She received ten dollars a week plus expenses, and spent most of her time arranging meetings and speaking tours for the leading lecturers—Abby Kelley Foster, Elisabeth Jones, and Lucy Stone, as well as Garrison and Phillips. Occasionally she filled in by speaking herself. In 1857 she wrote with exhilaration of her recent campaign: *"My spirit has grown in grace,* and the experience of the last winter is worth more to me than all my Temperance and Woman's Rights labors—Though the latter were the school necessary to bring me into the Anti Slavery work. . . ."* Reversing the more typical path of the early abolitionist women, she had gone from other reforms into antislavery, seeing that cause as the culmination of her efforts.[70]

Though she would become better known in the postwar period, the patterns of Anthony's personality and thought were already clear in the 1850's. Basically serious and modest, she was, like Lucy Stone, so fired with the desire to right the wrongs suffered by women and slaves that she took unconventional stands which brought her ridicule and abuse. Because of her own unmarried state, she was especially vulnerable when she argued for woman's independence in sexual relations. Like all the feminists, she felt that women's economic dependence led to unhappy marriages and prostitution, but her discussion of these delicate questions shocked her audiences. In her temperance speeches in 1853, for example, she urged women to separate from intemperate husbands and particularly not to allow drunken spouses to father children. The press predictably labeled her a bitter, jealous, man-hating spinster whose advice to women was "startling and disgusting." One newspaper, arguing with her assertion that wives could not love dissipated husbands, proclaimed that the most elevating and ennobling virtue of the sex was the *"persistency and intensity of woman's love for man."* "What," they asked, "does Miss Anthony know of the thousand delights of married life?"[71]

In spite of this special handicap, or perhaps because it helped her develop unusual resistance, Susan Anthony pursued her goals with a prosaic kind of doggedness that valued common sense over sentimentality. Her unromantic practicality, much like Lucretia Mott's, distinguished her from her more "ladylike" co-workers and sometimes brought her into conflict with them. At the 1852 New York state women's rights convention, she opposed the nomination of Elizabeth Oakes Smith for president because the latter was fashionably attired in a short-sleeved, low-necked dress. Anthony, who insisted that no one dressed that way could represent women of the state, won her point. For more than just puritanical reasons, she wanted women to appear as serious, not frivolous people. In another encounter she objected to women reading papers in weak, delicate voices which did not reach beyond the first few rows. Paulina Wright Davis argued that "ladies did not come there to screech; they came to behave like ladies and to speak like ladies." Anthony held her ground, declaring that the question of being ladylike was irrelevant; the business of anyone who read a paper was to be heard.[72] In all these cases Anthony, whether consciously or not, was trying to adapt traditionally feminine behavior to the demands of the new roles and greater independence which she envisioned for women. Like Sarah Grimké and Lucretia Mott, she felt strongly that equal rights implied equal duties and responsibilities—the old Quaker doctrine at work again.

Anthony's lack of sentimentality also led her to question the so-called natural differences between the sexes that were accepted even by most feminists. In a letter to Stanton asking her for a speech to be delivered to a teachers' convention, Anthony reminded her that "in the schoolroom more than any other place, does the difference of sex, *if there is any,* need to be forgotten." In a speech given in 1854, she suggested that if women received the same education as men, they might find that the present differences were not God-ordained; given the same opportunities, women might become capable of the same kind of intellectual efforts as men. Backing up somewhat, she went on to assure her audience that "woman will be woman still, be her position what it may," pointing to a woman like Elizabeth Blackwell, who was no less "pure, chaste and kindly affectioned" for all her achievements. Anthony's tendency was clearly away from the prevailing romantic view of true womanhood.[73]

Having rejected marriage in order to work for reform, Susan Anthony was impatient with her friends who, in her view, were diverting their energies from their true work by marrying and having babies. Always feeling a personal inadequacy as a speaker, she constantly bewailed the fact that more eloquent orators were often unavailable. To Stanton she wrote in 1856: "Those of you who have the talent to do honor to poor—oh! how poor—womanhood, have all given yourself over to baby-making; and left poor brainless me to do battle alone. It is a shame. Such a body as I might be spared to rock cradles. But it is a crime for you and Lucy Stone and Antoinette Brown to be doing it." When Antoinette disappointed her by not only marrying but also having two daughters in a row, Susan sent her a typical friendly scolding: "Now, Nette, *not another baby*, is my *peremptory command, two* will solve the *problem* whether a *woman can* be anything *more* than a *wife* and *mother* than a half dozen or *ten* even."[74] She either assumed that her friends knew more about contraception than they actually did, or was suggesting that they should practice abstention. Unfortunately for historians, modesty prevented her from being more specific.

Anthony expressed her own reasons for remaining single with characteristic directness. When told by a minister in 1854 that she should marry and have children instead of going door to door with petitions, she replied: "I think it a much wiser thing to secure for the thousands of mothers in this State the legal control of the children they now have, than to bring others into the world who would not belong to me after they were born." Many years later, after seeing scores of co-workers marry and drop out of the movement, she wrote: "I would not object to marriage, if it were not that women throw away every plan and purpose of their own life, to conform to the plans and purposes of the man's life. I wonder if it is woman's real, true nature always to abnegate self."[75] She was still asking relevant questions but failing to offer solutions. Her own panacea, suffrage, proved inadequate.

Anthony's increasing preoccupation with suffrage in the postwar period limited her naturally broad outlook. In 1868 she organized a Working Woman's Association in New York City, which failed because her goal was at odds with the more urgent needs of the laboring women she was trying to help. (Her genuine interest in working women throughout her life had always been flawed by her middle-class perception of their problems.) Anthony even came to resent the competition created by the movements for temperance and social purity, and she deplored Stanton's *Woman's Bible* project as diversionary and harmful to the cause. Stanton continued to argue that bigotry had to be overcome before suffrage could be of use; Anthony countered that women had to be enfranchised before they could be emancipated from their superstitions. She pushed so hard for a Sixteenth Amendment that it became known as the Susan B. Anthony Amendment. In 1872, she created a *cause célèbre* by voting in an election and then standing trial for this illegal act. Her desire to take the case to the Supreme Court was frustrated by a judge who, though he found her guilty and imposed a fine, refused to enforce payment.

Though Anthony became narrow and remained middle-class in her views, she was not as elitist as Stanton and continued to oppose the limitation of suffrage by property or educational qualifications. "Those who have the least," she said, "are the ones who suffer most from the legislation of the rich, and need the ballot for self-protection." Her tolerance and belief in personal liberty also overrode practical considerations when put to a crucial test. In 1896, the National American Woman Suffrage Association convention was faced with a resolution to disassociate itself from Stanton's *Woman's Bible;* passage would, in effect, condemn the project. Anthony left the chair to plead not for her friend or the *Bible,* but for free speech and toleration of diversity: "When this platform is too narrow for all to stand on, I shall not be on it." "If you fail to teach women a broad Catholic spirit," she went on, "I would not give much for them after they are enfranchised. . . . You had better organize one woman on a broad platform than ten thousand on a narrow platform of intolerance and bigotry."[76]

It was Susan Anthony's fate to play a secondary role in the women's movement during most of her life. In spite of her enormous admiration, even worship, for her co-worker (they always called each other "Mrs. Stanton" and "Susan," though the latter was only five years younger), Anthony always felt overshadowed. On a lecture tour in the 1870's, she wrote home: "I miss Mrs. Stanton, still I cannot but enjoy the feeling that people call on *me.*" At Susan's seventieth birthday celebration, Mrs. Stanton gave the major address, brilliant and humorous as always, and paid tribute to her friend's role in prodding her to action. "Dear friends," she said, "I have had no peace for forty years. . . . She has kept me on the warpath. . . ."[77]

Though Mrs. Stanton had playfully begged for a few quiet years free from Susan's tyranny, she died first, leaving Susan still feeling inadequate after fifty years: "I am too crushed to speak. If I had died first she would have found beautiful phrases to describe our friendship, but I cannot put it into words."[78] She continued active and, at eighty-four, made her second trip to Europe to help organize an international conference of women. In 1906 she attended her last woman suffrage convention and left her message for the future: "Failure is impossible." She died that year at eighty-six, having achieved worldwide recognition but not her lifelong goal.

In the lives of these three women are reflected all of the influences that converged in the antebellum period to provide the impetus for a women's movement: the tenets of liberal theology, which emancipated women (and men) from the restraints of orthodox Protestantism; efforts at social, political, and economic reform, which produced high expectations and greater opportunities for women, as well as feminist consciousness-raising; and, most important, radical abolitionism, which provided a powerful human rights argument as well as a crucial support group. The careers of the three also indicate how gifted and motivated women can channel frustration and anger into organized protest in an era when the possibility of social change exists.

All three women were able to become leaders in reform because they avoided the enslavement of the traditional marriage relationship—Anthony by shunning marriage, Stone and Stanton by choosing non-traditional husbands. By combining family and public work, the latter two set new patterns for future generations of women. All three shared their society's belief that woman's primary responsibility was to the home, but insisted that she have equality in that home, as well as access to the broader world.

A closer look at the beliefs of the three also provides insights into the divisions and subtle differences in the movement. Sharing a common feminist ideology, the leaders differed in style and personality. Stanton, who understood the need for a radical upheaval of social customs and attitudes, was always too bold for her times. Stone, sensitive to the oppression of women by orthodox religion and conventional marriage, came close to Stanton's analysis; she backed away from a direct confrontation on these issues, however, and was more driven by a romantic faith in the moral regeneration of her society. This view placed her in the mainstream of her generation of feminists. Anthony, more willing than Stanton to limit her goals and narrow her focus, was also more practical and realistic than Stone. Of the three, she adjusted best to the demands of the postwar era. None of the three, coming to feminism with middle-class perceptions, dealt seriously with the obstacles which women faced because of class and economic situation, rather than sex. Only Stanton, tilting against windmills in her increasingly conservative society, sensed that abolishing the slavery of sex would be an even more formidable task than ending chattel slavery.

NOTES

1. Elizabeth Cady Stanton's description of herself in her youth; interview, *Sunday Herald*, Jan. 22, 1899, copy in Elizabeth Cady Stanton Papers.

2. Samuel May, Jr.'s eulogy, *Woman's Journal*, Jan. 22, 1887.

3. Rev. A. Battles, quoted in *Lily,* Mar. 15, 1855.

4. *Blackstone Chronicle,* in Blackwell Family Papers, LC; *National Anti-Slavery Standard*, Dec., 1853.

5. Blackwell, *Stone*, pp. 282, 90.

6. Lucy Stone speeches, in *Lily,* Feb. 15, 1856, and "Workers for the Cause," ca. 1888, Blackwell Family Papers, LC.

7. *History of Woman Suffrage,* 1:165.

8. Blackwell, *Stone,* p. 20.

9. Lucy Stone to Francis Stone, Aug. 31, 1838, Blackwell Family Papers, LC; Stone to Stephen and Abby Foster, Mar. 25, 1846, Kelley-Foster Papers, AAS.

10. Antoinette Brown to Lucy Stone, "Winter '46 or '47," and A. B. Blackwell Autobiography, Blackwell Family Papers, RC.

11. Lucy Stone to Antoinette Brown, 1850; reminiscences of Mary Head, a former servant, Blackwell Family Papers, LC.

12. Blackwell, *Stone,* p. 65.

13. Lucretia Mott to Richard and Hannah Webb, May 14, 1849, Garrison Papers, BPL; Lucy Stone to Antoinette Brown, June 9, 1850, Blackwell Family Papers, LC; Stone to Lucretia Mott, 1850, Alma Lutz Collection.

14. Lucy Stone, address to Friends Moral Reform Society, 1850, and early, undated essay, "The Province of Woman," both in Blackwell Family Papers, LC; *Liberator,* Apr. 20, 1849, May 27, 1853.

15. Lucy Stone's "Speech to Colored People," Oct. 28, 1853, in Cincinnati *Daily Times,* copy in Blackwell Family Papers, LC.

16. Lucy Stone to S. B. Anthony, Mar. 3, 1854, and Stone to H. B. Blackwell, Oct. 22, 1854, Blackwell Family Papers, LC.

17. Lucy Stone speeches: "Woman's Duties and the Relation of the Sexes," *Chicago Tribune,* Nov., 1853; "Woman's Rights," Cincinnati *Daily Times*, Oct. 28, 1853; "Woman's Rights," *New York Tribune,* 1852; copies of all in Blackwell Family Papers, LC.

18. Lucy Stone speech, "Woman's Sphere," *Lily*, Dec. 15, 1855; speech to committee of Massachusetts Senate, Mar. 6, 1857, Blackwell Family Papers, LC.

19. Lucy Stone to H. B. Blackwell, Jan. 4, 1857, Blackwell Family Papers, LC; Elinor Rice Hays, *Morning Star; A Biography of Lucy Stone, 1818–1893* (New York: Harcourt, Brace & World, 1961), pp. 144–45.

20. The description is in Thomas Wentworth Higginson, *Letters and Journals of Thomas Wentworth Higginson, 1846–1906*, ed. Mary Thacher Higginson (Boston: Houghton Mifflin, 1921; reprinted, New York: Da Capo Press, 1969), p. 60. See also Elinor Rice Hays, *Those Extraordinary Blackwells* (New York: Harcourt, Brace & World, 1967).

21. H. B. Blackwell to Lucy Stone, Aug. 24, 1853, Jan. 3, July 12, May 6, 1854, Blackwell Family Papers, LC.

22. H. B. Blackwell to Lucy Stone, July 12, Jan. 22, Dec. 22, Jan. 3, 1854; Lucy Stone to H. B. Blackwell, 1854?, all in Blackwell Family Papers, LC.

23. Hays, *Stone*, pp. 121–22; Lucy Stone to H. B. Blackwell, Apr. 26, 1856, Blackwell Family Papers, LC.

24. Lucy Stone to H. B. Blackwell, Oct. 22, 1854, Blackwell Family Papers, LC; Higginson, *Letters*, pp. 60–63; protest is in Blackwell Family Papers, LC.

25. Robert Dale Owen (1832) and John Stuart Mill (1851) had made similar protests; see *History of Woman Suffrage*, 1:294.

26. A. B. Blackwell Autobiography, Blackwell Family Papers, RC.

27. Lucy Stone to E. C. Stanton, Oct. 22, 1855, Elizabeth Cady Stanton Papers.

28. Lucy Stone to S. B. Anthony, Sept. 7, 1856, and Stone to H. B. Blackwell, May 1, 1893, Blackwell Family Papers, LC.

29. The press comment on Blackwell is quoted in Lucy Stone to S. B. Anthony, May 30, 1855, ibid.; *Lily*, June 1, 1855.

30. Lucy Stone to S. B. Anthony, July 30, 1856, July 20, 1857, Aug. 26, 1858, Blackwell Family Papers, LC.

31. *History of Woman Suffrage*, 1:554.

32. Blackwell, *Stone*, p. 285.

33. Aileen S. Kraditor, *The Ideas of the Woman Suffrage Movement 1890–1920* (New York: Columbia University Press, 1965), p. 7.

34. M. C. Wright to Elizabeth McClintock, Jan., 1850, Wright Family Papers, SC; *History of Woman Suffrage*, 1:464; cf. Theodore Tilton's essay on Stanton in Parton et al., *Eminent Women*.

35. H. B. Stanton to Elizabeth Cady, Jan. 1, 1840, Elizabeth Cady Stanton Papers. See Stanton, *Eighty Years and More*, and Alma Lutz, *Created Equal, a Biography of Elizabeth Cady Stanton, 1815–1902* (New York: John Day, 1940).

36. Stanton, *Stanton*, 2:11.

37. Stanton, *Eighty Years*, pp. 20, 74.

38. Lutz, *Stanton*, p. 96; S. B. Anthony to Elizabeth Smith Miller, Mar. 2, 1901, Smith Family Papers, New York Public Library. Harriet Stanton Blatch and Alma Lutz, *Challenging Years; the Memoirs of Harriot Stanton Blatch* (New York: G. P. Putnam's Sons, 1940), pp. 16, 18.

39. Stanton, *Eighty Years,* p. 44; Stanton, *Stanton,* 2:40, 318.

40. See Weld et al., *Letters,* 1:53, and Lucretia Mott to Oliver Johnson, Dec. 30, 1839, Garrison Papers, BPL.

41. *History of Woman Suffrage,* 1:407; Lucretia Mott to Elizabeth Cady Stanton, Mar. 23, 1841, Elizabeth Cady Stanton Papers.

42. See Lydia Maria Child to E. C. Stanton, Mar. 24, 1863, Elizabeth Cady Stanton Papers; and Hallowell, ed., *Mott,* p. 211.

43. H. B. Stanton to E. C. Stanton, Feb. 15, 1851, Elizabeth Cady Stanton Papers.

44. Stanton, *Eighty Years,* p. 147; cf. Andrew Sinclair, *The Better Half; The Emancipation of the American Woman* (New York: Harper & Row, 1965), pp. 58–59.

45. Stanton, *Stanton,* 2:21.

46. E. C. Stanton to S. B. Anthony, Apr. 2, 1852 (Stanton, *Stanton,* 2:41), and June 10, 1856, Elizabeth Cady Stanton Papers; Lutz, *Stanton,* p. 102; E. C. Stanton to S. B. Anthony, June, 1859, Elizabeth Cady Stanton Papers.

47. Stephen Foster to E. C. Stanton, Aug. 21, 1860, Elizabeth Cady Stanton Papers. For a typical speech, see *Liberator,* May 18, 1860.

48. See H. B. Stanton to E. C. Stanton, Jan., 1861, and her 1860 speech "The Slave's Appeal," Elizabeth Cady Stanton Papers. The tour is described in Harper, *Anthony,* 1:211; *Liberator,* May 26, 1865; E. C. Stanton to W. L. Garrison II, Dec. 5, 1899, Garrison Family Papers, SC.

49. Elizabeth Cady Stanton speech on "Free Speech," Feb., 1861, Elizabeth Cady Stanton Papers.

50. *Revolution,* Feb. 4, 1869; E. C. Stanton to Elizabeth Smith Miller, Oct. 22, 1852, Elizabeth Cady Stanton Papers; Stanton, *Stanton,* 2:67; E. C. Stanton to E. C. Stanton, Jr., May 3, 1880?, and Stanton to Martha C. Wright, Apr. 22, 1863, both in Elizabeth Cady Stanton Papers.

51. Stanton, *Stanton,* 2:60, 72; E. C. Stanton to S. B. Anthony, Dec. 23, 1859, Elizabeth Cady Stanton Papers.

52. Harper, *Anthony,* 1:66; Stanton, *Stanton,* 2:35–36; E. C. Stanton to Lucy Stone, Feb. 23, 1854, Blackwell Family Papers, LC.

53. Martha Wright to Elizabeth McClintock, Jan., 1850, Wright Family Papers, SC; E. C. Stanton to Margaret, Dec. 1, 1872, and interview by Haryot Holt Cahoon, 1898, both in Elizabeth Cady Stanton Papers.

54. *Lily,* Nov., 1851.

55. Lutz, *Stanton,* p. 244.

56. Stanton, *Stanton,* 2:210, 183.

57. See E. C. Stanton speech to electors of the Eighth Congressional District, Elizabeth Cady Stanton Papers.

58. Lutz, *Stanton,* p. 202.

59. Harper, *Anthony,* 2:665; Lutz, *Stanton,* pp. 296–97, 233; Funeral Address by Moncure Conway, 1902, Elizabeth Cady Stanton Papers.

60. *Revolution,* June 30, 1870.

61. Harper, *Anthony,* 3:1601; *Revolution,* June 30, 1870.

62. See Sinclair, *Better Half*, pp. 74–76.

63. *History of Woman Suffrage*, 1:461; S. B. Anthony to Elizabeth Smith Miller, Mar. 2, 1901, Smith Family Papers, NYPL.

64. Harper, *Anthony*, 1:204.

65. Ibid., 2:921–23; Susan B. Anthony Diary, Apr. 9, 13, 1854, Susan B. Anthony Papers, RC; Stanton, *Eighty Years*, p. 161.

66. S. B. Anthony to her mother, Mar. 7, 1849; Anthony Diary, Apr. 2, 1854, Susan B. Anthony Papers, RC.

67. A. B. Blackwell Autobiography, Blackwell Family Papers, RC; Harper, *Anthony*, 1:84–85.

68. Lutz, *Stanton*, p. 74; Harper, *Anthony*, 1:157, 100.

69. S. B. Anthony speech on temperance, given summer and autumn, 1852, Susan B. Anthony Papers, Radcliffe.

70. Harper, *Anthony*, 1:272, 133, 154; S. B. Anthony to Abby and Stephen Foster, Apr. 20, 1857, Kelley-Foster Papers, AAS.

71. Anthony speech, "Woman's Rights," 1854; speech on temperance given to Woman's N.Y. State Temperance Society, Winter, 1853, Susan B. Anthony Papers, RC; Harper, *Anthony*, 1:84.

72. A. B. Blackwell Autobiography, Blackwell Family Papers, RC; Harper, *Anthony*, 1:75.

73. S. B. Anthony to E. C. Stanton, June 5, 1856, Elizabeth Cady Stanton Papers (emphasis mine); Anthony speech, "Woman's Rights," 1854, Susan B. Anthony Papers, RC.

74. S. B. Anthony to E. C. Stanton, June 5, 1856, Elizabeth Cady Stanton Papers, and Anthony to A. B. Blackwell, Apr. 22, 1858, A. B. Blackwell Autobiography, Blackwell Family Papers, RC.

75. Harper, *Anthony*, 1:108, 2:644.

76. Ibid., 2:899; Lutz, *Stanton*, p. 304.

77. Lutz, *Stanton*, p. 318; Harper, *Anthony*, 2:667.

78. Lutz, *Stanton*, p. 318.

4

The Feminist-Abolitionists in Profile

ELIZABETH CADY STANTON, writing in 1870 about her former friends in the "other" wing of the newly reorganized women's movement, referred to them as "daughters of the Puritans."[2] Though her tone was sarcastic, her observation was a precise acknowledgment of the importance of cultural roots. To understand the origins and the broad sweep of ninteenth-century feminism, one must go beyond its few major leaders to a larger group of women activists and look for patterns that link their personal histories to their public roles as reformers. How did family, early environment, and religion combine to shape their social vision? To what extent were inherited beliefs and childhood values transformed by the forces of mid-nineteenth-century society? What shared characteristics defined them as a unique group?

Fifty-one women have been chosen for study in order to answer these questions. All were members of the "first generation"—those feminist-abolitionists who initiated the first public defense of women's rights in the antebellum period, organized the first associations, called the first conventions. All but five were born before 1825.[3] The large majority were active as organizers and propagandists; thity-seven were among the conveners of the 1850's conventions.[4] Several, like Lydia Maria Child, had assumed leadership roles earlier and now remained on the sidelines;[5] others were important initially as women in new roles.[6] Nine of the group —including important suffragists like Mary Livermore, Harriet Robinson, and Isabella Beecher Hooker, all of whom had earlier been involved with antislavery and other reforms—became leaders of the women's movement only in the 1860's.

These women constitute a representative, but not all-inclusive, group of feminists active in antebellum reform. Many interesting women are excluded because of inadequate biographical sources. Important feminists like Frances Wright and Margaret Fuller remain outside the scope of this study because they were not involved in the organized movement and died just as it was taking off. The exclusion of other antebellum reformers like Mary Gove Nichols, whose free-love ideas shocked and alienated her feminist contemporaries, is consistent with their exclusion from the movement.[7] No black women have been included because they played only a peripheral role in organized feminism, although they were important as abolitionists (and several came from backgrounds similar to those of their white counterparts).[8] No attempt has been made to achieve homogeneity; the two women whose backgrounds are strikingly different serve to accentuate the strong similarities that mark the remainder of the group.

A group portrait of the feminist-abolitionist women must start with the influence of their Puritan-Yankee heritage. Many of their lifelong values, and prejudices, derived from their early upbringing and inherited traditions. Most early feminists traced their ancestry back to seventeenth-century Puritan and Puritan-derived Quaker families. The idea of a "city upon the hill" was part of their cultural heritage. Their grandparents belonged to the generation of the Revolution, and the granddaughters were brought up with great reverence for the ideal of a Christian Republic in which educated, virtuous citizens exercising responsible benevolence would be the mainstay of the nation.[9] Like most nineteenth-century reformers, they had abiding faith that the world could be brought closer to perfection, and that they were the ones chosen to effect this transformation.

Of the fifty-one women chosen for this study, thirty-three could claim New England ancestry, all but one reaching back to the seventeenth century. Twenty-four of this group were actually born in New England; seven hailed from New York, and one each from Ohio (Frances Gage) and Canada (Laura Haviland). Of the eighteen non-New Englanders, five came from old New York and New Jersey families and five from families who settled Pennsylvania. (Four were Quakers and a fifth, Jane Swisshelm, came from a Scotch-Irish family.) Four women came from the South: the Grimké sisters migrated to Philadelphia as young women; Sarah Pugh's Quaker mother moved the family from Virginia to Philadelphia in 1803, when Sarah was three; Amanda Way's family, also Quakers, left South Carolina in 1817 for Indiana, where Amanda was born. Two women were born in England: Elizabeth Blackwell migrated with her family to New York in 1832, at the age of eleven; as an adult Elizabeth Comstock moved first to Canada, then to a Quaker anti-slavery settlement in Michigan.

The two atypical feminists are Mathilde Anneke and Ernestine Rose, both born in Europe and the only non-Protestant members of the group. Anneke, born into a German Catholic family, came to Wisconsin in 1849 with the "Forty-Eighters," refugees of the 1848 revolution. Rose, from a Jewish Eastern European background and the daughter of a rabbi, came to New York in 1836. Both renounced their religion to become freethinkers, thus strengthening their anomalous position among their sister reformers.

The feminist-abolitionist women enjoyed not only a solid ancestry, but also a comfortable class position, although their involvement in reform often meant a fall in both status and income. The fathers of seventeen were wealthy businessmen or professional people. The large majority, twenty-nine, came from comfortable middle-class or upper-middle-class homes: the fathers of four were ministers, two were teachers, the remainder farmers, mechanics, and small merchants and shopkeepers. Only four were raised in relative poverty—three because of the early deaths of their fathers (Harriet Robinson, Sarah Pugh, Jane Swisshelm); the fourth because her father was a chronically poor reformer (Abby Hopper Gibbons).[10]

The women in this group expressed pride in belonging to "the better class," although they took care to remember that this entailed responsibilities as well as privileges. This consciousness of class embraced both a nationalistic pride in their Yankee roots and a Puritan sense of duty; it was an important element in their psychological makeup, as well as in their ideas and rhetoric. Their sense of heritage gave them an aura of righteousness and superiority, but it also contributed to feelings of security and self-confidence which enabled them to survive in the face of hostility and disapproval. Though they lived in a period of social upheaval, they generally appeared optimistic and confident, rather than anxious or threatened. While others of their class spent considerable time deploring the passing of old customs and values, the feminist-abolitionists directed their energies to creating a republic consistent with the ideals of their ancestors. Conservative in upholding old virtues—such as the importance of the family as the central institution of society—in a time of change, they were radical in demanding changes consistent with these virtues—such as the emancipation of women as a means of elevating family and society.

Their diaries, memoirs, and letters reveal this sense of heritage and special mission. Their language is peppered with references to "the best people" and appeals to "the noblest class of men and women." Quaker families often tried to overcome this elitism in their children; Lucretia Mott's parents sent her to a public school in order to "mingle with all classes without distinction and avoid 'class pride.'" Class pride, however, remained a distinguishing characteristic of this group. Harriot Hunt, brought up in Boston's North End in the first decades of the century, recalled in 1856 that her life had begun "at a period in the republic when substance had not given way to shadow; when the distinction between wealth and happiness was seen and accepted; when prudence, intelligence, and economy were considered household virtues." After visiting the family of Antoinette Brown in western New York, she expressed gratitude that "out of such noble homes, and from such true parentage had arisen advocates of the woman movement; these homes of freedom are like the shadows of rocks in a weary land." Hunt saw these "noble" men and women not as a disappearing class, but as harbingers of new happiness and freedom for "the weary land."[11]

To these reformers, New England (and especially Massachusetts) was, in the words of Angelina Grimké, "the moral lighthouse of our nation." This ideal was carried over from earliest antislavery days into the postwar suffrage movement. In the first issue of the *Liberator,* Garrison explained that he had chosen to raise the banner of emancipation in the most likely place, "within sight of Bunker Hill and in the birthplace of liberty." Maria Weston Chapman, speaking to a group of Massachusetts antislavery women, admonished, "Let us all feel the responsibility which devolves upon the advanced guard of humanity." Lydia Maria Child, whose ancestors settled in Massachusetts in 1636, wrote to Elizabeth Cady Stanton during a dark period of the Civil War, asserting that she trusted in God and comforted herself with the thought that "he did not bring the Mayflower here for nothing. The spiritual cargo it brought was leaven for a Continent. . . ."[12]

Above all, Massachusetts was expected to be in the forefront of the battle for women's rights. As Henry Blackwell predicted in 1858, "There, where the standard of womanhood is highest, where *character* is most prized because most developed, where human rights are household words, and where the revolutionary spirit burns most brightly, there we will *win for women absolute equality before God and the law.*" This optimistic prophecy was not fulfilled, and Massachusetts became a bulwark of antisuffragism in the post-war period.[13]

The early feminists also shared nineteenth-century America's romantic vision of the West as a place of freedom and promise. Elizabeth Cady Stanton, working for suffrage in Kansas in 1867, wrote to her husband that life there was open and free, not like the "contracted eastern existence."[14] Nineteen of the fifty-one women actually joined the national migration and lived in the West during at least part of their lives. Most moved west because their families sought greater economic opportunity; Elizabeth Blackwell's father, for example, moved his family to Cincinnati after serious losses in the depression of 1837. A few, like Mary Livermore and Clarina Howard Nichols, went to Kansas with the antislavery migration of New Englanders in the 1850's.

When they moved west, the feminist-abolitionists brought their New England prejudices with them. Frances Gage, who moved from Ohio to Missouri in 1853 (and returned home in 1860), praised the West as a place with "much less of conservatism and rigid adherence to the old-time customs of law and theology." She never forgot, however, that New England was the birthplace of antislavery. She liked to say that her role in the West was "to arouse woman there to her duties and responsibilities, that she may sympathize more fully with her Eastern sisters, who caught the first glow of the sunrise hours of our great reform movement." Jane Elisabeth Jones, who migrated to Ohio in the 1840's to work for antislavery, also felt that Westerners were backward in terms of duties and responsibilities.

She told Abby Kelley that they were *"mean,* destitute of principle, unstable . . . they can never be depended upon. . . ." Even the antislavery people, she wrote, were "mere half-abolitionists."[15]

A few New Englanders returned happily to their mecca after their sojourns in the West. Mary Livermore, whose family started for Kansas in 1857 but settled in Chicago, urged Garrison to come to a suffrage convention in 1869 by reminding him: "We look to Massachusetts as the brain and conscience of the country. . . ." The following year the Livermores returned to Boston. Lucy Stone, contemplating a return to Massachusetts after years of residence in Cincinnati and New Jersey, wrote Antoinette Blackwell: "You know I belong there, body, soul, and estate." Caroline Severance, born in western New York and exiled to the frontier town of Cleveland when she married in 1840, eagerly seized the opportunity to move to Boston in 1855 so that her children could have the "best schools" and she could have the company of "noble women." Massachusetts, she said, had been the "home of my heart always."[16]

The class consciousness of the feminist-abolitionist women combined with their genuine humanitarian concerns to produce a paternalism which spurred them to work for the poor and oppressed, but also hindered their understanding of the problems of the working classes. Elizabeth Buffum Chace, whose husband was a well-to-do Rhode Island mill owner, concerned herself with the living conditions of Chace's mill girls, even insisting on the establishment of part-time schools. She lectured on the working conditions of New England factory operatives and argued that it was the responsibility of the manufacturers' wives and daughters to "raise up" these girls. The "better class" of factory workers should also help those less fortunate. In the 1870's, when there was talk of striking for a ten-hour day, however, Mrs. Chace viewed this demand as "ungrateful" behavior on the part of "ignorant" people.[17]

Susan B. Anthony also took an interest in her father's female employees. Although she was more sympathetic than most feminists to the grievances of working women, even Anthony carried with her the values and attitudes of the upper classes. At eighteen, when her father's business collapsed after the panic of 1837, she wrote in her diary: "I do not think that losing our property will cause us ever to mingle with low company." In 1862 she urged Elizabeth Cady Stanton to send her children to the public school, where they could mix with the lower classes and learn "to resist evil" at an early age: "I believe those persons stronger and nobler who have from childhood breasted the commonalty."[18] Several years later, she tried unsuccessfully to convince a group of New York City working women that suffrage was a more important demand than shorter hours or improved working conditions. In the case of Anthony, as well as Chace and most other feminists, their sense of responsibility toward what they perceived as inferior classes combined with their feminist concern to produce an attitude of "maternalism," rather than paternalism.

At its worst, the Yankee chauvinism of the feminists often bordered on nativism, although this was seldom translated into action. The undemocratic tendencies of the later suffragists have been publicized, but similar biases existed in the earlier generation as well, although not as pervasively. For the most part, the feminists' strong sense of justice and sympathy with the oppressed led them to oppose all efforts to harass foreigners and restrict immigration; their language, nevertheless, revealed their prejudices. Amelia Bloomer, who in the 1850's moved first to Ohio and then to Iowa, had high praise for Council Bluffs because "the people who settle here are mostly from the east, and are nearly all Americans; subsequently we have an intelligent, well-ordered community."[19]

Mary Livermore's attitudes were also typical. Born in Boston's North End, she grew up in a family which cherished the sacred memories of the fight for the Republic. Her father had been born at the close of the Revolution and was brought up with "ecstatic love of country." The language of her autobiography, written in 1899, betrays the attitudes acquired in her youth and is in conflict with her lifelong crusade for democratic ideals: the mill town of Fall River, where she lived briefly after her marriage, "was a more desirable place of residence than now, for the people were almost wholly Americans." Of the campaign for a state liquor law in the 1850's, she said that only "exceptional women, the low and foreign born, the illiterate," were opposed to it. Livermore was one of the few in the group who publicly supported immigration restriction when it became a controversial issue in the 1890's; she asserted that "the constant overflow of European nations of their undesirable citizens into the country was a constant menace to our republic." She also talked of the "genius of Anglo-Saxons" in one of her most popular lectures, arguing that Anglo-Saxons were one of the "strong races" because they had proved their character and endurance. Elsewhere she described her utopia, where the Golden Rule would govern all relations: "It will then be possible for an inferior race to live comfortably amid dominant Anglo-Saxon people, with no danger of being enslaved or destroyed by them."[20]

Another Yankee reformer who worried about threats to Anglo-Saxon dominance was Elizabeth Blackwell. Opposed to birth control as immoral and unnatural, she also viewed it as a danger to the nation. One effect of the rapid spread of "Neo Malthusianism," she wrote to Lucy Stone in the 1880's, was "checking the growth of what may be called legitimately the native American race—so that ne-groes and foreigners are gradually supplanting the better stock."[21]

Elizabeth Cady Stanton was more open on the subject of birth control, and more typical of the group in continuing to oppose legislation which would restrict immigration. In her last years, however, she supported American imperialism in the Philippines, once more creating friction among the old abolitionist group. William Lloyd Garrison, Jr., chastised her for "vaunting of the Anglo-Saxon supremacy" and showing the "barbarism of our forefathers with their Calvinistic conceit and bigotry." In defense, she cited the superiority of Anglo-Saxon civilization and asked rhetorically: "What would this continent have been if left to the Indians?"[22] The prejudices of feminist-abolitionists were undoubtedly height-ened in the conservative atmosphere fostered by late nineteenth-century Social Darwinism, but those sentiments had their roots in the culture in which the women were raised.[23]

The group's attitudes toward the Irish illustrate the tensions and conflicts in their ideology. Their egalitarian impulse and romantic defense of the oppressed were here at war with their class paternalism and evangelical Protestant distaste for Catholicism. Although the feminists usually succeeded in overcoming their anti-Catholic feel-ings, and they supported the Irish nationalist movement in the 1830's and 1840's, religious and class differences ultimately stood in the way of true rapport. They also opposed vigorously all forms of Know-Nothingism in the antebellum period. Their language, how-ever, often revealed the basic mistrust of the Catholic church that characterized so much of Protestant America in the nineteenth century. Abby Hopper Gibbons, nursing the wounded during the war, thanked God for Protestant women who could sympathize with suffering humanity and deplored "the cold intercourse of Catholic nurses, who are the machinery of an Institution, and do not minister to the broken-down in spirit."[24] There was also an element of racism in their attitude toward the Irish, who were perceived as foreign and non-Anglo-Saxon, as well as Catholic and lower class. This combination of prejudices imposed an enormous strain on the women's humanitarian ideals.

In their daily lives, the feminist-abolitionists came into contact with the Irish mostly via the latter's role as servants to the growing urban middle class. Here again, their genuine concern for the victims of poverty and injustice coexisted with the women's impatience with the apparent ignorance and intractability of the lower classes. The "servant problem" was important to women who tried to manage large households and also lecture on antislavery and women's rights, and the reformers' letters frequently referred to the trials involved in supervising their "Irish girls." Elizabeth Cady Stanton felt responsible for alleviating poverty in Ireland as well as at home, and she acted the lady bountiful among the Irish of Seneca Falls, who were "always ready to serve me." She complained constantly, however, about "some stupid Hibernian" who had burned the pudding or the "daughters of Erin" who were more trouble than her children.[25]

There was, of course, diversity in their responses. Angelina Grimké deplored the "feeling of aristocracy" visible even among Friends, and she disapproved of the "aristocratic arrangement" which separated servants from the family. All the abolitionists' efforts to elevate the poor had failed, she wrote in 1838, because "we visit them as unfortunate *in*feriors, not as our *suffering equals*." In the 1840's Abby Kelley agonized about the "inhuman" treatment accorded Irish servants, and the state of slavery to which they were often reduced. Her husband, however, writing a few years later, expressed extreme reluctance about allowing an Irishwoman to clean the house "without some person of taste and order to oversee." He was also looking for a "Yankee man" to help with the farm because the Irish, though plentiful, were incompetent.[26]

The *Woman's Journal* in the postwar years incorporated these personal prejudices into its feminist philosophy. Advocating enlightened family leadership as a means of elevating society, it pleaded for

American women to go into domestic work because "the ignorant, foreign help now occupying the field are a positive element of demoralization and barbarism in a household." Mary Livermore edited the *Journal* in this period and shared the views of the Stone-Blackwell family and the majority of the feminist-abolitionist group; she became interested in the idea of cooperative housekeeping as a way of avoiding immigrant servants who were "ignorant, thriftless, wasteful, insubordinate, unteachable."[27]

In contrast to their anti-Irish prejudices, the views of the feminist-abolitionists toward black Americans were enlightened by nineteenth-century standards. Elizabeth Buffum Chace, aristocrat supreme, objected to the marriage of the black abolitionist William Wells Brown to an Irishwoman because she was beneath him socially. Chace and her daughter later resigned from the Rhode Island Woman's Club because it excluded black women. The Grimkés made a point of planning Angelina's wedding as an interracial affair and, in later years, openly acknowledged and supported three black nephews, illegitimate sons of their brother Henry. Lydia Maria Child was one among many abolitionist women who publicly protested the Massachusetts law barring racial intermarriage; her own friendships and associations crossed racial lines. Lucretia Mott's group of Philadelphia antislavery women included members of the middle-class free black community, and Abby Hopper Gibbons was, in 1841, the only white member of the black female Manhattan Anti-Slavery Society.[28]

The ties of friendship between blacks and whites in the antislavery movement were strengthened by the parallel positions of blacks and women (though such ties were strained in the postwar period). Elizabeth Cady Stanton explained that her empathy with the Negro was based on the common oppression of women and slaves. On the death of Frederick Douglass, who had been a close friend and early supporter of the feminists, Stanton wrote, "Suffering myself from the slights cast upon me because of my sex, I loved him as he loved me because of the indignities we both alike endured." Earlier, in 1884, Stanton had courted unfavorable publicity by publicly congratulating Douglass on his controversial marriage to a white woman. Only Susan B. Anthony's more cautious stance prevented Stanton from reading her letter to Douglass at the women's rights convention that year.[29]

These liberal racial views were not, however, free from the feminists' New England sense of superiority and self-righteousness. The many women who worked with freedmen after the war were expressing strong humanitarian concern, but their sympathy was tinged with the desire to mold the ex-slaves in the New England image. Lydia Maria Child, discussing the importance of land for the freedmen, typically expressed the hope that it would be sold to them rather than given away because "it is more salutary to all classes of people to *earn* a home than to have it *given* to them." Even the most compassionate women tended to act as patronizing benefactors. Sallie Holley, praising the war work of her friend Emily Howland, wrote of "your poor, precious contrabands."[30] The Puritan upbringing of the Garrisonians helped make them the conscience of the nation, but it also inclined them to conservative economic views and limited their social vision.

The feminist-abolitionist women were products of family influences and childhood experiences, as well as of class and culture. The data support some generalizations about the group and provide a few (albeit inconclusive) clues to explain their drive toward reform.

As one might expect, a large number of the women—twenty-two of the fifty-one—grew up in families which were sympathetic to antislavery and other radical social reforms. Many feminist-abolitionists were the daughters of well-known antislavery men whose involvement in the movement began early—Arnold Buffum, Gerrit Smith, Isaac Hopper, Myron Holley, and Daniel Anthony. The father of Mary Frame Thomas and Hannah Longshore was a descendant of an old Pennsylvania Quaker family, and was associated with Benjamin Lundy in pre-Garrison antislavery days; he moved his family from Maryland to Ohio in 1833 to escape the proslavery environment.[31] (The group of fifty-one women under study includes Thomas and Longshore, who were half-sisters, and three other pairs of sisters.) Usually, the entire family was involved with antislavery and other reforms for a good part of their lives. Maria Weston Chapman's three sisters as well as Henry Chapman's family; Elizabeth Buffum Chace's parents, her two sisters and their husbands; Susan B. Anthony's parents and sisters; the families of Betsy Cowles, Abby Hutchinson, Abby May, and others all participated in reform movements.

Since these antislavery homes were meeting places for reformers from all parts of the country, the women grew up with spirited discussions of reform and religion as their daily fare. More than most young people of the middle class, they learned sharing and sacrifice, and witnessed Christian principles in daily practice. Their earliest memories invariably included the experience of sheltering fugitive slaves. For this group, the mandate to resist injustice was inherited along with the family Bible.

One would expect abolitionists (like the parents of Susan B. Anthony and Antoinette Brown) to be sympathetic to their daughters' aspirations and to support their feminist activities. With a few important exceptions, this was true. (Lucy Stone's father subscribed to the *Liberator* and the *National Anti-Slavery Standard* but refused to send his daughter to college. Mary Grew's father was an abolitionist but an antifeminist who opposed the seating of his daughter and other women at the 1840 London meeting.[32]) Matilda Joslyn Gage's father, a physician who was a constant host to intellectuals and abolitionists in his New York home, directed the education of his daughter, an only child, and encouraged her precocious tendencies. He personally taught her mathematics, Greek, and physiology, and then sent her to a private institute to complete her formal education. Caroline Dall's father also taught his daughter from an early age —she was reading at two—until tutors and private schools took over. When they lived in Maryland, Mary Frame Thomas's father regularly took his daughters to the capital to listen to political debates. Harriot Hunt and her sister Sarah, who also became a physician, were encouraged by their parents to read widely, to take an interest in public affairs, and to educate themselves to their highest potential.[33]

Among the group as a whole, about half received some parental support for their feminism, even though the families of some of those women were not active in reform themselves. Six families are known to have objected to their daughters' reform activities. At least two women, Child and Stanton, received encouragement from other relatives. Lydia Maria Child's older brother Convers Francis, a Unitarian minister, was the most important family influence in her early life; she lived and studied in his home for a number of years and probably converted to Unitarianism under his guidance. Elizabeth Cady Stanton was drawn into reform through the influence of her cousin Gerrit Smith, and the Smith family continued to be a source of support and inspiration to Stanton, as well as to Susan B. Anthony and other reformers.[34]

While such an impression is difficult to document in detail, the fathers and mothers of these feminists seemed to play equally important roles in their families. The typical nineteenth-century family was undoubtedly more like Lucy Stone's, with the mother playing a subservient role while the father made most of the decisions. One would expect the fathers of these women to play a more influential role in their lives, by virtue of their dominant role in the family. Elizabeth Cady Stanton's father, for example, was a strong force in the family and in her life. More typically, however, the feminist-abolitionists remember mothers as well as fathers as being strong influences and active participants in family decisions, a pattern which the daughters generally repeated in their own families. Mary Livermore recalled that her parents shared family responsibilities, and that her mother was consulted on all important matters. Her father, a devout Baptist, prayed daily to "bless the united heads of the family." The religion which Mary ultimately chose, Universalism, was closer to the creed of her mother, who believed that morality was practical good living.[35]

This observation is not as surprising as it may seem at first glance. The feminist women inherited intelligence and personality traits from both parents. The mother of Abby and Julia Smith was described as a remarkable woman, an amateur poet, linguist, mathematician, and astronomer. (The Smiths' father was also a distinguished scholar.) Frances Gage recalled that her mother and grandmother were interested in reform and encouraged her as a girl to aid fugitive slaves. The large number of families expressing sympathy for abolitionism and feminism also indicates that those husbands might be expected to view their wives as equals, and impressionistic evidence seems to confirm this possibility.[36]

The fifteen feminists who grew up in Quaker homes—eight of which were active abolitionist families—were provided with the role models generally denied to other women. They were accustomed to seeing women speak in church on an equal basis with men, and to watching them play a more active role in the home as well. Quaker women ministers were permitted to travel about the country without their husbands, an unusual display of female independence.[37] By providing these early examples, Quakerism became an important training ground for feminism. Abby Hopper Gibbons's mother was a Quaker minister, and Laura Haviland's mother was an elder in the Society of Friends. The Quaker mother of Lucretia Mott and Martha Wright was a Nantucket fisherman's wife who managed both family and business during her husband's extended absences. Mott attributed her feminism to this double heritage of self-reliance: "I grew up so thoroughly imbued with women's rights," she said many times, "that it was the most important question of my life from a very early day."[38]

Quakerism was a training ground for feminism in other important ways. Quaker parents, unlike most of their middle-class contemporaries, believed in educating their daughters and training them for usefulness. Lucretia Mott, Abby Kelley, and Susan B. Anthony supported themselves by teaching while still in their teens. This was only one of the many ways in which Quaker girls gained the early experience of being part of an unconventional, and unpopular, minority. Partly because of external pressures, Quaker children were raised with a strong sense of community and group consciousness, no small help in facing the hostile world as reformers. Elizabeth Buffum Chace recalled that she and her sister attended a public school in Connecticut, where they were jeered by other children for their plain clothes and speech. Even the teachers were disapproving when, following Quaker custom, they refused to curtsy to their elders.[39] The Quaker emphasis on fidelity to conscience encouraged the women's self-reliance and "strong-mindedness" as adults.

Other women grew up with widowed mothers who supported their families and also served as models of self-reliance. Harriet Hanson Robinson's mother was an impressive woman, a Universalist with liberal ideas in her youth and an active suffragist in her later years. Harriet, following her mother's example of independence, went to work in the Lowell mills at the age of ten to help support the family; she was the only one of this group of feminists to have this experience. A few mothers, such as Harriot Hunt's, went beyond the role of model and actively supported their daughters' careers. Others were themselves active in reform. As a young woman in the 1830's, Jane Swisshelm helped her widowed mother obtain signatures on petitions to abolish slavery in the District of Columbia.[40]

Many of the mothers were obviously independent-thinking persons with whom their daughters could identify. Others, however, like Lucy Stone's mother, played very traditional roles. The diversity in these patterns is again a reminder that the individual qualities of the feminists must be considered at least as important as their early environments. Their life experiences after childhood were also influential in shaping their decisions. Many gained freedom and encouragement for their feminism in their marriages. The unmarried women (and many of the married as well) found support in close female friendships. All the women were sustained by their feminist-abolitionist network.[41]

The one generalization that can be made is that all fifty-one women were remarkably educated for women growing up in the mid-nineteenth century. The economic position of most of their families made private education possible at a time when public schooling beyond the early grades was not yet widely available for women. Many families obviously placed a high value on their daughters' education. Perhaps most important was the fact that all of these women were of above-average intelligence and strong willed. Most were precocious as children. Those whose parents were reluctant to finance their schooling either overcame these parental objections or acquired an education on their own, with the same dogged determination they exhibited in their reform work.

Of the fifty-one women, forty-one are known to have acquired above-average educations. Many had tutors and attended female seminaries which were generally conservative in their goals but which usually offered a good classical education. Mary Livermore, for example, studied French, Latin, and metaphysics at a private Baptist seminary. The fifteen who were Quakers received their educations in Friends' schools noted for their emphasis on a high standard of education for both sexes.[42] Only Stone and Antoinette Blackwell graduated from college, but six others—Elizabeth Blackwell, Hannah Tracy Cutler, Hannah Longshore, Clemence Lozier, Ann Preston, Mary Frame Thomas—attended professional medical schools. Three women—Amelia Bloomer, Frances Gage, Jane Swisshelm—are known to have received only limited formal schooling but were undoubtedly self-taught, because they were among the twelve who became important editors and writers in the women's movement. There is scant information about the early schooling of seven, but these, too, show evidence of having acquired good educations. Harriet Robinson, for example, read omnivorously while working in the mills as a child, and she attended school when she could. She later worked for reform as an editor and writer; her literary efforts include memoirs of her Lowell years and a history of the suffrage movement in Massachusetts, as well as novels and plays.

All of the women hungered for more education than was easily available to them and found ways of acquiring it. Hannah Tracy Cutler studied Latin with the family doctor while she was in her teens. Thwarted in her desire to attend Oberlin and pushed into marriage at eighteen, she subsequently studied theology and law with her first husband. After his death (at the hands of an anti-abolitionist mob while helping a fugitive slave), she supported her children by writing and teaching. At the age of thirty-one she finally enrolled in Oberlin and studied there while also running a boardinghouse. Later, after a second marriage, she earned a medical degree and practiced medicine. This extraordinary level of motivation and persistence was typical of the whole group.[43]

Though most of the women were well educated and grew up in comfortable homes, a striking number had youthful experiences which made them acutely aware of the limitations of women's roles. Most were characterized as "rebellious" and "strong-minded" because they insisted on sharing in their brothers' play and work. They were, as Louisa May Alcott described herself, "born with a boy's spirit under my bib and tucker."[44] Bright and achieving, most had been told by a parent: "What a pity you were not a boy!" This is a constant theme running through their reminiscences of childhood. Mary Livermore's father, observing his daughter playing at being a preacher, commented that if only she were a boy, he would educate her for the ministry. Frances Gage liked to tell her audiences that, as a girl, she had been mechanically inclined, but her father, seeing her at work making barrels with the cooper on their farm, sent her into the house to do woman's work. His comment: "What a pity that you were not born a boy, so that you could be good for something."[45]

Lucy Stone was not the only "disappointed woman" from her first years. Sarah Grimké wrote to Harriot Hunt in 1852 that "the powers of my mind have never been allowed expansion; in childhood they were repressed by the false idea that a girl need not have the education I coveted." Her father denied her request to study law, while commenting that she would have made a great jurist "if only she had been a boy." Emily Howland, precocious and intellectual, was forced to leave school at sixteen and take over the household because of her mother's poor health. Bored and frustrated, she complained, "I am as a bell that cannot ring," and once signed a letter "Emily Howling." Elizabeth Oakes Smith, who became an important writer as well as a feminist, was an unusually precocious child who started school at the age of two, read the Bible fluently at five, and had a mental breakdown from overwork at six. Trained to duty and obedience in a "Puritan childhood," she gave up her dream of attending college and, at her mother's insistence, married at sixteen. After marriage she rose early each morning to read and study. Smith "folded my wings," she wrote later, but never recovered from this deprivation. She was happy that her children were boys, because girls' lives must always be "arrested" and "abridged." She attributed her own feminism, and indeed the whole suffrage movement, to the "compression" suffered in a submissive, Puritan upbringing.[46]

Certainly it is not surprising that propagandists for women's rights emphasized this type of early experience and pointed to it as the source of their feminist indignation. But it also was natural for bright and determined young women to have hopes and ambitions that would not be fulfilled, especially in a period of social change and great expectations for the country as a whole. The young Elizabeth Cady, unhappy because the laws were hard on married women, could dream of changing these laws because other institutions were toppling and other groups were experiencing new power and opportunity. Lucy Stone, frustrated at her failure to merit the same education as her brothers, could aspire to a college education because it was now a possibility. This generation of women faced unique opportunities, as well as traditional obstacles.

The pattern of frustration and opportunity appears again and again in the lives of the feminist-abolitionist women, with these opposing forces serving to reinforce each other. Women like Susan B. Anthony, who were raised in supportive and egalitarian families, were first exposed to the reality of being female when they left the shelter of home, usually to teach. At least half of this group taught for some part of their lives, usually on completion of their education and before marriage (the pattern for most women teachers), but often in order to finance further education. This employment opportunity existed because of the burgeoning public school systems in mid-nineteenth century. Invariably, though, the experience of being paid a good deal less than men for the same work made the women acutely aware of their low status (a status which ultimately affected the whole teaching profession because of its association with women). Lucretia Mott was paid half the salary received by the men in her school; recalling her indignation, she said later: "I early resolved to claim for myself all that an impartial Creator had bestowed." Most of the feminists gave up teaching because they found it narrow and unsatisfying, as well as low paying. They tended to move to reform or to other work still considered in the male domain. Harriot Hunt, who turned from teaching to medicine, complained that the stigma attached to the former work prevented a woman from doing her job well and left her "pinched, degraded, condemned, accused, weary, and miserable." Here again, frustration resulted from opportunity, and in turn led to a further expansion of woman's role.[47]

A number of forces were clearly impelling unusual women into new roles. However, the religious impulse of these women caused them to become reformers, rather than to assert their independence and individuality in other ways. No other element is as important in understanding the motivation which sustained them through long careers. This absorption with religion appeared early in their lives; many ventured out of woman's proper place even as children by playing at being preachers, as if preparing themselves for lives as missionaries of reform. Mary Livermore enjoyed delivering sermons to her playmates or, in their absence, addressing logs arranged in rows in the woodshed. Abby May corralled her brothers and sisters into sitting through Sunday afternoon services which she conducted from an improvised pulpit and which included hymns, prayers, and sermons.[48]

Ironically, reform became the main religion for most of them, replacing formal church-going as a means of expressing their faith. This process was hastened by the hostility of the churches to abolitionism and feminism. The relationship of religion and reform was spelled out in a typical abolitionist appeal to American women: "We are born into the world for a *purpose* . . . we are here to do good as we have opportunity: to save what was lost . . . this is our religion, and it is all the religion we have." The goal of their religious faith was the redemption of society. Abby Hutchinson, who was part of a well-known singing family that toured the country for antislavery, avowed that "the best religion is that which makes the best society." Susan B. Anthony was the outstanding illustration of this marriage of reform and religion. Single-mindedly devoted to her cause, in her later years she told an interviewer that work and worship had been one with her. She prayed every second of her life, she said, but with her work rather than on her knees. "My prayer is to lift woman to equality with man."[49]

The beliefs of the group tended to be eclectic, rather than narrow and doctrinal. From their Puritan forebears they inherited a sense of mission and devotion to duty. The evangelical fervor of the period in which they grew up served to remind them of this mission, and of the urgent need for redemption from sin. From the small but growing liberal faiths like Unitarianism they learned that men and women could come close to perfection in *this* world, and that the salvation of society was as imperative as individual redemption. All responded warmly to the Quaker preference for the dictates of inner conscience over external dogmas and rituals. Many were also influenced by the Transcendentalists' romantic vision of the divinity in human beings, and of the power of men and women to transcend their human limitations and strive for the ideal. Their actions and beliefs were a response to the complex dynamics of mid-nineteenth-century thought, and the growing availability of alternative religious paths.

A striking fact about this group of feminists is that they subjected traditional Protestant beliefs to intense scrutiny and repeated re-examination. As a result of this skepticism, they moved consistently away from orthodox Protestantism in all its forms, making no distinction between evangelical and other sects, and toward more liberal denominations and beliefs. They particularly rejected the Calvinist doctrine of infant damnation and the traditional scriptural view of women. This liberation from orthodox dogma, and from their society's evangelical emphasis on sin and damnation, was a crucial element in the development of the women's movement (as is confirmed by a recent study documenting the close correlation between the evangelical beliefs and antifeminism of a group of non-Garrisonian antislavery women).[50] Also typical was the feminist-abolitionists' estrangement even from more liberal sects because of their radical activities.

This pattern of change is evident in the women's personal histories. Fifteen came from Quaker homes, and six were already Unitarians or Universalists, the adopted churches of their families. The largest group, of twenty-seven, grew up in orthodox or evangelical faiths.[51] Of this number, only one—Clemence Lozier, a Methodist—is known to have remained active in her father's church. Twenty-one rejected orthodoxy; the course of the other five is not known. Of the twenty-one, nine affiliated with Universalism or Unitarianism. The Grimkés became first Quakers, then non-churchgoers. Amelia Bloomer avoided much of the harshness of Calvinism by moving from Presbyterianism to an Episcopalian affiliation. Nine either remained without formal affiliation (like Elizabeth Cady Stanton) or joined a radical religious group (like Caroline Severance, who left the Presbyterian church and, with her husband and other antislavery people, organized an Independent Christian Church). This pattern is repeated in the broader feminist-abolitionist movement.[52]

Some generalizations can be made about all the women, regardless of doctrinal affiliation. All felt "called" to a special vocation, usually at an early age. This sense of mission set them apart from their contemporaries, often even from their families. Even those who severed all formal religious connections did so for Puritan reasons —the church had not kept faith with its ideals. The Puritan belief that men and women are born into the world for a purpose was a central element in these feminists' world-view. That belief had special meaning for urban, middle-class women in mid-nineteenth century because the work that had occupied their grandmothers was now being done by others in factories and schoolrooms, and by servants at home. The prospect of fashionable idleness was revolting to women who took seriously the dictum that work was the way to serve God. This became a rallying cry of the movement—women must have useful work to do, even if this meant upsetting traditional ideas. As Susan B. Anthony was fond of saying, "Woman must take to her soul a purpose and then make circumstances to meet that purpose."[53]

The purpose which the feminist-abolitionists chose, and the work to which they devoted a good part of their lives, was no less than the regeneration of the world. The Grimkés epitomized this sense of calling and special mission. Angelina wrote, for instance, in 1836: "I feel as if I was given up to travel in the Cause. . . ." Others expressed the idea as well. Harriot Hunt felt that she had been called to practice medicine and wrote in her autobiography: "I saw God's appointed designs wonderfully worked out in my life." In the 1840's Clarina Howard Nichols told Susan B. Anthony of her involvement in the women's rights cause: "I knew, *I always feel*, that God has set me apart for this service: all the providences of my life have conspired to qualify me for & place me in the very van of these reforms." As a young widow, Elizabeth Comstock kept a shop to support herself and her child, but she gave it up after several years because "I feel I have a call for other work than shopkeeping." A Quaker minister, she traveled the country as a missionary in all good causes—on behalf of slaves, women, prisoners, the poor, soldiers during the war, and freedmen afterward.[54]

Religious crises, especially following the death or illness of a close relative, were often significant turning points in the women's reform careers. Sarah Grimké left her home for Philadelphia shortly after her father's death. Abby Kelley vowed to devote greater effort to reform following the death of her father, and Sallie Holley, in similar circumstances, moved to find a more serious purpose in life. Lucretia Mott preached for the first time following the death of a child, and Elizabeth Buffum Chace plunged into antislavery work after the death of her first five children. Harriot Hunt saw her sister's recovery from a serious illness as a sign that they were to devote their lives to curing the sick.

The feminists all had confidence that their work was part of a benevolent, divine plan. Elizabeth Buffum Chace, recovering from a nearly fatal illness, wrote, "My faith in the good purpose that runs through all, so perfectly satisfied me, that I was sure that whatever became of *me*, would be just what was best for me." Lucy Stone, who might have been speaking for the group, requested that these lines be part of her funeral service: "Not on a blind and aimless way/ The spirit goeth."[55]

Though all of the women rejected orthodox dogma, they retained a Calvinist absorption with duty and an evangelical sense of life as a battle with evil. Mary Livermore viewed her life as a long struggle: "There has always been some good thing to strive for and to win; or some evil to be suppressed or rooted out." Lucy Stone, explaining her decision to be an antislavery lecturer, wrote to her mother: "There are no trials so great as they suffer who neglect or refuse to do what they believe is their duty." She ackowledged that the trials of reformers were great also, but added: "But 'without the shedding of blood there is not remission for sin.' " Lydia Maria Child, who vehemently protested the hashness of Calvinist doctrine, nevertheless wrote: "Whoso does not see that genuine life is a battle and a march, has poorly read his origin and his destiny. . . ."[56]

The reminiscences of John Hooker, husband of Isabella Beecher Hooker and a well-known reformer himself, illustrate how Puritan indoctrination can persist even after orthodox theology has been rejected. Hooker describes in great detail how he gave up belief in the Trinity and adopted "liberal Christianity." He came to see God as a loving Father, he said, and Christ as a human being with special spiritual qualities. The Bible became legend and history to him, rather than the Word of God. His sole requirement as a declaration of faith was belief "in the Fatherhood of God and the Brotherhood of Man." At the same time, he explained that God had chosen, in his wisdom, not to create perfection in the world because "it is for man's highest good that he *work out* his own salvation. If everything were done for us, we should always remain mere children." "Man" was to be saved, after all, by his character, and the key to this salvation was a life of duty and earnest work: "God meant that we should all suffer together, as if we were one large family, thus imposing upon us all the duty of looking out for our fellowman and his needs."[57] Here is the eclecticism of the typical reformer: the Puritan sense of duty, the evangelical zeal for salvation, and the Universalist belief that all men and women are to help each other to salvation as one family under the benign direction of a loving God.

Although the women retained strong remnants of Puritanism, the orthodox churches became anathema to most of them for several reasons. One grievance was shared by members of all denominations—the failure of the churches to take a stand against slavery. Seven of the fifteen Quaker women left their church for this reason, including Abby Kelley and Martha Wright (who were expelled) and Elizabeth Buffum Chace and Abby Hopper Gibbons (who resigned). Others, like Lucretia Mott and Susan B. Anthony, were alienated from the Friends but never formally resigned. Even the liberal churches were found lagging, although in general they offered the most support for both abolitionism and feminism. Frances Gage was the only one in the group who actually broke with the Universalist church over the slavery issue. The Free Will Baptists, as well as the Unitarians and Universalists, also provided a home for many of the first women ministers.[58]

The orthodox tenets relating to women, as reflected in both the theology and the institutional aspects of the church, made early rebels out of many of the feminists. They were especially offended by the relegation of their sex to an inferior place in spiritual and moral matters. Orthodoxy was intolerably narrow and binding on the spirits of all people, but especially on women. Elizabeth Oakes Smith felt that her whole life was shaped by her childhood as a "Puritan maiden" trained to marry early and serve her husband; she had been expected to bury all passion under "a vast substratum of Duty." Paulina Wright Davis was never happy, she said, until "I outgrew my early religious faith, and felt free to think and act from my own convictions."[59]

The women who grew up in orthodox homes felt most enslaved by the Calvinist belief in hell and human depravity. The spectre of infant damnation was especially burdensome in a period of high infant mortality. Coming to maturity in a period of widespread revivalism, the feminists were exposed to an intense barrage of hellfire and doom and grew up with feelings of guilt and inner torment. Each went through a period of doubt and religious crisis, and was ultimately emancipated by the discovery of more liberal faiths. Their reminiscences reveal again and again this process of torment, questioning, and then release. Caroline Severance remembered that, as a child, she was constantly haunted by visions of torture of those doomed to eternal punishment. Her marriage into an antislavery family freed her from "bondage to authority, dogmas, and conservative ideas."[60]

Mary Livermore's recollection of her conversion experience was more detailed but typical. Her father's preoccupation with sin and salvation left her with anxiety and guilt. She brooded over the possibility of damnation, and was tormented about the prospects for her three siblings who died in infancy. The death of a close sister when Mary was eighteen proved a pivotal point in her life. Out of a desperate need for comfort, she turned to the Bible, and with great relief marked passages that seemed to refute the doctrine of eternal punishment. With characteristic resoluteness she intensified her study of Greek in order to read the New Testament in the original and confirm her discoveries. Of this period she wrote: "I hardly dared to breathe it to myself, for I supposed I was the only person in the world who doubted the accepted belief." Her final release came when she wandered into Boston's Universalist church and came to know the man she later married, the Reverend Daniel Parker Livermore, who preached the goodness of man and the lovingness of God.[61]

Antoinette Brown's case was a special one. She was one of five women in the group who became ministers, but while the others were Quakers, she was ordained in an orthodox faith. Growing up in a warm, accepting family that practiced a compassionate brand of Calvinism, she had experienced relatively little conflict or need for rebellion. When she assumed her duties as the first female Congregationalist minister in 1853, she found that she could neither accept nor preach eternal punishment and infant damnation. This situation brought on her religious crisis, relatively late in life (she was twenty-eight). Voluntarily resigning her pulpit after only a year, she spent several years in emotional and intellectual turmoil, looking for rational arguments to replace religious dogma. During part of this period she worked with Abby Hopper Gibbons, helping the poor in the slums of New York City and in prisons and hospitals of the area. She eventually rejected orthodoxy and found a new faith built, as she described it, on "belief in *practical service,* in *justice,* and *a few moral principles.*" She ultimately became a Unitarian minister and a convert to "the law of love."[62]

Their new beliefs freed the women to take responsibility for their own actions and opened a realm of new possibilities. Though they were responsive to the Quaker belief in the inner light, they tended to reject the Quaker exaltation of spirit over reason. They were attracted instead to the Unitarian emphasis on human rationality and free will. Reflecting the influence of Enlightenment ideas on liberal religious thought, most feminists believed that God was revealed through natural laws, and that, through knowledge of these rational forces governing the universe, men and women could perfect themselves and their society and do God's will. Lucretia Mott preached, for example, that intellectual light was a guide to spiritual truth.[63] The women's passion for self-improvement through knowledge and reason helps to explain not only their faith in education, but also their involvement with causes, like phrenology and spiritualism, which seem more irrational. They were all viewed as a means of extending the boundaries of knowledge and helping men and women to achieve their highest God-given capabilities.

The doctrines of the liberal churches were also more compatible with the concept of Christian Republicanism. The Universalist church particularly emphasized the belief that Christ had died for all men and women, not only for the few elect. The democratic assumptions implicit in this creed were especially appealing to women who had found the traditional churches oppressive. In their reform work they stressed the idea of citizens voluntarily joining together to eliminate the evils and imperfections of their society. This emphasis reflected their religious beliefs, as well as their faith in the Republic.[64] The eclecticism of their ideology was, inevitably, not without its tensions. Their faith in democratic religion was at war with their sense of divine calling, but this conflict generally went unexamined. The feminists were activists, not philosophers.

Like others in the nineteenth century who gave up orthodoxy, the feminists felt liberated from worry about the hereafter and were free to focus their energies on this life. An incident involving Sallie Holley, who converted from Methodism to Unitarianism, reveals this sense of spiritual security. A woman in her audience expressed encouragement for women lecturers: "We shall one day be where the wicked cease from troubling and the weary are at rest." "Oh," Holley responded, "I'm there already; I've arrived." Virtually all the feminist-abolitionists (excepting Ernestine Rose) believed in the immortality of the spirit and thought of "the other side" as a place of happy reunion. Antoinette Brown Blackwell said she was "as sure of this as of life itself." Toward the end of their lives, they comforted each other with this belief. Mary Livermore wrote to Elizabeth Chace: "It is good to have no fear of death." Just before her own death, Sarah Grimké wrote that she believed there would be room for her immortal spirit to make progress, even in heaven —a true reformer to the end.[65]

The feminists' rejection of the concept of infant damnation also helped them to bear what was a constant trauma for nineteenth-century parents: the death of children. For unmarried women, the death of nieces and nephews brought similar sorrow. Few in the group were spared this grief, but the blow was softened by faith that God was loving and would care for their children until they could be reunited. Daniel Livermore comforted bereaved parents by reminding them that God had "infinite wisdom and love"; he asked parents to think of their children not as dead, but as alive unto God, living in heaven, "waiting our arrival there."[66] The indomitable optimism of these men and women helped them to survive and pour still greater energies into reform.

Theodore Parker, the Unitarian minister and reformer who was close to the Transcendentalist circle in Boston,[67] personified the religious beliefs of the group and exercised a strong personal influence over the many who attended his sermons and came to know him as a friend. Abby May, who was brought up in Unitarianism, considered Parker the strongest influence in her life. He made a deep impression on Mary Livermore in her period of conversion, and Elizabeth Buffum Chace also credited him with helping her abandon her belief in hell. Julia Ward Howe, who was a "zealous Calvinist" until her marriage but later attended Parker's church, said of him: "Truly he talked with God, and took us with him into his divine presence." Sallie Holley called herself a "Theodore Parker Unitarian."[68]

After Parker's premature death, a number of his followers, including several in this group, organized the Free Religious Association to continue his teachings. Caroline Severance described as the purpose, "to unite all honest searchers after the essentials of the universal, in religion and in life." Lydia Maria Child, who found all religions too narrow and sectarian, left a bequest to the Free Religious Association in order to "continue to help a little the cause of truth and freedom." Lucretia Mott addressed the first session, along with Ralph Waldo Emerson and Robert Dale Owen. Exhorting her listeners to preach the truth, she predicted that in time all religions would be one, "and there will come to be such faith and such liberty as shall redeem the world."[69]

Theodore Parker's ideas on women further illuminate the attraction of liberal religions for feminists. In 1853 he gave a lecture on "The Public Function of Woman," in which he asserted his belief that woman "has the same nature, right, and duty, as man" and therefore the same right to "use, shape, and control" the four institutions of "Family, Community, Church and State." The "popular theology" (i.e., orthodoxy) suffered, he said, from the lack of the feminine influence; no woman would ever have preached infant damnation or supported the idea of human depravity or even clerical celibacy. Because women had been cut off from participation in the church, theology had left "nothing feminine in the character of God"—a circumstance which he deplored. Parker liked to think of God as embodying both feminine and masculine attributes, a concept very amenable to his feminist followers. In her reminiscences Julia Ward Howe praised him as the first minister "who in public prayer to God addressed him as 'Father and Mother of us all.' "[70] The concept of a "Father-Mother God" was used by Elizabeth Cady Stanton and other feminists as an argument for woman's equality with man, especially in response to the common antifeminist claim that Eve's fall had doomed all women to a subservient position.[71]

Not only Theodore Parker but also Emerson, Margaret Fuller, Bronson Alcott, and others of the Transcendentalist group were important influences. The feminists were attracted by their idealistic vision of man (and woman) as a free, responsible individual called to a life of high purpose by the spirit of God within him (or her). Lydia Maria Child, a close friend of Fuller's, rejected the Bible as the source of all truth: "If we want truth, we must listen to the voice of God in the silence of our own souls as he [Christ] did." She praised Transcendentalism for going beyond Unitarianism, and for not only demolishing old falsehoods but also striving "to build anew." Emerson's stress on self-reliance and the need for all men and women to be free to reach their highest capabilities was highly compatible with feminism, as was his belief in women's special moral sensibilities. Lucy Stone confessed to reading Emerson's essays over and over again, finding them "full of light, of beauty, and of glorious truth."[72] Margaret Fuller especially was looked on as a heroine because of her accomplishments and her commitment to the women's cause; her death in 1850 frustrated many feminists' hopes that she would become a leader of the women's movement.[73]

Quakerism proved to be an even stronger religious influence on the feminist-abolitionists, and the fifteen women who were raised in Quaker families had a special kind of preparation for their careers. Lucretia Mott, Laura Haviland, Elizabeth Comstock, and Amanda Way became ministers. (Ironically, at least one, Laura Haviland, was attracted as a young girl to local revival meetings in western New York; she attended against the wishes of her parents, who desired her to be moved by "settled principle not mere excitement."[74]) The Quaker women were spared the need to rebel, as other women had, against a fundamentalist interpretation of the Scriptures. Quakers were accustomed to seeing women preach in meeting and were taught that, spiritually, at least, women were equal with men. Women had an equal claim to ministry in the church and took reciprocal vows as part of the marriage covenant.[75] The Quaker belief that "in Christ Jesus there was neither male nor female" was the earliest argument used in defense of the rights of abolitionist women. The spirit and beliefs of the Friends were important in the antislavery movement, but were even more relevant to the feminist cause.

Feminists brought up in other faiths often attended Quaker services and were impressed with the roles women were allowed to play. After Harriot Hunt, a Universalist, heard Lucretia Mott speak at a Yearly Meeting of Friends in 1851, she wrote, "I shall never forget this gathering and it impressed me with the power and capacity of woman, and convinced me that she was able to legislate for herself." Gerrit Smith was similarly moved: "The Quakers are the best people I have ever known . . . no people make so little difference as they do, between man and woman." Because of compatible beliefs, all of the Garrisonians felt closer to their Quaker compatriots than to any other group. Lydia Maria Child noted, "In many respects my own views are so similar to the Friends, that I can have better sympathy with them than with any others." Quaker leaders were constantly pointed to when the movement required examples of women who had long been accustomed to acting outside their domestic sphere without losing their womanly qualities. Susan B. Anthony, in an 1854 speech, reminded her audience that Quaker women had discharged their duties as ministers and elders since the founding of the Society. Were they, she asked rhetorically, "any less decorous in their manners, less affectionate in their natures, or less christian in their daily lives . . .?"[76]

The influence of Quaker religion among feminists went beyond the example of its women. Most important was the concept of "inner light," making the individual, rather than the church, the center of moral authority. Lucretia Mott liked to speak of "the inward monitor which speaks in the name of God." Women as well as men were encouraged to take stands as individuals when their religious principles were threatened; this enabled them to "come out" of their churches and rely on the force of their own consciences. Garrison, Abby Kelley, and others who led the movement out of the church were acting on the Quaker principle of inner light. Susan B. Anthony, responding to widespread condemnation of Garrison as a heretic, noted that he was "the most Christ like man I ever knew" because he practiced Christian benevolence instead of being "bound to creed and dogma."[77]

Though the Society of Friends was superior to other religions in its respect for women, it was not perfect, as many feminists learned when they attempted to take part in the decisions of their church. Abby Hopper Gibbons, who announced her resignation publicly after her husband and father were expelled for their antislavery work, condemned the meeting also because women were being ruled by "Men Friends." The Grimkés, when attacked by the Congregationalist ministry, chose to base their defense on human rights, rather than on Quaker tenets. As Angelina explained, Quakers regarded women "as equal to men on the ground of *spiritual gifts,* not on the broad ground of *humanity.* Women may *preach:* this is a *gift;* but woman must *not* make the discipline by which *she herself* is to be governed."[78]

Elizabeth Comstock, an outspoken Quaker minister, was in close touch with her sister in England and encouraged the latter to assume greater responsibility in her church. Upon hearing that the English group had only one Yearly Meeting, a men's meeting (rather than two "equal" meetings for men and women, as was the American custom), she was appalled: "For our Society, of all others, to allow the self-styled 'Lords of the Creation' to arrogate so much to themselves, is *outrageous.* We profess to be the only pure democracy in the world—men and women being *one*—on an absolute equality in the Lord Jesus, is one of our fundamental doctrines." In a speech in England in 1874, she exhorted the women to stop deferring to men and to "take their proper places, and use the gifts that God has given them."[79]

Lucretia Mott also complained that Quaker women had to obey laws made by men, but she realized the importance of the church as a training ground for women. Writing to Abby Kelley, who objected to the separation of the sexes in general meetings, she sympathized with her friend's grievance but concluded: "And yet their meetings of women, imperfect as they are, have had their use, in bringing our sex forward, exercising their talents, and preparing them for united action with men, as soon as we can convince them that this is both our right and our duty."[80] As usual, her perceptions were clear and prescient, and her influence an inspiring yet moderating one.

An interesting aspect of the group's tendency to see a oneness of religion and reform was the gravitation of many toward spiritualism, a very popular "ism" in the mid-nineteenth century. The feminist-abolitionists wanted to believe that communication with spirits was possible, and therefore they were generally interested in and open to this suggestion, a heretical idea to orthodox believers. Of the fifty-one, only Ernestine Rose took a known stand in opposition, although Lucretia Mott was uninterested in the hereafter and unromantic about its possibilities. Most found it appealing, and a few were ardent followers. Following the approach of Robert Dale Owen, the best-known convert to spiritualism in this country, the women justified the inquiry as a rational effort to extend the limits of knowledge. In addition, Owen saw that spiritualism could serve as a powerful lever of reform by encouraging self-improvement in anticipation of eternal rewards, presumably reinforced by communication with the spirit world.[81] To the feminist-abolitionists, spiritualism also offered the happy possibility of continuing their efforts to make the world better from the other side.

Lydia Maria Child, like many in the group, was fascinated by spiritualism but wavered between skepticism and belief. Unhappy with even the more liberal faiths, she was constantly searching for a belief that would satisfy her religious and reform yearnings. A self-proclaimed "free spirit," she sought in spiritualism a literal confirmation for the freedom of the spirit. In the early 1850's, because Garrison had finally become convinced of the reality of the spirit world after receiving messages from an old friend, Child asked him to put her in touch with a reliable medium so she could observe a "fair test." Several years later she described the satisfying results of such a test: she was "cheered by 'gossip' from the Spirit world" but still "distrustful, to an extreme degree." Spiritualism was "tantalizing to the yearnings of the soul," however, and her own yearnings continued. She suggested to Garrison that perhaps they could view the progress of the world better from yonder, "and perhaps be enabled to *help* better, too." In 1877 she was still trying to investigate the subject rationally; she was certain that there were universal laws governing spiritual phenomena that had occurred, but unsatisfied with the explanations she had thus far seen.[82]

Most of the feminist-abolitionists were eager to believe but, like Abby Kelley and Stephen Foster, approached spiritualism cautiously. After a séance in 1857, Stephen was impressed but still "not prepared to acquiesce in the correctness of that theory." Abby consulted a clairvoyant about an illness of Stephen's, and followed her prescriptions because they seemed "so reasonable." Others were more easily convinced. Like non-reformers, many feminists took up spiritualism after a bereavement. Elizabeth Buffum Chace hoped to communicate with her "lost babes." All the Blackwells were interested in the phenomenon, and after Lucy's death Henry Blackwell sat night after night, hoping in vain for a message from her. Mary Livermore became an enthusiastic spiritualist in her later years and wrote a friend that people everywhere "are hungering and thirsting for a *certainty* of knowledge about the other life." After her husband's death she was comforted by the prospect of hearing from him, and a year later she was satisfied that she had received, through a medium, an authentic communication. Paulina Wright Davis had similar experiences.[83]

Two of the most ardent and proselytizing spiritualists were Isabella Beecher and John Hooker. The two became converts in the 1870's, possibly because of the death of their son, and regularly reported receiving communications from friends on the other side. They considered the movement of supreme importance to the progress of the world. In a paper on "Spiritualism and Good Morals," written in 1897, Isabella Hooker argued that spiritualism went far beyond orthodox Christianity in deterring vice and encouraging good deeds. The suffering and remorse reported by the spirits of deceased sinners had a "practical effect" on the living. At the same time, the spirits were not condemned to everlasting punishment, because they, too, could reform themselves, with help and encouragement from the living. Reform and religion were inseparable, even in the next world.[84]

The world-view of all the feminist-abolitionists, whether spiritualists or not, embraced both religion and reform. The most concrete statement of this philosophy was made by Julia Ward Howe at the end of her long career. In her journal she recounted a vision which came to her one night, of the great work which women were to do in the regeneration of the world. Aided by good men, they would work like bees "to unwrap the evils of society and to discover the whole web of vice and misery and to apply the remedies." In the glow of the light born of human endeavors, she saw "the men and the women, standing side by side, shoulder to shoulder, a common lofty and indomitable purpose lighting every face with a glory not of this earth." Then she saw the victory. All evil and misery were gone, and mankind "was emancipated and ready to march forward in a new Era of human understanding."[85] This was not the raving of an eighty-nine-year-old woman, but the religious philosophy which guided her and her compatriots from antislavery days.

This first part of the investigation into the lives of these "daughters of the Puritans" reveals a striking series of common characteristics. The earliest force in their lives, the heritage of their New England ancestors, exerted a pervasive influence on their lifelong beliefs and attitudes. They inherited a sense of duty as well as superiority, and an identification with the revolutionary vision of a Christian Republic. The women's early training inclined them toward humanitarian endeavors and defense of human rights; however, it also tended to make them a conservative elite which was dedicated to upholding the traditions of family and community and which behaved condescendingly toward those of a different class and background. Paradoxically, their humanitarian zeal and strong sensitivity to injustice also inclined the women toward an impressively liberal racial attitude, although this, too, was tinged with the usual paternalism of reformers. Because their racial attitude embodied a romantic view of the oppressed slave, the parallel they saw between the fates of women and slaves created a natural, sympathetic bond.

Since most New Englanders did not become either abolitionists or feminists, other cultural forces were also clearly at work on those who did. As this group of women grew up in mid-nineteenth-century America, they were affected by both positive and negative influences. Their parents tended to be supportive and to permit them an unusually good education. The atmosphere of social change and exciting new opportunities for the average man offered encouragement, and the widespread religious revivalism provided inspiration. New opportunities for women in the teaching profession were also available, and some small hope existed that higher education would soon open its doors to the female sex.

These very circumstances also proved a source of frustration for ambitious, strong-minded, and talented young women. The feminists experienced rejection, even by their own families, when they stepped too far out of woman's sphere. They experienced humiliation at the hands of the orthodox churches, and disappointment in the low pay and inferior status accorded women teachers. The opportunities in higher education were token ones, and the growing professions were clearly becoming male enclaves. Such obstacles confronted all women who tried to broaden their place in society.

This particular group of feminists reacted uniquely to these challenges. From an early age, they resolutely believed that they had been "called" to a role that transcended the domestic sphere. They displayed extraordinary persistence and determination to free themselves from the constraints imposed by society, exhibiting unusual initiative in liberating themselves from the harshest doctrines of Calvinism and in searching for faiths more compatible with their optimistic beliefs. They were aided in this quest by the example of their Quaker colleagues, who served as models of female independence while they offered a faith that glorified the force of inner conscience over external dogma. The Universalist and Unitarian churches provided a rationalistic and optimistic view of God and humanity that encouraged the women to seek perfection in the present, as well as in the hereafter. The Transcendentalists further reinforced the feminists' romantic belief in the divine possibilities within all men and women. The inherent tension between the democratic aspects of their chosen faiths and their own elitist tendencies went unexamined in their active pursuit of their personal and social goals.

Ultimately, the religious needs of the feminist-abolitionists were met by their work—reform became their religion. During emotional crises and career difficulties, they were sustained by a belief in the rightness of their cause and a faith in their own special mission. They were secure in the knowledge that all sacrifices were justified by their ultimate goal—the regeneration of the world.

NOTES

1. "A perfect woman, nobly planned/ To warn, to comfort, and command," from William Wordsworth's "She Was a Phantom of Delight," was much quoted by the feminist-abolitionists to describe their ideal woman.

2. *Revolution,* Feb. 3, 1870.

3. See preface for complete list. All are profiled in *Notable American Women;* biographical information is from this source unless otherwise indicated.

4. *History of Woman Suffrage,* vol. 1 *passim.*

5. The Childs were active briefly during the drive for a Sixteenth Amendment; see Caroline Severance to L. M. Child and D. Child, 1868, Child Papers, BPL.

6. Elizabeth Blackwell, Hannah Longshore, and Clemence Lozier were practicing doctors in the 1850's; the latter two became active suffragists later.

7. See Harriot K. Hunt, *Glances and Glimpses* (Boston: John P. Jewett, 1856; reprinted, New York: Source Book Press, 1970), p. 140, and Joseph G. Gambone, ed., "The Forgotten Feminist of Kansas: The Papers of Clarina I. H. Nichols, 1854–1885, Part II," *Kansas Historical Quarterly* 39 (Summer 1973): 232.

8. See Sarah Parker Remond, Charlotte Forten, and Sarah Mapps Douglass in *Notable American Women* and Gerda Lerner, ed., *Black Women in White America* (New York: Pantheon Books, 1972).

9. See Lois W. Banner, "Religious Benevolence as Social Control: A Critique of an Interpretation," *Journal of American History* 60 (June 1973): 23–41.

10. Little is known of Ernestine Rose's early life.

11. Hallowell, ed., *Mott,* p. 35; Hunt, *Glances and Glimpses,* pp. 2, 300.

12. Angelina Grimké Weld to Anne W. Weston, July 15, 1838, Weston Family Papers; *Liberator,* Jan. 1, 1831, Mar. 15, 1839; L. M. Child to E. C. Stanton, May 24, 1863, Elizabeth Cady Stanton Papers.

13. H. B. Blackwell to L. Stone, May 1, 1858, Blackwell Family Papers, LC.

14. E. C. Stanton to H. B. Stanton, Oct. 9, 1867, Elizabeth Cady Stanton Papers.

15. *History of Woman Suffrage,* 1:656; J. E. Jones to S. Foster and A. K. Foster, Apr. 18, Jan. 23, 1848, Kelley-Foster Papers, AAS.

16. Mary A. Livermore to W. L. Garrison, Aug. 16, 1869, Livermore Correspondence, Boston Public Library; Lucy Stone to A. B. Blackwell, Feb. 10, 1869, Blackwell Family Papers, LC; Parton et al., *Eminent Women,* p. 381.

17. Wyman and Wyman, *Chace,* 2:146–59, 44.

18. Harper, *Anthony,* 1:34, 221.

19. Bloomer, ed., *Life and Writings,* p. 226; see also David Brion Davis,

"Some Ideological Functions of Prejudice in Antebellum America," *American Quarterly* 15 (Summer 1963): 115–26.

20. Mary A. Livermore, *My Story of the War* (Hartford, Conn.: A. D. Worthington, 1889), p. 87, and *The Story of My Life* (Hartford, Conn.: A. D. Worthington, 1899), pp. 473, 398, 686. *Melrose Reporter*, Mar. 30, 1895, Livermore Collection, Melrose Public Library.

21. Elizabeth Blackwell to Lucy Stone, Aug. 4, Dec. 28, 1888, Blackwell Family Papers, LC.

22. W. L. Garrison, Jr., to E. C. Stanton, July 26, 1899, Elizabeth Cady Stanton Papers; E. C. Stanton to W. L. Garrison, Jr., July 27, 1899, Garrison Family Papers, SC. For her views on immigration restriction, "expansion," and educated suffrage, see Stanton, *Stanton*, 2:294, 341; her article in *American Woman's Journal* (Mar.-Apr. 1895), Elizabeth Cady Stanton Papers; and Lutz, *Created Equal*, p. 314.

23. See Barbara Miller Solomon, *Ancestors and Immigrants: A Changing New England Tradition* (Cambridge: Harvard University Press, 1956).

24. Abby Hopper Gibbons, *Life of Abby Hopper Gibbons. Told Chiefly Through Her Correspondence*, ed. Sarah Hopper Emerson (New York: G. P. Putnam's Sons, 1896–97), 1:347–48; see also Gilbert Osofsky, "Abolitionists, Irish Immigrants and the Dilemmas of Romantic Nationalism," *American Historical Review* 80 (Oct. 1975): 889–912.

25. Stanton, *Eighty Years and More*, pp. 105, 146; E. C. Stanton to Elizabeth Smith Miller, June 20, 1853, in Stanton, *Stanton*, 2:52, and letter dated "1852," Elizabeth Cady Stanton Papers.

26. Angelina Grimké to Abby Kelley, Apr. 15, 1837, Kelley-Foster Papers, AAS; Weld et al., *Letters*, 2:524 (emphasis hers); Abby Kelley to Stephen Foster, Mar. 11, 1845; S. Foster to A. K. Foster, Apr. 16, 1854, Kelley-Foster Papers, AAS.

27. *Woman's Journal*, Apr. 16, July 9, 1870.

28. Wyman and Wyman, *Chace*, 2:99; Lerner, *Grimké Sisters*, pp. 358–66; Lydia Maria Child's statement to Massachusetts legislature, in Western Anti-Slavery Society Papers; Gibbons, *Life*, 1:99.

29. Stanton Diary, Feb. 14, 1897, in Stanton, *Stanton*, 2:323; Harper, *Anthony*, 2:586.

30. Lydia Maria Child to Abby Kelley Foster, Mar. 28, 1869, Kelley-Foster Papers, WorHS; Sallie Holley to Emily Howland, July 30, 1863, Emily Howland Papers, Cornell University.

31. Biographical sketch of Mary Frame Thomas, *History of Woman Suffrage*, 1:314.

32. Blackwell, *Stone*, p. 17; *History of Woman Suffrage*, 1:379–83.

33. *History of Woman Suffrage*, 1:466, 314; Caroline H. Dall, *Alongside* (Boston: T. Todd, 1900); Hunt, *Glances and Glimpses*, pp. 126–28.

34. See L. M. Child to E. C. Stanton, May 24, 1863, Elizabeth Cady Stanton Papers; S. B. Anthony to Elizabeth Smith Miller, Mar. 10, 1875, Smith Family Papers.

35. Livermore, *Story of My Life;* quotation on p. 40.

36. Elizabeth G. Speare, "Abby, Julia, and the Cows," *American Heritage* 9 (June 1957); *Notable American Women,* 2:2.

37. Cf. Janis Calvo, "Quaker Women Ministers in Nineteenth Century America," *Quaker History* 63 (Autumn 1974): 75–93; see also Sheila M. Cooper, "Quaker Women and the Nineteenth Century Women's Movement: A Social-Historical Perspective" (paper given at Thomas More College Conference on Women in World and American History, Apr. 24, 1976).

38. Laura S. Haviland, *A Woman's Life-Work* (Cincinnati: Walden & Stowe, for the author, 1881; 5th ed., Grand Rapids, Mich.: S. B. Shaw, "c. 1881"); Gibbons, *Life;* Cromwell, *Mott,* p. 125.

39. Elizabeth Buffum Chace and Lucy Buffum Lovell, *Two Quaker Sisters; From the Original Diaries of Elizabeth Buffum Chace and Lucy Buffum Lovell,* ed. Malcolm R. Lovell (New York: Liveright, 1937).

40. See Harriet Robinson Scrapbook, Harriet Hanson Robinson Papers; see also Philip S. Foner, ed., *The Factory Girls* (Urbana: University of Illinois Press, 1977), pp. 1–16. Hunt, *Glances and Glimpses,* pp. 126–28; *Woman's Journal,* Aug. 27, 1870.

41. See Judith Colucci Breault, *The World of Emily Howland* (Millbrae, Calif.: Les Femmes, 1976).

42. See Thomas Woody, *History of Women's Education in the United States* (New York: Science Press, 1929).

43. See Hannah M. Tracy Cutler's Autobiography, *Woman's Journal,* Sept. 19, 26, Oct. 3, 10, 17, 1896.

44. Louisa May Alcott, *Louisa May Alcott; Her Life, Letters, and Journals,* ed. Ednah Dow Cheney (Boston: Roberts Brothers, 1890), p. 85; see also Reminiscences of Abby Kelley Foster, Jan. 26, 1885, Kelley-Foster Papers, WorHS.

45. Livermore, *Story of My Life,* p. 70; *History of Woman Suffrage,* 2:224; see also Gage's letter, *Woman's Journal,* Mar. 31, 1883.

46. Anne Firor Scott, *The Southern Lady: From Pedestal to Politics 1830–1930* (Chicago: University of Chicago Press, 1970), p. 64; Birney, *Grimké Sisters,* p. 229; *Notable American Women,* 2:230; Mary Alice Wyman, ed., *Selections from the Autobiography of Elizabeth Oakes Smith* (Lewiston, Me.: Lewiston Journal, 1924), pp. 42, 45, 46.

47. Hallowell, ed., *Mott,* p. 38; Hunt, *Glances and Glimpses,* p. 104.

48. Livermore, *Story of My Life,* p. 70; Lucretia Crocker and Abby W. May, *Memoirs of Lucretia Crocker and Abby W. May,* ed. Ednah Dow Cheney (Boston: By the Editor for the Massachusetts School Suffrage Association, 1893).

49. *Anti-Slavery Bugle,* Nov. 28, 1845; Carol Brink, *Harps in the Wind: The Story of the Singing Hutchinsons* (New York: Macmillan, 1947), p. 273; Harper, *Anthony,* 2:859.

50. Swerdlow, "Abolition's Conservative Sisters." James McPherson, commenting on this paper, suggested "modernization" as a useful conceptual framework for both abolitionism and feminism.

51. Two in the group were not Protestant; the affiliation of Jane Elisabeth Jones is not known.

52. See esp. Lucy N. Colman, *Reminiscences* (Buffalo: H. L. Green, 1891).

53. S. B. Anthony to A. B. Blackwell, n.d., Blackwell Family Papers, RC.

54. Melder, "Beginnings," p. 199; Hunt, *Glances and Glimpses,* p. 126; Gambone, ed., "Papers of Clarina I. H. Nichols," *Kansas Historical Quarterly* 39 (Spring 1973): 14, note 8; C. Hare, ed., *Life and Letters of Elizabeth L. Comstock* (London: Headley Brothers, 1895), p. 59.

55. Wyman and Wyman, *Chace,* 2:231; Lucy Stone's quotation is from a poem by Whittier; Blackwell, *Stone,* p. 285.

56. Livermore, *Story of My Life,* p. xi; Lucy Stone to Hannah Stone, Mar. 14, 1847, and Stone to Alice Stone Blackwell, Sept. 7, 1882, Blackwell Family Papers, LC; Lydia Maria Child, *Letters from New York,* 3rd ed. (New York: C. S. Francis, 1845), p. 21.

57. John Hooker, *Some Reminiscences of a Long Life* (Hartford, Conn.: Belknap & Warfield, 1899), esp. "My Theology"; quotations on pp. 241–43.

58. See *Anti-Slavery Bugle,* Mar. 20, 1846; *Revolution,* Feb. 5, 1868; *Woman's Journal,* Nov. 21, 1874, Jan. 8, 1870.

59. Wyman, *Elizabeth Oakes Smith,* p. 42; Paulina Wright Davis Reminiscences, *History of Woman Suffrage,* 1:284.

60. Caroline M. Severance, *The Mother of Clubs: Caroline M. Seymour Severance,* ed. Ella Giles Ruddy (Los Angeles: Baumgardt, 1906), p. 55.

61. Livermore, *Story of My Life;* quotation on p. 142.

62. A. B. Blackwell Autobiography, Blackwell Family Papers, RC; see also A. L. Brown to W. L. Garrison, Sept. 19, 1854, Garrison Papers, BPL.

63. From a Mott sermon, 1836; Cromwell, *Mott,* p. 41.

64. See Ernest Cassara, *Universalism in America, a Documentary History* (Boston: Beacon Press, 1971).

65. Holley, *Life for Liberty,* p. 127; A. B. Blackwell to Mary Booth, July 18, 1876, Alma Lutz Collection; for Rose, see also S. B. Anthony Diary, Dec. 6, 1853, RC; Wyman and Wyman, *Chace,* 1:297; Birney, *Grimké Sisters,* p. 300.

66. Daniel Parker Livermore, *Comfort in Sorrow* (Chicago: The New Covenant, 1866), p. 14.

67. See Daniel Walker Howe, *The Unitarian Conscience; Harvard Moral Philosophy, 1805–1861* (Cambridge: Harvard University Press, 1970), esp. introduction.

68. May is quoted in Alcott, *Alcott;* Livermore, *Story of My Life;* Wyman and Wyman, *Chace,* 1:103–4; Howe, *Reminiscences,* p. 167; S. Holley to Emily Howland, July 22, 1857, Emily Howland Papers.

69. Severance, *Mother of Clubs,* p. 61; L. M. Child to T. W. Higginson, Feb. 21, 1871, Higginson Correspondence, Boston Public Library; Cromwell, *Mott,* p. 207.

70. Parker's speech, in pamphlet form, is in Garrison Family Papers, SC, also in *History of Woman Suffrage,* 1:277, 282; Howe, *Reminiscences,* p. 166.

71. See Lutz, *Stanton,* pp. 24, 299; Harper, *Anthony,* 3: 1264; cf. Barbara Welter, "The Feminization of American Religion: 1800–1860," in *Insights and Parallels, Problems and Issues of American Social History,* ed. William L. O'Neill (Minneapolis: Burgess, 1973), pp. 305–31.

72. Child, *Letters,* p. 78; L. M. Child to Convers Francis, Jan. 8, 1841, Child Papers, CU; L. Stone to A. Brown, 1850, Blackwell Family Papers, LC; see also Helene G. Baer, "Mrs. Child and Miss Fuller," *New England Quarterly* 26 (June 1953): 249–55; for Emerson's address to an 1855 women's rights convention, see Harper, *Anthony,* 1:132, and Holley, *Life for Liberty,* p. 149.

73. See *National Anti-Slavery Standard,* Mar. 20, 1845; Holley, *Life for Liberty,* p. 146; L. M. Child to Louisa Loring, Feb. 8, 1845, Child Papers, RC; *History of Woman Suffrage,* 2:921.

74. Haviland, *Woman's Life-Work,* p. 17.

75. See L. Mott to E. C. Stanton, Mar. 16, 1855, Elizabeth Cady Stanton Papers; see also Woody, *History of Women's Education,* pp. 43–51.

76. Hunt, *Glances and Glimpses,* p. 274; *History of Woman Suffrage,* 1:497–98; L. M. Child to Ellis Gray Loring, Jan. 30, 1836, Loring Family Papers; Anthony Speech, "Woman's Rights," 1854, Susan B. Anthony Papers, RC.

77. Hallowell, ed., *Mott,* p. 109; Anthony Diary, Apr. 28, 1854, Susan B. Anthony Papers, RC.

78. Gibbons, *Life,* p. 118; Lerner, *Grimké Sisters,* p. 201.

79. Hare, ed., *Comstock,* pp. 272, 323.

80. L. Mott to E. C. Stanton, Mar. 16, 1855, Elizabeth Cady Stanton Papers; Mott to Abby Kelley, Mar. 18, 1839, Kelley-Foster Papers, AAS; see also Stanton's comments in *Revolution,* Aug. 27, 1868.

81. Richard W. Leopold, *Robert Dale Owen, a Biography* (Cambridge: Harvard University Press, 1940), pp. 330–31.

82. Garrison and Garrison, *Garrison,* 2:374–77; Lydia Maria Child to W. L. Garrison, Feb. 1, 1857, July 7, 1865, Garrison Papers, BPL; Child to Henrietta Sargent, Nov. 19, 1861, and to Lucy Osgood, Apr. 10, 1860, Child Papers, CU; Child to Louisa Loring, Dec. 10, 1866, Loring Family Papers; Child to T. W. Higginson, June 20, 1877, Higginson Correspondence.

83. S. S. Foster to A. K. Foster, Sept. 5?, 1851, A. K. Foster to S. S. Foster, Dec. 2, 1851, Kelley-Foster Papers, AAS; Wyman and Wyman, *Chace,* 1:106–8; Blackwell, *Stone,* p. 287; M. A. Livermore to "Lillian," Aug. 4, 1899, Dec. 11, 1900, Livermore Correspondence, BPL; *Notable American Women,* 1:445.

84. Hooker, *Reminiscences,* pp. 247–65; see also *Notable American Women,* 2:213; Harper, *Anthony,* 2:665; Isabella Beecher Hooker, "The Last of the Beechers: Memories on My Eighty-third Birthday," *Connnecticut Magazine* 9 (Apr. 1905): 286–98.

85. Laura E. Richards and Maude Howe Elliott, *Julia Ward Howe, 1819–1910* (Boston: Houghton Mifflin, 1915), pp. 421–22.

5

The Feminist-Abolitionists
as Universal Reformers

ELIZABETH BUFFUM CHACE, the quintessential feminist-abolitionist, explained her lifelong philosophy in an article written in
the 1870's. She had learned early that the best way to live in the
world was to avoid things that were wrong in practice and in
principle. She had chosen to associate in moral fellowship with
reformers, because they were people "who, living in the world, have
yet, in a certain sense, lived apart from it, bearing before it, in their
lives, a continual testimony against its evil habits."[1]

The feminist-abolitionists were "universal reformers" who saw
themselves as part of a worldwide effort to improve the race by
freeing all people to realize their highest potential. Their missionary zeal led them into campaigns for temperance, social purity,
world peace, educational reform, progressive child-rearing, reform of health and medical practices, and diverse efforts to liber-
ate oppressed peoples. Though they shared this world-view with
a broader group of nineteenth-century reformers, the feminist-
abolitionist women brought to their many campaigns a unique
perception of women's needs and problems, and a heightened
sense of women's responsibilities. They also encountered the burdens and obstacles faced only by female reformers, and possessed
a female experience that even their most sympathetic male colleagues were unable to share. This combination of perfectionist
zeal and female-oriented vision was reflected in their personalities, in their day-to-day activities, and in their lifelong involvement

with good causes. All aspects of their lives were touched by their romantic dream of creating a world free of evil, and by their belief that women had a special role to play in this battle. They were spurred to even greater commitment by the knowledge that women had numerous obstacles to overcome before they could join the liberated human family.

Several distinctively feminist themes permeated the feminist-abolitionists' efforts at reform. Self-improvement, the secular counterpart of the radical abolitionists' faith in individual salvation, was central to these efforts. Women especially needed to develop their innate talents to compensate for years of uselessness and educational neglect. In appealing to women to join them in work, the reformers invariably stressed the beneficial effects of reform activities on their own growth and development. Self-development and reform were two sides of the same coin; both were at the heart of most of the feminists' work. Emily Howland, who lived to age one hundred and one as a feminist and reformer, summed up this credo in the epitaph she requested: "I strove to realize myself and to serve."[2]

Their view of woman's moral superiority and responsibilities also helped shape the philosophy and direct the reform efforts of this first generation of feminists. All moral reformers felt an obligation to the human family, but women, destined to be the guardians of family virtue and the domestic order, felt a special calling. Sisterly obligation to women in all types of bondage was also a constant theme in their thought and rhetoric. Their involvement with the temperance campaign, for example, was aimed not only at eliminating evil, but also at protecting their sisters who were victims of male cruelty and lust.

The feminist-abolitionists were driven by faith that the removal of all obstacles to individual development would lead to a better world—a philosophy more in tune with the romanticism and religious revivalism of the antebellum years than with the harsher realities of the postwar period. Nevertheless, they were able to blend the spirit of their early feminism and abolitionism with the social gospel movement of their later years. Their faith in human goodness was not total; indeed, lurking behind their optimism was the firm knowledge of the baser human instincts. Their reform careers quickly made them realize that it was essential to create the proper environment if men and women were to be elevated to their highest moral plane. Men, especially, needed to have temptations like liquor removed from their paths. Though initially the feminist reformers relied on moral suasion, they joined most radical abolitionists in coming to accept the need for compulsory measures to emancipate women as well as slaves. After the war they were able to adjust to the increasing emphasis on institutionalized methods of social control, because such methods had always been an element in their own approach. Their romantic faith in progress through individual effort, however, outweighed their Calvinist distrust of human nature. They had confidence that, given the right environment and the proper controls, men and women would conquer their lower natures and elevate society through education and self-improvement. Women, as they saw it, were the natural leaders in this effort.

Members of this first generation exhibited many personality traits typical of reformers of all ages: the self-righteousness and superior attitude of the "true believer," the seemingly limitless and often humorless determination to overcome all obstacles, the self-definition as a special group. Abby Kelley Foster's daughter described her mother's single-minded perseverance and childlike faith in her cause: "Whatever was right and just she firmly believed to be possible." Amelia Bloomer's husband explained her over-earnest and humorless manner by the fact that "she concentrated so much on the cause of women."[3]

Though as "true believers" these reformers resembled their male counterparts, as women they were forced to develop a unique pattern of attitudes and behavior. In assuming roles as public agitators, they defied custom and deviated from social expectations, and they were more vulnerable than male reformers to public censure and abuse. Because the feminist-abolitionists attempted to combine traditional female tasks with new and unprecedented roles, they lived with conflict, guilt, and uncertainty, meeting these challenges with a variety of adaptations and defenses.

Because they were constantly criticized as unsexed and unwomanly, the feminists took great care to maintain the appearance of femininity and extreme respectability. Such an accommodation was not difficult, for most of them naturally gravitated to simple, demure clothing and matronly manner; the normal demeanor was warm and motherly, and only infrequently does the stereotypical battle-ax appear. The grandmotherly Lucretia Mott in her Quaker garb was typical, as was Clarina Howard Nichols, a pleasant-looking woman who regularly knitted while traveling to speaking engagements, presenting a "disarming image of domesticity" to other railway passengers. A typical dress for public appearances was made of black silk, with white lace collar and cuffs. A group of feminists attending a party for Susan B. Anthony was described by a friendly observer as so tastefully dressed—nothing *"mannish* or *clannish"*—that none would suspect them to be "strong-minded" women.[4]

The few women who appeared in more adventurous outfits, like Elizabeth Oakes Smith, were frowned on. The bloomer outfit, worn for a few rebellious years in the early 1850's, was the major departure from the norm; those feminists who adopted it did so mostly on principle. Occasionally, a more fashionable image was defended (or rationalized), also on principle. Paulina Wright Davis was an unusually beautiful woman whose elegant clothes and stylish manners contrasted with the plain, prim appearance of her co-workers and even irritated a few of them—Lucy Stone complained of Davis's "vanity and jealousy." Davis defended the exercise of charm and grace in the crusade for women's rights, and declared herself "determined to do my utmost to remove the idea that all the woman's rights women are horrid old frights with beards and mustaches who want to smoke and swear." She insisted that lecturers like Abby Kelley antagonized their audiences with their severe appearance and manner, and declared that such feminists placed an unnecessary burden on the movement.[5]

The unpopularity of the women's unconventional careers also affected their personalities. Probably few developed, or required, the tough outer shell that protected Abby Kelley Foster from abuse. All inevitably became more independent and less vulnerable to criticism, reinforcing their original image as rebellious and strong-minded women. Mary Livermore was typical in developing a resilient self-confidence that was buoyed by past successes and the constant approval and support of her husband and friends. Comparing herself to a more "lovable" friend, she explained that people did not take to her as well because "I am more positive—more independent—more unlovely, and I probably care less for the opinions of people than she." Antoinette Brown Blackwell was also forced to become more self-reliant because of the lonesome path she chose. First as a theology student and later as an ordained minister facing intense opposition, she learned to stand alone and not look to others for support. To Susan Anthony she wrote that *"every soul had to live absolutely within itself."* [6] All feminist-abolitionists were bolstered by their belief that their cause was God-ordained, and therefore right and just.

This sense of mission was a source of psychic energy, but it often produced self-righteousness and stubborn inflexibility, traits unheard of in a "true woman." To unsympathetic observers who expected greater feminine modesty and deference, the feminists appeared inexcusably self-important and holier-than-thou. Despite the obvious sincerity of Susan B. Anthony or the ladylike demeanor of Antoinette Brown, it was difficult for many people to accept moral truths from female sources of authority.

The feminists expected resistance from the less enlightened, and they declared themselves fully prepared for suffering and sacrifice until truth and right would ultimately prevail. Such self-denial was seen as an especially female obligation, although the feminists turned it to the cause of woman's advancement, rather than accepting it in the more common spirit of female passivity. Lucy Stone constantly assured her friends of her "quiet faith in the *certain triumph of the right*"; acts of "venom and ill nature" would only make her stronger and better able to carry on the battle. Paulina Wright Davis, surviving a period of self-doubt after the death of her husband and partner in reform, pointed to the strength she had gained by leaning on principle and resisting "influences around her." Jane Grey Swisshelm, old and in poor health after a lifetime of fighting for good causes, could still write: "Oh but it is good to have lived and suffered and worked. To know that the Lord is overall, and that nothing can go wrong with us if only we are right." [7]

Like most of their male co-workers, the feminist-abolitionist women were primarily doers rather than thinkers. Their full energies were devoted to agitating, propagandizing, and pioneering in new roles. Few took the time to analyze their positions intellectually or to consider the broader implications of their crusade. Even those who were capable intellectuals, like Elizabeth Cady Stanton, were geared almost intuitively to producing arguments for the cause. Subtleties and contradictions tended to be submerged in rhetoric and hyperbole. Most of the women forged ahead in a blaze of constant activity and achievement, leaving introspection for the more philosophically inclined. Harriet Stanton, Elizabeth's daughter and a reformer herself, caught this quality in Susan Anthony. "You are completely swallowed up in an idea, and its a glorious thing to be," she wrote to her. "Carlyle says, 'The end of man is an Action, not a Thought,' and what a realization of that truth has your life been . . . you are possessed by a moral force, and you act. You are a Deed, not a Thinking."[8]

Despite the truth of these broad generalizations, there was room for some differences in style and personality. Martha Coffin Wright was a suffragist leader who, like Elizabeth Cady Stanton, brought rare humor and wit to the women's movement. Unlike her more serious older sister, Lucretia Mott, Martha used her talents to write children's poems and nonsense limericks, as well as feminist speeches and serious poetry. Letters to family and friends were often in verse form. Her personal charm and warmth enabled her to act as a respected intermediary between hostile factions of feminist-abolitionists.

Because of their single-minded devotion to their cause and their overriding faith in progress, one looks in vain for signs of disillusion or discontinuity in these women's long reform careers. Most of them were active well into the late nineteenth century, a period of rapid change and uncertainty that could be expected to leave even the most determined reformers with some uneasiness or confusion. While some in the group may have been so affected, evidence points in the other direction. Occasionally Susan B. Anthony would privately express impatience with women who were apathetic about their own enfranchisement, but this mass apathy only made her work even harder. Again, there were varying degrees of commitment and determination, and not all feminists were as single-mindedly devoted to the cause as Anthony. Nevertheless, their collective record of persistence and achievement indicates extraordinary faith, as well as unusual courage and ability.

The perfectionist thrust of the antislavery campaign carried over into the postwar years. The feminists' involvement remained intense, with only the names of the battles changing. Efforts for emancipation were transformed into concerns for the freedman;

work for temperance and moral reform was expanded to include social welfare work and campaigns for social purity. As the reformers' causes multiplied in the 1880's and 1890's, the survivors of early feminist-abolitionism joined Nationalist Clubs and Christian Socialist Societies, enlisted in "Friends for Armenia" and "American Friends of Russian Freedom," and spoke out for Indians and other oppressed groups that came to their attention. Feminism and abolitionism continued to be only parts of a broad crusade for human liberation. Stephen Foster expressed this view when he wrote in 1870 that the antislavery struggle would not be ended until "all shall have an *equal chance* in the great struggle of life." "We may fight under another banner," he wrote, "but the enemy is the same."[9]

A brief look at the reform careers of two typical feminist-abolitionist women illustrates the scope of their movement, as well as its feminist dimension. Elizabeth Buffum Chace, who lived ninety-three years (1806–99), was a woman of extraordinary vigor and determination. A leader in antislavery, women's rights, and prison reform, Chace was also involved in work for temperance, peace, child welfare, health and diet reform, and other causes too numerous to list. Her letters and diaries paint a portrait of a strong-willed aristocrat of inflexible moral convictions, a woman whose achievements gained her enormous admiration among reformers, but who found it difficult to relate to people outside reform circles. Her children, who respected her humanitarian accomplishments, complained that she was arrogant, narrow in her interests, and domineering.

Elizabeth Chace's first reform efforts were typical. An important member of the Garrisonian abolitionist group in Rhode Island, she was a signer of the call to the first national women's rights convention in 1850. After the war she was a founder and first president of the Rhode Island Woman Suffrage Association, a post she held until her death. Chace became deeply involved with improving the state's welfare and penal institutions; she worked for equal treatment of women in prisons and for special consideration of female inmates' needs, including women matrons. She pushed for the appointment of women to the state prison board, arguing that only women could properly determine the needs of other women, and citing the particular suitability of the female sex for "reclaiming" fallen men and women. She succeeded in being named to the Women's Board of Visitors, an advisory group. Though she resigned in protest after six years because the board's reports exposing abuses in the prisons had been ignored, she was later persuaded to return after some reforms were instituted.[10]

Chace's interest in the causes of poverty and crime also led her to investigate a broad array of other state welfare institutions —almshouses, insane asylums, homes for dependent children—as well as working conditions for factory women and girls. She ultimately came to the conclusion that the foremost cause of pauperism and crime was alcohol. Here, too, her chief concern was for women and girls who were forced to live in an immoral environment. In a speech on "Factory Women and Girls of New England," given in 1881, she told an audience of suffragists that "the vice of intemperance is a terrible curse to these people"; the problem of protecting the virtue of young girls was particularly severe under such troublesome circumstances.[11] Bolstered by her investigations, she threw herself with even greater vigor into the battle for temperance, and renewed her efforts for woman suffrage as a means to achieve liquor control (as well as for other reasons).

The reform career of Abby Hopper Gibbons was a New York counterpart to Chace's Rhode Island example, though Gibbons was more a model than a leader in the suffrage movement. Like Chace, she came from a Quaker Garrisonian abolitionist family and married a reformer. She also maintained a lifelong interest in the care and rehabilitation of women prisoners and was a mainstay in an organization founded in the 1840's by her father, Isaac Hopper, to shelter female ex-convicts. Throughout her life Gibbons lobbied for special treatment of women, and she reached a major goal in 1892, when the state created a women's reformatory. She appeared before the state legislature to speak for the reformatory bill at the age of ninety-one, a year before her death.

Abby Hopper Gibbons was also involved in personal welfare work in the New York City tenements and believed strongly in the benefits of private charity to both the donor and the recipient. "There will always be the rich and the poor," she wrote in 1892, "and how liberally the former dispense to the latter." Like many feminists, she was active in the social purity movement of the late

FEMINIST-ABOLITIONISTS AS UNIVERSAL REFORMERS

nineteenth century, seeing it as women's special business. As head of the New York Committee for the Prevention of State Regulation of Vice, she worked against bills for state licensing and inspection of prostitutes, and she opposed all other measures that would perpetuate an institution seen as morally evil and exploitative of women.[12] Like her colleagues, Gibbons combined a Puritan-Quaker sense of duty and individual responsibility with a willingness to work through social agencies, when necessary, to create the proper environment for personal self-improvement. Her moral stance typified that of the feminist-abolitionists as a group, in that it remained consistent and relatively unchanging from early antislavery days, only shifting targets as the needs changed. The special needs of women were always central to the feminist reformers' concern.

The reform interests of the feminist-abolitionists had an international scope that dated from the close ties between the Garrisonians and their English counterparts in the 1830's. The abolitionists' motto, "Our country is the world, our countrymen are all mankind," carried over into the women's rights movement. At the 1853 national convention, a committee was appointed to prepare an address "to the women of Great Britain and the continent of Europe, setting forth our objects, and inviting their co-operation in the same." This same convention heard a passionate message from Mathilde Anneke, a refugee of the 1848 revolution in Germany. Anneke, who later became the editor of a women's rights journal in Milwaukee, declared that German women were looking to their American sisters for encouragement and sympathy in their fight for emancipation. In 1856, the national convention passed a resolution of sympathy for the "noble women in England" who were struggling against even greater wrongs than those experienced by American women.[13]

The feminists maintained an active correspondence with reformers in England and circulated reports of achievements on both sides of the Atlantic. Harriet Martineau, a close friend of Maria Weston Chapman and an important link between the two groups, helped the American feminists to remain informed about their English counterparts. The English writer and feminist Caroline Norton, whose long struggle to reclaim her children from her estranged husband was the *cause célèbre* which led to reform of England's marriage and divorce laws, received expressions of support from American conventions.[14]

The feminist-abolitionists also kept in touch with their counterparts in religious groups and in temperance and peace organizations. Several were involved in the Friendly Address movement of the 1840's, an Anglo-American effort to exchange peace propaganda which was carried on mostly by Quaker groups. This peace movement, viewed as women's special province, was given added impetus by the horrors of the Civil War, and it continued as an international women's effort in the postwar period. Julia Ward Howe served as a one-woman world peace crusade. Her "Appeal to Womanhood Throughout the World" (1870) was translated into five languages and resulted in the organization of a World's Congress of Women. Addressing the opening session, she pleaded with women to "help others, and you help yourselves." At home she worked for woman suffrage as a means to world peace, declaring that women were under "a sort of military subjection to Man—captive of his bow and spear" and must free themselves to exercise their superior moral force for peace.[15] The thrust of her efforts bore a striking resemblance to earlier appeals for women to free themselves in order to work against slavery.

Many of the women traveled to England and the Continent both before and after the war, spending up to six months away from home. After such a trip in 1859, Caroline Dall reported to the New England Woman's Rights Convention on the achievements of the English movement. Paulina Wright Davis visited Europe in 1859 and again in 1871, and developed close ties with English women reformers. Hannah Tracy Cutler went as a delegate to a World Peace Convention in London in 1851, developed friendships with feminists there, and stayed to give a series of women's rights lectures in London and other cities. Elizabeth Comstock delivered addresses on temperance and women's rights during her extended visit with British Quaker groups in 1874.[16]

Elizabeth Blackwell was the personification of Anglo-American ties. Born in England, she migrated to the United States as a child. After receiving her medical degree, she returned to her native land in 1849 to study and practice medicine, and she became closely associated with English reformers. In 1869 Blackwell settled in England permanently, establishing a practice and becoming professor of gynecology at the London School of Medicine for Women. She was an important force in encouraging English women to enter the field of medicine, and she became a central link in the continuing Anglo-American reform network.[17]

After feminism and abolitionism, the cause most ardently supported by this group of universal reformers was temperance. Of the fifty-one women under study, thirty were definitely involved in the temperance movement, and the actual figure is probably much higher. Many first worked for temperance in the 1830's and 1840's, when the influence of religious revivalism caused the crusade to abandon a gradualist approach, and instead to press an "immediatist" demand for total abstinence, following a tactical path similar to that of abolitionism.[18]

Again, the feminist-abolitionist women brought a unique, female-oriented vision to their temperance efforts. Drunkenness was seen as almost entirely a male habit, with women the chief victims. Married women were viewed as slaves to their drunken husbands, just as slave women were helpless victims of their masters. Temperance was a means of protecting women and emancipating them from still another form of bondage.

This feminist aspect of the temperance movement has been largely overlooked by historians, who have tended to view the movement as primarily a means of social control.[19] The desire of women to rescue their sisters was always an element in the movement, although in the 1840's and 1850's the feminist-abolitionist crusade was only on the periphery of the largely male-dominated movement. In the 1870's temperance underwent a revival as largely a "woman's war," and the movement was institutionalized in 1874 with the formation of the Women's Christian Temperance Union. Just as Susan B. Anthony, in the early 1850's, had demanded the broadening of woman's sphere so that she could carry out her "woman's mission" of attacking the "monster evil," so Frances Willard later described the women's temperance movement as "the home going forth into the world."[20] A theme which appeared first in the antislavery movement, of woman exercising her special moral responsibility to aid her sisters in bondage, remained important in the temperance crusade throughout the nineteenth century.

The feminists' view of drunkenness as primarily a male habit was partly a middle-class judgment and was closely related to the popular idealization of woman as a delicate, refined lady, a being less subject than men to control by the "lower passions." There is also evidence that middle-class women responded more enthusiastically than men to the crusade for total abstinence. Women not only gave up drinking, but they also abandoned the use of alcohol in cooking, a practice which had not been uncommon before. In organizing groups like the Daughters of Temperance in the 1840's and 1850's, women "took the pledge" to totally abstain from the use of alcohol and to influence their husbands and sons to do likewise. It was assumed that daughters would be as virtuous and self-controlled as their mothers.[21]

The feminist-abolitionists emphasized that heavy drinking among men led to debauchery, brutality, the degradation of women, and the desecration of marriage. The reformers' language in temperance speeches, exhorting men to exercise "self-control" and urging young people to resist the "seductions" and "temptations" of alcohol, reveals the close connection they saw between intemperance and uncontrolled sexuality. The desire for strong drink was regularly described as "the most uncontrollable and destructive passion that has ever cursed humanity," and temperance speeches railed against "the carnal nature of the confirmed drunkard." In a typical address, duplicated thousands of times in the movement, Elizabeth Cady Stanton described a "young, pure, beautiful" girl who "heedlessly united her destiny with some fine looking man given to low pleasures, and gross associations." After marriage, "His animal nature runs to excess, in every way." Soon the mother and her little ones are "helpless, abused, outraged, hungry, cold, and in rags," forced by a drunkard to live "a life of degradation and peril." Who, she asked rhetorically, would tell this woman to cling to "that moral monster—that vulgar, gross, imbruted nature?" The holiest instincts of our nature, she concluded, cry out "shame, shame, shame, thus to desecrate the solemn sacrament of marriage!" This dramatic outpouring, strikingly similar to the appeals on behalf of slave women, was as much an argument for legal rights for married women as for prohibition of strong drink.[22]

The temperance crusade of the feminist-abolitionists went beyond a Victorian distaste for excessive sexuality and a rejection of the woman's subservient role in marriage. Recent studies have documented the high level of alcohol consumption in the 1830's and 1840's and have confirmed the feminists' observation that drunkenness was a widespread condition.[23] All the reformers reported numerous case histories of abused and neglected wives. Since married women had few legal rights, the crusade for total abstinence became, for the feminists, a movement for the protection of women and led to their first demands for easier divorce. Though all feminists put a high value on the sanctity of marriage, most of them considered divorce a necessary expedient until liquor control could be achieved.

All feminists supported the temperance movement, but this support was not wholly reciprocated. The evangelically inclined women of the small towns where the temperance movement sprang up in the 1870's were more interested in the improvement of men than in the emancipation of women. To the feminists, temperance was only one aspect of the broader reform of society; however, such a vision was threatening to many temperance women, whose goal was simply to abolish the liquor traffic. Still, the latter did share with the more radical urban feminists the perception that this was a woman's duty and a woman's fight.[24] Though the two movements were strategically in conflict (the threat that suffrage would close the saloons turned many men against the woman's cause, and the actions of the more radical feminists encumbered moderate temperance advocates), the movements were ideologically close in their emphasis on woman's moral superiority and special mission to reform society, and in their view of women as the chief victims of alcoholism. The feminists could not reject their more conservative sisters in the temperance movement without ideologically hurting their own cause.

Temperance and feminism were linked in still another important way. Though for many temperance women the goal undoubtedly remained narrow, others gained a first intimation of what women could do if they were given power, just as the antislavery movement had broadened women's vision in an earlier period. A woman wrote to the *Woman's Journal* in 1874, asserting that the arrest of forty-three temperance ladies in her hometown of Cincinnati had aroused public sentiment to an unprecedented degree. "Women are being brought forward in a way they little expected," and were ennobling not only themselves but all womanhood. "We can never go back to where we were on this subject," she concluded.[25] Temperance proved to be still another training ground for feminism.

Closely related to their work for temperance was the feminists' involvement in the postwar movement for social purity. The abolition of prostitution (and opposition to the legal regulation of this "social evil") was one major goal. In 1895 seven of the fifty-one women under study were members of the executive board of the American Purity Alliance, a body which also included husbands and children of others in the group. They and all other moral reformers viewed prostitution as a sin and a major blot on society to be eradicated as slavery had been. Indeed, the emancipation of the "white slave" was a new stage in the old abolitionist campaign. When the New York Committee for the Abolition of Regulated Vice closed its parlor meetings, members often sang the "Battle Hymn of the Republic." The nation, redeemed in battle for the sin of slavery, had to endure still another ordeal of cleansing.[26]

The feminists' concerns went beyond the elimination of social evil. While other "new abolitionists" were concerned primarily with the effect of prostitution on society, the feminists focused on the harm done to women—an important difference in emphasis. They also argued that prostitution was an evil resulting from woman's economic dependence as well as from man's "abnormal passion" and lack of self-control, again broadening significantly the more prevalent reform view. To the feminist-abolitionists, the crusade for moral reform had always been inseparable from efforts to emancipate women and slaves. Abby Kelley Foster, speaking to a convention of spiritualists in 1860, commended them on their stand to abolish prostitution and went on to remind them that American women could not be elevated until those who were presently compelled to live as prostitutes in slavery were also freed.[27] To Foster, all these causes were one cause, and all involved the universal emancipation of the human family.

Because of their unique analysis of its causes, the feminists' program for elimination of prostitution also differed from that of other moral reformers. It included education and training for women, greater economic opportunities, and suffrage for protection, as well as moral education for the next generation (a cause which all reformers favored). Feminists advised parents to train boys to the same standards of purity and refinement as their sisters, and they constantly condemned the "false ideas of sex" which laid the groundwork for society's double standard of morality. Like all moral reformers, they were interested in the purification of society, but their greater stress was on the means to this end: the emancipation of women and the elevation of both sexes to a single standard of morality.[28]

None pursued the path of moral education more diligently than Elizabeth Blackwell. Like all the moral reformers, she preached that chastity and sexual restraint could only be achieved by early sex education—a progressive and controversial solution for her day. Like all the feminists, she linked moral reform with the woman's cause: prostitution was the greatest obstacle to the progress of the race, and victory in the battle with licentiousness was crucial for the emancipation of woman. That victory would strike off "the chains of thought in which women have been so long shackled." Blackwell called herself a "Christian physiologist" and lectured to women on "moral hygiene." She stressed the need for women to be informed about the relationship between sexual physiology and Christian morality, because they had been "warped, perplexed or blinded by the one sided male physiology which is ruining society." The chief purpose of encouraging women physicians, as she saw it, was the advancement of a higher morality. If the medical movement on the part of women were "simply a small imitation of men, or a struggle for bread and butter," it would be "a pitiful failure."[29]

Moral education was an element in another crusade which occupied the feminist-abolitionists and touched on their daily lives. Since they believed that the elevation of both women and men began in early life with the proper training of children, reform of child-rearing practices was a pivotal link in the reform of society. They also shared in the nineteenth century's romanticization of childhood as a state of purity and innocence, and the idealization of the child as the embodiment of the spirit of the republic. The influence of the mother in shaping the child's character came to be viewed as a holy mission. Feminists accepted this as woman's responsibility, although they also emphasized the parallel responsibilities of the father.

The need to reform child-rearing practices was closely related, in the feminists' view, to women's need for education and self-development. Society's increasing emphasis on the child reinforced their demand that women be given better preparation for motherhood. In a series of "Letters to Mothers" in the *Lily,* Jane Swisshelm deplored the fragility and poor health of most mothers. America was becoming noted for its disobedient children, she declared, and "No reformation can be wrought in the mode of managing children that does not commence in the physical and mental education of mothers."[30] Disobedience and other undesirable traits in children were constantly attributed to the inadequate education of mothers.

The importance attributed to child-rearing practices is reflected in the way the feminists raised their own children. The sketchy evidence suggests certain patterns. In keeping with their romantic view of the child as savior, they took great care to protect the innocence of their children and yet to help them realize their full potential. The reformers tended to reject physical punishment as a disciplinary measure, and to rely on reason and appeals to conscience. James and Lucretia Mott were typical in their belief that the process of "making the world better" began at home. They exhorted others to instill in their children the principles of peace, and at home tried to rear their own children with kindness and love. Their granddaughter confirmed that they indeed "taught by gentleness."[31]

In raising their daughter Alla, Abby and Stephen Foster made every effort to substitute reason for the use of parental authority. They extended to family government their belief in non-resistance. Alla was assured, for example, that hard work in school would serve to make her "happy and useful in future life." Apparently their method was successful, because Alla was both gifted and dutiful. She explained to a cousin: "My mother lets me do just as I please. If she wants me to do a thing I generally do it." Alla also absorbed her parents' ideas on women's rights and lived up to the feminism of her namesake, Paulina Wright Davis. Lydia Maria Child reported that at the age of nine, Alla had raised a real objection to ending all prayers with "Amen" and none with "Awomen."[32]

Other feminists were also permissive in their child-rearing, practicing at home what they preached in their lectures on self-improvement and women's rights. Antoinette Brown Blackwell shocked her sisters-in-law by the freedom she allowed her five daughters and, in her novel, made clear her objection to parents badgering their children. The offspring of Elizabeth Buffum Chace also described her child-rearing as permissive. Elizabeth Cady Stanton boasted of using reason in raising her seven children, but admitted that occasionally a spanking worked better. Martha Wright also tempered her idealism with practicality. Like Stanton, she concluded that expecting children to be obedient without any punishment at all was unrealistic, and bluntly informed her sister Lucretia that "you can't do it."[33]

Abbey Hopper Gibbons gave typical advice to her children at school. Her college-aged son was regularly reminded to abstain from even a drop of alcoholic beverage, and to be moderate in all things. Friends should not be permitted to smoke in his room, so he could avoid inhaling the "poison weed." "You may have your good times on gingerbread and cold water," she added. The inequality of women was on her mind a great deal, for Abby also reminded her son that smoking and drinking were part of the way in which men made drudges of their wives and denied them the appreciation and sympathy they deserved.[34]

To her daughters (who "have come up their own way pretty much"), Abby Hopper Gibbons wrote that she feared they might be misled by their young men into thinking that wives ought to be submissive. To her sister she expressed her anger that her daughters, and all women, were denied the opportunity to "have intercourse with the intelligent world" and so to become men's equals. While grieving about woman's lot, she still conscientiously instructed one daughter to interest herself in "the art, trade and mystery of household affairs" and to become "skillful in all matters pertaining to housewifery." Gibbons and others were fairly consistent in their private and public utterances, although their children obviously did not "come up their own way" without a great deal of parental advice and moralizing.[35]

All of the feminists conscientiously watched over their childrens' development. They put a high value on the education of girls as well as boys, personally assuming much of this responsibility in the early years and choosing their children's later teachers with great care. At one point in her life, Mary Livermore reported spending three hours a day teaching a daughter who was apparently retarded; she felt that only education could "perfect her cure, and develop her mind."[36]

The feminist-abolitionists believed that rearing children was the highest duty of fathers as well as of mothers. Theodore Weld's anxiety over the proper training of his children, for example, is detailed in a series of long letters written when he was away from home. Those letters constitute, in themselves, a manual on child-rearing. Weld especially emphasized the learning of self-control and the "cultivation of gentle, forbearing, benevolent affections." The first lesson to be instilled, he reminded his wife, was *always* and *everywhere DARE TO DO DUTY."* Elizabeth Cady Stanton reported several years later that the Weld children were charming, highly intelligent, and free from all orthodox restraints and rituals. Their father, she wrote, taught them himself.[37] Male and female reformers viewed the child as one of the most important keys to the improvement of society, with both sexes playing equally important roles in both generations.

The feminist-abolitionists' belief in universal reform and self-improvement took still other forms, all embraced with the enthusiasm of the missionary and the true believer. As young women they had organized self-improvement societies in their home towns; in the postwar period they joined the lyceum movement and lectured throughout the country on woman's self-improvement and related reforms.

Even the group's widespread interest in phrenology was related to their desire for woman's self-improvement. Viewed by many in retrospect as a fad at best and quackery at worst, phrenology was taken seriously by many nineteenth-century reformers, especially at the movement's height in the 1840's and 1850's. These reformers saw phrenology as part of the scientific search for natural laws by which men and women could improve themselves. Phrenologists not only associated parts of the brain with special behavioral traits; in addition, they taught that, by proper exercise, one could consciously cultivate the good faculties and inhibit the harmful ones. This theory had democratic implications for all—men and women could elevate themselves and become more equal by careful training—but it had special potential for women because they were most in need of development. Lucretia Mott was fond of responding to criticisms of women by saying, "Let Woman's intellect be cultivated for a few generations, as man's has been, and then judge." She believed that the study of phrenology held great promise.[38]

Feminists were also hospitable to phrenological theory because it emphasized the "feminine element" in human development; i.e., the role of feelings, sentiments, and affections, as well as the importance of the mother's influence in early childhood. The health regimen recommended by phrenologists—fresh air, exercise, simple diet, loose clothing, the use of cold water—also coincided with the advice given by feminists to their audiences. Above all, the concept that the welfare of the body was related to that of the mind and the soul seemed a progressive approach. As Sarah Grimké observed, phrenological theory seemed "so perfectly consistent with the other works of God and with enlightened reason and religion." Anthony, Stanton, Livermore, and other feminists submitted to phrenological examinations and took the diagnoses seriously. Stanton, usually one of the most intellectually skeptical of the group, felt that the results of her exam were strikingly accurate and expressed enthusiasm for the "evident science of the system."[39]

Health reform itself, of course, was a central concern. All of the women were involved in the crusade to instruct women on physiology and hygiene, whether through lectures, journal articles, or local physiological societies. On one level, this constant and persistent interest was part of the broad reform movement, begun in mid-nineteenth-century America, to improve and extend social services. More specifically, it was a feminist response to the deplorable state of women's health. Interest in health reform also involved rebellion against the standard treatment of women's illnesses by the male medical profession, and an effort to reform medical practices. Chronic illness and frailty were widespread among women, at least among the middle-class women who left records of their nervous disorders, frequent dyspepsia, headaches, and general indisposition. The mid-nineteenth-century proliferation of health cure resorts to treat women's diseases confirms the prevalence of such problems. Feminists attributed ill health to female ignorance about physiology and proper health habits, as well as to indifference and incompetent treatment by male physicians. They also associated the poor state of women's health with the narrow, useless lives that so many of their sex endured.[40] Female self-development would lead to an improvement in physical health, as well as to other gains.

The careers of Paulina Wright Davis and Jane Elisabeth Jones in the 1840's were typical of the feminist movement to enlighten women. Davis, who earned a reputation as a "Fanny Wright woman," set the precedent for Jones and others to follow. Using manikins and engravings, feminist lecturers explained the parts of the body and their proper care. Judging from the large audiences to which the reformers spoke, they filled a dire need. If the state of Abby Kelley Foster's knowledge was any indication, the ignorance of even educated women was deplorable. In a letter to Lucy Stone shortly after Abby was married, she referred to rumors of her pregnancy thus: "If I am not mistaken in physiological facts, I never can be a mother while I work so hard in the cause."[41]

Contributing to this ignorance was the prevailing modesty and delicacy that kept women from discussing their complaints with their doctors, or even with their husbands. Davis reported that when she uncovered her manikin in her first lectures in 1844, some ladies dropped their veils, others fled the room in horror, and a few delicate souls fainted on the spot. These reactions were at least partly the result of the attitudes of doctors who, even more than most men, saw ignorance as woman's natural state. Harriot Hunt's patients complained that their regular physicians usually dismissed their questions by assuring them that women were better off not knowing about themselves because it would make them nervous.[42]

One obvious solution to the problem of inadequate care was to encourage women to study medicine. It was necessary to press for the creation of female medical schools, since urging the acceptance of women by regular medical colleges seemed a hopeless cause. Both lines of attack were pursued with great vigor, despite the intense prejudice against women doctors. To many people, "female physician" meant a woman abortionist, making the term doubly obnoxious.[43]

As early as the 1840's, Amelia Bloomer's *Lily* urged women to study medicine and so to avoid "a great amount of suffering and death" due to ignorance and women's unwillingness to visit male doctors. The *Lily* sympathized with this reluctance—"There is always something abhorrent in the thought of having to send for a *man*"—and complained that "men have too long usurped the sole right to practice medicine." Sounding the battle cry of the feminist health crusade, the journal went on: "We have too long been subjected to the impositions of Quacks, and quack medicine, and the sooner we learn enough of physiology to take care of ourselves, instead of trusting to them, the better will it be for mankind at large." As a final argument, the writer added that, as everyone knew, "women are naturally better calculated to watch over and nurse the sick than men." Opening medical education to women, the *Lily* argued in a later series of articles, would also afford women an "honorable, profitable and useful employment." The medical movement clearly was intended to fill several urgent needs.[44]

Seven of the fifty-one women responded to this call; their independence and determination were notable, even among this group of strong-minded achievers. Elizabeth Blackwell's name has survived because she was the first to receive her degree, and because of her famous family and long career; nevertheless, the others were as influential in their time, and were more important in the women's movement.

Harriot Hunt was practicing medicine as early as the 1830's after studying privately because no college would accept her.[45] An ardent feminist, she took time from her busy practice to participate in the early conventions and attracted national attention by her annual tax protest. Noted for her charm and lively personality (Martha Wright called her "the laughing little Doctor"), Hunt was important to feminist-abolitionists both as activist and as model, especially for those women who chose reform careers over marriage. Unlike the prim, righteous Elizabeth Blackwell, whose career was probably at least partly a means of avoiding marriage, Hunt's choice was a positive, life-embracing action. Seeing herself "wedded" to medicine, she celebrated her "silver anniversary" after twenty-five years of practice. (Martha Wright wondered, with sharp but affectionate wit, whether "if some Boston Adonis of mature age should be accepted someday, it would be considered *bigamy,* and whether succeeding patients would be less *legitimate* than previous ones."[46])

Like Susan B. Anthony, Harriot Hunt contributed to a new image of the unmarried woman and helped to counter the prevailing belief that a woman's only opportunity for usefulness and fulfillment was in marriage. Hunt appropriately paid tribute to her good friend Sarah Grimké as her ideal. In dedicating her autobiography to

Grimké, Hunt praised her for her principles and the example she had set for other women reformers—another reminder of the importance of models, especially for women entering new territory.

Unlike Harriot Hunt, four of the women entered formal medical training relatively late in life, after marrying and raising families. These women had longtime interests in medicine and had studied informally with close relatives. Hannah Longshore had studied with her brother-in-law while raising two children. She entered the newly founded Philadelphia Female Medical College in 1850 at the age of thirty-one and received her degree a year later. (Ann Preston, thirty-seven and an unmarried feminist-abolitionist and health lecturer, was a classmate of hers.) Longshore's half-sister, Mary Frame Thomas, studied with her husband for a number of years while raising her family; she started her formal training in 1856 at thirty-seven, and graduated from Pennsylvania Medical University in Philadelphia at forty. Clemence Lozier studied with a brother before entering Syracuse Medical College and also became a physician at the age of forty in 1853. Hannah Tracy Cutler, who lectured on physiology in the 1850's and did important work for married women's property laws in the West, graduated from Women's Medical College in Cleveland in 1869 at the age of fifty-four. All four combined marriage with active medical careers as well as with reform work, although Lozier eventually divorced her husband.[47]

All four were strong feminists keenly aware of their influence on other women. Mary Thomas sent a letter to the first women's rights convention in her home state, Indiana, urging girls to enter the trades and professions. "Although a wife, mother, and housekeeper, with all that that means," she wrote, "I am studying medicine, and expect to practice, if I live." In 1857, while in school, she acted as president of a similar convention and told her audience: "By my example, as well as my words, I have tried to teach women to be more self-reliant, and to prepare themselves for larger and more varied spheres of activity."[48]

These women faced ridicule and harassment when they began practicing medicine in the 1850's, much as the early abolitionist women had suffered because they were "out of their sphere." They were fired by their determination to provide the medical care and education they felt women so desperately needed. All were bolstered by their religious faith, and by the support of the newly organizing and growing women's movement. All felt they were doing work for which they were uniquely fitted. Clemence Lozier was following in the footsteps of her Quaker mother, who had practiced an informal medicine, using healing arts learned from Indian tribes; the daughter felt that she also had been given the gift of healing. Her successful career in New York City followed her brother's and preceded that of her son (whose wife also was a graduate of a medical college). [49]

For those who could not study medicine, the next-best thing was to become one's own physician. Like all nineteenth-century Americans, the feminists had good reason to distrust the current state of medical knowledge, and their first health rule tended to be, "Stay away from doctors." Caroline Severance was moved to study health reform tracts after the early deaths of her husband's parents and brothers. Her family became "largely emancipated from the physicians and learned to trust nature to do her own work by her own remedies." Like all the feminists, she preached the use of simple, plain food, fresh air, exercise, and comfortable clothing. Elizabeth Blackwell taught seven basic rules of health: the first six emphasized moderation, balance, and simplicity; the seventh was, "Shun drugs and doctors!"[50]

The loss of children particularly turned women against medicine and toward other panaceas. All of Elizabeth Buffum Chace's children had died while under medical care, causing her to reject conventional medicine and turn to magnetic treatment, water cures, and spiritualist medicine. Lucy Stone wrote to a friend that her brother's little children were both dead, "killed we think by the Drs." "I do believe," she wrote, "they kill more than they cure." Feminists related the high death rate of young children to maternal ignorance, and to the fact that the medical profession was "too exclusively in the hands of men."[51]

One of the particular interests of feminists was the influence of the mind on the body—Elizabeth Blackwell, in a lecture in 1889, called it "psycho-physiology." This concern was not unique to women reformers, but they stressed it because it seemed so obviously relevant to the state of women's health.[52] Elizabeth Cady Stanton constantly preached that woman's physical emancipation and mental freedom went hand in hand. Women would escape "much cruel bondage of mind and suffering of body" when she "takes the liberty of being her own physician of both body and soul!" To this end

Stanton advocated a whole series of reforms, ranging from the bloomer dress and short hair (to avoid "over-heated, aching heads"), to natural childbirth, to giving up sewing and embroidery (which injured the eyes). Women's social habits kept them delicate and helpless and were "so at variance with the highest good of the race." In one of her most popular lyceum lectures, "Our Young Girls," Stanton argued that women were feeble in body and mind because they were forever in a condition of tutelage. When they became independent and self-sufficient, they would be rid of their aches and pains.[53]

Harriot Hunt developed a special interest and expertise in psychosomatic medicine. In her long years of healing women of all classes and conditions, she often found "physical maladies growing out of concealed sorrows." Her method of treatment was unorthodox for the time, often bordering on modern psychotherapy. She eschewed medication, taught the patients simple rules of hygiene and health, and listened to their troubles. She felt strongly that only women could understand and treat other women, who could not explain their sufferings to a male doctor or expect sympathetic advice from him. Hunt's constant theme was "woman as physician to her sex," and she carried on a lifelong campaign to teach women to care for themselves and for each other.[54]

As one would expect, the feminists, like all nineteenth-century reformers, also linked physical and moral health. One of the main attractions of the popular Graham diet (which eliminated tea, coffee, meat, all spicy foods, and—of course—alcohol) was its alleged success in subduing the carnal passions. Not all reformers followed this regime as avidly as the Welds or the Fosters, who lived quite ascetically, but all believed that moderation was the key to good moral and physical health.[55] Cold water was one of the most popular panaceas, prescribed for everything. Lydia Maria Child sat in it to cure her headaches, Abby Foster plunged her baby in it every morning, and everyone drank it instead of more harmful beverages. Harriet Robinson enjoyed a dramatic improvement in her health and her easiest childbirth experience after she gave up all medicines and used only cold water to drink, to bathe in, and in local applications. Susan Anthony was an enthusiastic convert and went regularly for rest and treatments at water-cure resorts. Hannah Longshore's thesis for her medical degree concerned the treatment of neuralgia by the use of water.[56]

An intriguing and relevant question relating to this group of fifty-one women concerns the state of their own health. At first glance, their remarkably long lives seem to support the validity of the health rules they preached and practiced so avidly. The average age at death was eighty years. According to the best available statistics, a twenty-year-old white Massachusetts woman in 1850 could expect to live until the age of sixty, a forty-year-old until about seventy.[57] Obviously, this group far outlived these expectations. Forty-one lived past the age of seventy, twenty-eight past eighty, and nine lived past ninety years, including Emily Howland, who died at the age of one hundred and one. (Though showing physical effects of age, Howland was still mentally alert and giving speeches at suffrage meetings.[58])

Longevity was often the natural result of unusual good health. Seventeen of these reformers were known to be unusually healthy and vigorous. (Only seven were considered frail. Eight had a normal mixture of illness and good health, and the health of nineteen is not known.) In a period when "true women" were expected to be fragile and delicate, Mary Livermore (who was active until her death at eighty-five) boasted of her "magnificent health and vigor" and her "power of persistent unflagging work that could hold sleep in abeyance until my task was completed." Maria Weston Chapman, who lived to seventy-nine, expressed thankfulness at weathering the strain of abolition work for thirty years without an end in sight, and decided it was "all a matter of health in a great measure."[59]

Many in this group also enjoyed the advantages of good heredity. Susan Anthony's mother and grandparents on both sides were octogenarians, and the family included some centenarians. Her own unusually good health was bolstered by careful attention to diet, fresh air, and exercise. At sixty she hiked about Europe on a sightseeing trip; she returned to the Continent at eighty-four for an international conference she helped organize, and lived to eighty-six. Elizabeth Cady Stanton, who also lived to eighty-six, boasted that her father had served on the bench until eighty-four, the oldest judge in the country.

The feminists themselves, geared at all times in private as well as in public to promoting woman's emancipation, insisted that useful work kept them healthy and alive. They prided themselves on living according to the laws of nature, but they put the most emphasis on keeping mind and body geared to a noble purpose. Considering the longevity of the group, as well as the knowledge we now have of psychosomatic medicine, their arguments are quite convincing. Stanton, in "The Pleasures of Age," a lecture written when she was seventy, told her audiences that women who lived a full life in middle age would also enjoy a full old age. "Good health, moral purpose, and mental vigor are keys to the good life," and women, she declared, "were never too old to find useful work." She herself was still writing furiously at eighty-one, although her eyesight was poor. She had turned out so many obituaries that she felt like "a sort of spiritual undertaker for the pioneers of the woman suffrage movement." She was thinking of her funeral and wanted "some common-sense woman" to conduct it, but declared she was "not ready to go yet." Vigorous to the end, Stanton dictated a letter urging woman suffrage to President Roosevelt just hours before she died.[60]

Harriot Hunt, who lived only to sixty-nine, kept on her desk a vase inscribed with a poem by Elizabeth Barrett Browning. This stanza is particularly appropriate:

> The honest earnest man must stand and *work*,
> The *woman* also;—otherwise she drops
> At once below the dignity of man,
> Accepting serfdom. . . .

These lines expressed the sentiments of the whole group on woman's need for work to achieve personal dignity and freedom.[61]

Antoinette Brown Blackwell, who lived to a healthy and active ninety-six (her father lived to ninety-four), was one of the foremost advocates of physical and mental work to prolong health and life. In 1872 she involved herself in a controversy over a book by Dr. Edward H. Clarke, *Sex in Education.* To the disgust of the feminists, Clarke advised that schoolgirls be given ample time off to rest on a regular basis because of their delicate condition. Blackwell responded with a series of six articles on "Sex and Work," published in the *Woman's Journal;* she condemned idleness and advocated the same physical regimen for both sexes at all ages. On health in old age she wrote: "Work! Work! In nothing else is there hope for man, or beast, or vegetable that would continue to live." Let every woman comprehend fully, she warned, that inactivity is death.[62]

Blackwell pursued her cause happily at every opportunity. She congratulated Stanton on her seventieth birthday (she herself was ten years younger) and urged her friend to "strike for a hundred." "It is grand that all of our lifetime workers refuse to grow old," Blackwell wrote; "They make splendid illustrations of the goods results which come from the steady use of brains—especially of 'pluck' and will." Like many of her friends, Blackwell worked even harder as she got older because there were so many things she had yet to accomplish before she was ready to go. When she was eighty, she expressed this thought in a letter to her niece Alice Stone Blackwell. Thinking over her life, she concluded that she would work just as hard if she were to do it over; but perhaps she would try to find time for "rather more sociability," a luxury she had not allowed herself in this life. [63]

The argument that life can be prolonged by work and will power is even more convincing when one looks at the group of feminists who were always in fragile health but who managed long, active lives nevertheless. Lucretia Mott suffered frequently from dyspepsia and other ailments, but she lived to eighty-seven. At eighty-two she was still speaking "clearly and forcibly" at woman suffrage meetings. Her daughters, recalling that their mother had promised to stop speaking at sixty, noted that "mother takes a long time in being sixty." To her sister Mott confessed: "I mean to live as long as I can." Matilda Joslyn Gage was constantly burdened by feeble health but remained active in the women's movement and other causes until her death at seventy-two. Laura Haviland, occupied with antislavery before the war and with suffrage and temperance afterward, described frequent illnesses in her autobiography, but, driven by the urgency of her causes, she seemed constantly to will herself well. She lived to be eighty-nine. [64]

Others followed a similar pattern. Amelia Bloomer, who died at seventy-six, had persevered in spite of constant stomach trouble and other health problems. She once gave a woman suffrage speech while recuperating at a water-cure establishment. Her husband gratefully noted that her energetic pace slowed a little as she got older, and for the first time he was easily able to keep up with her on their walks. Despite chronic headaches and periods of depression, Lucy Stone never slowed up; she lived to seventy-five. Hannah Longshore had a "delicate constitution" but improved in health and endurance after establishing her medical practice. This improvement she attributed to the active habits of her profession. Her practice, which she began in her thirties, lasted forty years with only two interruptions for illness. She died at eighty-two. Elizabeth Buffum Chace, describing herself as an "almost helpless invalid" at eighty-nine, kept busy painting pictures and dictating letters to the state legislature and the newspapers. Friends inquiring about her during a particularly serious illness found that she had rallied and was giving painting lessons to her nurse.[65]

Ann Preston, who graduated from medical school with Longshore at the age of thirty-eight, suffered from rheumatism and frail health but continued active in private practice for twenty years. She served as professor of physiology and dean of the medical college as well as consulting physician to the Philadelphia Woman's Hospital, which she helped found. Though she died young, at fifty-eight, she apparently survived to this age on the strength of sheer determination. Her own explanation serves for all the women: she was sustained "by the profound conviction that the cause was right and must succeed, that the study and practice of medicine are adapted to woman's nature, and that the profession and the world need her."[66]

The feminist-abolitionist women were motivated by the universal reformer's millennialist dream of emancipating the human family; in addition, they expanded that dream by their own female-oriented vision. Their romantic faith in truth and right and their strong sense of personal mission drove them on in the face of all obstacles. Other theories have been put forth to explain the motivation of reformers, such as the force of individual neurotic needs, and the desire of a displaced social group to regain status and exercise social control. Both appear as minor elements in the total picture but are unsatisfactory as major explanations—they underestimate the idealism and force of conviction with which these women set out to "make their world better."

This group of women viewed each crusade through a feminist prism which distinguished their perception from that of other universal reformers. Just as they had seen women as the chief victims of slavery, so they viewed the temperance and social purity campaigns as ways to emancipate women as well as to purify society. Health and medical reforms were the answers to the prevalence of women's illnesses and the neglect by the male medical profession. Education and child-rearing reforms were a means of elevating and training women, as well as of improving the next generation and ultimately perfecting the race.

In attacking evils which were particularly burdensome to women, the reformers also faced special obstacles because they themselves were women. Consequently they were forced to develop additional inner strengths and external defenses. Because the public condemned them as women neglecting their proper duties, they were compelled to work even harder in their domestic role. All of these forces united this group of women and separated them to some extent from even their closest male counterparts.

Though many of the feminists' demands have a contemporary ring (such as the right of women to know about their bodies), those demands must be viewed within the context of nineteenth-century society. Historically, the first generation of feminists stood between the early abolitionists, who were influenced by evangelicalism and romantic perfectionism, and a later generation of reformers who would institutionalize a more secular and pragmatic brand of social reform. The feminists' faith and optimism carried over unabated, and largely unexamined, into the complex postwar society. Though they were flexible about shifting to new means to achieve their millennialist ends, it was their moral fervor, rooted in the earlier era, which sustained them throughout their long careers.

NOTES

1. Wyman and Wyman, *Chace,* 2:63–64. The chapter's title is from Lucy Stone's last words, in Blackwell, *Stone,* p. 282.

2. Breault, *Howland,* p. 164.

3. Alla Foster's Reminiscences, in Howe, ed., *Representative Women,* p. 22; Bloomer, ed., *Life and Writings.*

4. *Notable American Women,* 2:626; Caroline Soule to her archbishop, Feb. 22, 1883, Caroline Soule Papers, New York Public Library.

5. Lucy Stone to Antoinette Blackwell, July 11, 1855, Blackwell Family Papers, LC; Paulina Wright Davis to Elizabeth Cady Stanton, "1852" and Dec. 12, 1852, Elizabeth Cady Stanton Papers.

6. Mary A. Livermore to Olympia Brown, June 13, 1869, Olympia Brown Papers; Antoinette Brown Blackwell Autobiography, Blackwell Family Papers, RC.

7. Lucy Stone to Margaret W. Campbell, Apr. 9, 1869, Blackwell Family Papers, LC; Paulina S. Wright to Maria Weston Chapman, Oct. 13, 1845, Weston Papers; *Woman's Journal,* Aug. 27, 1870.

8. Harper, *Anthony*, 2:544.

9. Stephen Foster to George Thompson, Jan. 15, 1870, Kelley-Foster Papers, AAS.

10. Wyman and Wyman, *Chace*, 2:65–66; her children's comments are on 1:126.

11. Ibid., 2:146; see also 67–68.

12. *Notable American Women*, 1:29; see also Gibbons, *Life*, and David J. Pivar, *Purity Crusade: Sexual Morality and Social Control, 1868–1900* (Westport, Conn.: Greenwood Press, 1973).

13. *History of Woman Suffrage*, 1:570–73, 644–45; see also Frank Thistlewaite, *America and the Atlantic Community* (New York: Harper & Row, 1959), and Betty Fladeland, *Men and Brothers: Anglo-American Antislavery Cooperation* (Urbana: University of Illinois Press, 1972).

14. *History of Woman Suffrage*, 1:226, 644–45, 706–7.

15. Richards and Elliott, *Howe*, p. 160; *Woman's Journal*, Nov. 5, 1870; see also July 6, 1872.

16. *History of Woman Suffrage*, 1:265–66, 283–89; Cutler Autobiography, *Woman's Journal*, Oct. 3, 1896; Hare, ed., *Comstock*.

17. See Elinor Rice Hays, *Those Extraordinary Blackwells* (New York: Harcourt, Brace & World, 1967), and Thistlewaite, *America and the Atlantic Community*.

18. See Alice Felt Tyler, *Freedom's Ferment* (Minneapolis: University of Minnesota Press, 1944).

19. See Herbert G. Gutman, "Work, Culture, and Society in Industrializing America, 1815–1919," *American Historical Review* 78 (June 1973): 531–88.

20. Susan B. Anthony Speech on temperance, 1852, Susan B. Anthony Papers, RC; Frances E. Willard, *Glimpses of Fifty Years* (Chicago: Woman's Temperance Publishing Association, 1889), p. 471; for "woman's war," see *Woman's Journal*, Mar. 21, Apr. 4, 1874.

21. See Janet Z. Giele, "Social Change in the Feminine Role: A Comparison of Woman's Suffrage and Woman's Temperance, 1870–1920" (Ph.D. dissertation, Radcliffe College, 1961), p. 54.

22. *History of Woman Suffrage*, 1:848; Stanton Temperance Speech, Jan., 1852, Elizabeth Cady Stanton Papers; *Lily*, May, 1852.

23. David Hackett Fischer, "America as Social History" (unpublished MS), ch. 8, pp. 5–11; Table of Alcohol Consumption, p. 30.

24. See Giele, "Social Change."

25. *Woman's Journal*, June 6, 1874.

26. Pivar, *Purity Crusade*, p. 71, Appendix A.

27. *Liberator*, Aug. 24, 1860.

28. See Anthony speech "Social Purity," in Harper, *Anthony*, 3:1004–12; Livermore speech "The Boy of To-Day," in *The Story of My Life* (Hartford, Conn.: A. D. Worthington, 1899), p. 648; Hunt, *Glances and Glimpses*, pp. 101–2.

29. Elizabeth Blackwell to Lucy Stone, n.d., Apr. 26, 1883, Dec. 28, 1888, Blackwell Family Papers, LC; Hays, *Extraordinary Blackwells*, pp. 181–82; see

also Elizabeth Blackwell's *Counsel to Parents on the Moral Education of Their Children* (New York: Brentano's Literary Emporium, 1881).

30. *Lily,* Mar., 1850.

31. Hallowell, ed., *Mott,* p. 429. See also James Mott, *Hints to Young People on the Duties of Civil Life* (New York, 1826), pamphlet in Garrison Family Papers, Smith College.

32. Holley, *Life for Liberty,* pp. 122–23, 84; Stephen Foster to Alla, Oct. 5, 1857, and Sallie Holley to A. K. Foster, July 19, 1856, Kelley-Foster Papers, AAS; Child is quoted in Pease, "Freshness of Fanaticism," p. 88.

33. Hays, *Extraordinary Blackwells,* p. 185; Wyman and Wyman, *Chace;* Stanton, *Stanton,* 2:91; M. C. Wright to L. Mott, Feb. 25, 1847, Wright Family Papers.

34. Gibbons, *Life,* pp. 151, 186–87.

35. Ibid., pp. 280, 192, 166.

36. Mary A. Livermore to Olympia Brown, Apr. 28, 1868, Olympia Brown Papers.

37. Weld et al., *Letters,* 2:898, 959, 892; Elizabeth Cady Stanton to Lucretia Mott, ca. 1848, Garrison Papers, BPL.

38. Lucretia Mott to Richard D. Webb, Feb. 24, 1870, Garrison Papers, BPL; see also John D. Davies, *Phrenology, Fad and Science; A Nineteenth Century American Crusade* (New Haven: Yale University Press, 1955).

39. Weld et al., *Letters,* 2:529; Stanton, *Stanton,* 2:46–47.

40. See Ann Douglas Wood, "'The Fashionable Diseases': Women's Complaints and Their Treatment in Nineteenth-Century America," *Journal of Interdisciplinary History* 4 (Summer 1973): 25–52; also Carroll Smith-Rosenberg, "The Hysterical Woman: Sex Roles and Role Conflict in 19th-Century America," *Social Research* 39 (Winter 1972): 652–78.

41. Davis Reminiscences, *History of Woman Suffrage,* 1:283; Pease, "Freshness of Fanaticism," p. 105.

42. *History of Woman Suffrage,* 1:37–38; Hunt, *Glances and Glimpses,* p. 152.

43. Hays, *Extraordinary Blackwells,* p. 62; see also p. 268.

44. *Lily,* Dec. 1, 1849, Oct. 2, 1854.

45. Hunt, *Glances and Glimpses;* see also Parton et al., *Eminent Women,* pp. 528–37.

46. The anniversary is described in *Liberator,* June 13, 1860; Martha Wright to Lucretia Mott, Jan. 29, 1856, and Wright to Elizabeth Cady Stanton, July 5, 1860, Wright Family Papers.

47. Parton et al., *Eminent Women,* pp. 537–44, 517–22; Frederick C. Waite, "The Three Myers Sisters—Pioneer Women Physicians," *Medical Review of Reviews* (March 1933), pp. 114–19; Reminiscences of Dr. Mary F. Thomas, *History of Woman Suffrage,* 1:306–10; Cutler Autobiography, *Woman's Journal,* Oct. 10, 17, 1896; Harper, *Anthony, passim,* for Lozier.

48. *History of Woman Suffrage,* 1:306, 308.

49. Parton et al., *Eminent Women,* pp. 517–22.

50. Severance, *Mother of Clubs,* p. 58; Elizabeth Blackwell, *How to Keep a*

Household in Health (London: Ladies' Sanitary Association, 1870).

51. Wyman and Wyman, *Chace,* 1:106–8; Lucy Stone to Samuel May, Jr., n.d., Blackwell Family Papers, RC; *History of Woman Suffrage,* 1:37.

52. Hays, *Extraordinary Blackwells,* p. 281; see also Edward Bliss Foote, *Medical Common Sense* (New York: By the Author, 1863), esp. p. 235.

53. Stanton, *Stanton,* 2:44; E. C. Stanton to M. S. Gove Nichols, Aug. 31, 1852, Elizabeth Cady Stanton Papers; Stanton, *Eighty Years,* pp. 419–20; *Lily,* July, 1851; Stanton speech "Our Young Girls," Elizabeth Cady Stanton Papers.

54. Hunt, *Glances and Glimpses,* pp. 155–57 and *passim.*

55. See Weld et al., *Letters,* 2:942–43, also Thomas H. Le Duc, "Grahamites and Garrisonites," *New York History* 20 (Apr. 1939): 189–91.

56. L. M. Child to Anna L. Dresel, Mar. 21, 1873, Loring Family Papers; A. K. Foster to S. Foster, Aug. 18, 1847, Kelley-Foster Papers, AAS; Harriet Hanson Robinson Diary, Oct. 6, 1854, Harriet Hanson Robinson Papers; Harper, *Anthony,* 2:134–135; *Notable American Women,* 2:426–28.

57. *Statistical History of the United States from Colonial Times to the Present* (Washington, D.C.: U.S. Bureau of the Census, 1965), p. 24.

58. *Notable American Women,* 2:231.

59. Livermore, *Story of My Life,* p. 490; Maria Weston Chapman to daughter Anne, Apr., 1857, Weston Family Papers.

60. Stanton speech "The Pleasures of Age," Elizabeth Cady Stanton Papers; Stanton, *Stanton,* 2:321, 316.

61. *Liberator,* June 13, 1860.

62. *Woman's Journal,* Apr. 11, 1872; also Mar. 14, 21, 28, Apr. 4, 18, 1872. See also Antoinette Brown Blackwell's *Sexes Throughout Nature* (New York: G. P. Putnam's Sons, 1875), pp. 211–18.

63. A. B. Blackwell to E. C. Stanton, Nov. 10, 1885, and Blackwell to Alice Stone Blackwell, Dec. 15, 1905, Blackwell Family Papers, RC.

64. Higginson, *Letters and Journals,* p. 272; Hallowell, ed., *Mott,* p. 395; *Notable American Women,* 2:4–6; Haviland, *Woman's Life-Work.*

65. Parton et al., *Eminent Women,* pp. 537–44; *Woman's Journal,* Dec. 23, 1899; Wyman and Wyman, *Chace,* 2:300.

66. Parton et al., *Eminent Women,* p. 547; *History of Woman Suffrage,* 1:389; *Notable American Women,* 3:96–97.

6

The Emergence of a Feminist Ideology

THOUGH "FEMINISM" AND "SUFFRAGISM" have been used interchangeably even by scholars, the central demand of feminists in the antebellum period was not the right to vote, but the right of woman to define her own sphere. Jane Elisabeth Jones, one of the important propagandists of the early movement, typically articulated the feminists' main grievance in an editorial in the Ohio *Anti-Slavery Bugle* in 1848, a week before the Seneca Falls meeting. The "lordly sex" had enslaved woman in a narrow sphere and condemned her as "unsexed" if she revealed any intelligence or creativity. Responding to this injustice, Jones wrote: "Sphere! No, 'circle' would be a better name for woman's present walk; for it is round, round, round, like a blind horse on a mill wheel." In 1860 she delivered a major address at the last antebellum national women's rights convention, with her text based on this resolution: "That woman's sphere can not be bounded. Its prescribed orbit is the largest place that in her highest development she can fill."[2]

Although the Declaration of Sentiments issued at Seneca Falls in 1848 has been the most publicized expression of nineteenth-century feminist ideology, the themes of the developing movement had been appearing in print for ten years before that, principally in the *Liberator,* the *National Anti-Slavery Standard,* and later the *Bugle.* The 1830's controversy over the right of women to play an equal role with men in antislavery had sensitized the feminist-abolitionist women to the need to assert their own rights in order to defend those of the slave. From the conflicts both within the antislavery movement and with antifeminists outside arose the principal themes of early feminism: the equal rights and responsibilities of women and men, the right of a woman to leave her prescribed "sphere" in order to do a "man's" job, and the parallel positions of woman and slave. Although the latter was partly a rhetorical device, it also represented the feminists' feeling of identification with all slaves, and especially with their black sisters in slavery. In speeches, articles, and stories, the feminist-abolitionists dwelled on the similarities between women and all enslaved peoples: the deprivation of human rights, the loss of identity, the enforced dependence, the denial of opportunity for self-development. Emancipation of all humankind, but especially of women, would be their lifelong goal.

To the feminist-abolitionist women, "emancipation" meant access to the world outside the home and freedom from psychological and economic dependence on men. Accepting woman's special responsibilities to home and family, they argued that she should not be limited to this role or forced into it against her will because the opportunity for self-reliance was denied her. "Woman is too large for the sphere in which society compels her to move," declared Elizabeth Oakes Smith; "marriage no more fills up the sum of her whole being than it does that of a man."[3] Woman's sphere should be limited only by her capacity, and all obstacles to her highest development should be removed. This argument, in the spirit of the early nineteenth-century democratic movement, had been advanced heretofore only on behalf of white males. The feminist-abolitionists attempted to extend it to the rest of the human family.

The most important obstacle to woman's emancipation was the widespread belief that the sexes, because of "natural" and divinely ordained differences, should occupy separate spheres. Though there were economic and political motives for maintaining inequality between the sexes, the commitment to keeping woman in her "proper" place transcended even these forces. Because the doctrine was so pervasive and so inimical to their own interests, the feminists were compelled to challenge it and to offer an alternative conception of sexual spheres. Significantly, Sarah Grimké's *Letters on the Equality of the Sexes* were originally published in 1837 as "Letters on the Province of Woman." This questioning of woman's natural "province" led inevitably to an inquiry into the differences between the sexes and the proper roles of women and men. The efforts of Sarah and Angelina Grimké and other abolitionist women to answer these questions led to the first coherent expression of a feminist ideology concerning the nature and rightful sphere of woman. The principal tenets of this belief system were expressed publicly before 1840; although they were expanded and embellished in the 1840's and 1850's, and carried over as assumptions into the later suffrage movement, very little was subsequently added or changed. This new concept of woman's sphere was at the heart of the feminists' major antebellum demands. Lucy Stone spelled out these demands in an 1853 speech: the right to education; the right to "honorable" independence so women would not be forced to marry; the right of wives to legal protection and personal freedom within marriage; the right to vote and be represented in government.[4]

The feminists drew on several sources to justify the broadening of woman's sphere. In their earliest arguments they turned to the Scriptures for authority, but they rejected the orthodox interpretation and relied instead on a Quaker-inspired, feminist reinterpretation strongly influenced by the romanticism and perfectionism of the times. Though they renounced the content and form of Calvinist doctrine and the current religious revivalism, they retained much of the evangelical spirit. The Puritan concept of duty, work, and suffering as means of serving God remained integral to their ideological framework.

Though their religious roots helped shape their developing ideology, they derived their principal arguments from secular sources —the Enlightenment ideology of human rights, and the republican ideals of the Revolution. For their rhetoric the feminists also drew heavily on radical abolitionism, which shared the same ideological origins. Finally, they took society's belief in innate psychological and spiritual sex differences, and in woman's moral superiority, and incorporated these elements into their own belief system, with important modifications.

Such beliefs were rarely presented in a formal or systematic way because the feminists were primarily activists and propagandists, not writers or philosophers. If they were aware of ideological tensions or inconsistencies, they optimistically assumed that all difficulties would be resolved when their ideal society was realized. Their ideas were fashioned mainly in writing articles and tracts or in delivering speeches, often extemporaneously. Few women approached their subject as scholars or sought the leisure to develop their ideas in greater depth, although most had the intellectual capacity to do so.

Nevertheless, feminists did develop an ideology which embraced a new conception of the relationship between the sexes, both within marriage and the family and in the world outside the home. An examination of their rhetoric in the period 1830–60, as well as of their private statements in correspondence and diaries (often more forceful than public utterances), indicates the shape of this emergent feminist ideology. Future feminists would turn repeatedly to these earlier models for guidance and inspiration.

The earliest coherent public defense of women's rights, promulgated by the Grimké sisters in 1837, relied on the authority of the Scriptures. Here personal belief and inclination coincided with expediency. Since their principal attackers were orthodox clergymen who cited the Bible as *their* source of authority, the sisters' tactic was a logical and useful one. Such a defense could not be dismissed as easily as the work of "infidels" like Mary Wollstonecraft or "free love women" like Frances Wright. The scriptural approach also represented the Grimkés' general feelings. As Sarah explained, their claim to equal rights came from "a conviction of duty based on the Scriptures." She would depend solely on the Bible to designate the sphere of woman because almost everything written on the subject was the result of opinions formed by men without reference to the simple truths developed in the Scriptures. Her *Letters on the Equality of the Sexes and the Condition of Woman* (1838) contained carefully developed arguments which continued to provide an important basis for feminist ideology throughout the nineteenth century and into the twentieth.[5]

Sarah Grimké argued that the Scriptures, properly translated and interpreted, taught that men and women had been created in perfect equality and should be granted the same rights, duties, and privileges. Adam and Eve fell from innocence but not from equality, since their guilt was shared. Conventional interpretations, based on false translations by men, incorporated male prejudices. For example, God's pronouncement upon woman, "Thy desire shall be to thy husband and he shall rule over thee," was meant as a simple prophecy rather than as a command—a prediction of the consequences of sin, rather than a divine endorsement of male superiority. The statement had been incorrectly translated from the Hebrew, she argued, by men who substituted "will" for the original "shall" because they were accustomed to exercising authority over their wives.

All the feminist-abolitionist women, and many of the men, drew on this basic argument in the antebellum period and applied it to the New Testament as well as the Old. Paul's edict, "Let your women keep silence in the churches," was one of the biblical quotations used most frequently by clerical antifeminists. The feminists countered it in a variety of ways. Lucy Stone, in a speech on "The Province of Woman" probably given in the 1840's, suggested alternative explanations. Paul's apparent injunction could be considered a contradiction to another edict of his to the whole church (women included) that *all* might prophesy. A more probable interpretation, she argued, was simply that women of biblical times were less educated than men and, given their first opportunity to question, were taking up too much of the congregation's time by asking questions which could be answered privately at home. Neither interpretation, according to Stone, implied woman's inequality.[6]

Antoinette Brown, more than Lucy Stone or other contemporaries, took up the scriptural defense of women's rights where Sarah Grimké left off. As a theology student at Oberlin in 1849, she published in the *Oberlin Quarterly Review* her feminist exegesis of Paul's interdiction on women speaking in church. Paul's advice had been written for women of that time and was not meant as a universal principle, she argued; it was also incorrectly translated—women were forbidden to babble, but they were not forbidden to teach or prophesy. In numerous later articles and speeches Brown refuted other apparent references to women's inferior position. Paul's injunction to Timothy that women not be permitted to teach or rule over men, for example, really was meant to prohibit dogmatizing or teaching in a dictatorial spirit, which was also forbidden to men. The Bible was "truly democratic" and recognized "neither male nor female in Christ Jesus." The Quaker influence on Brown, as on all the feminist-abolitionists, was here quite apparent.[7]

The proper interpretation of biblical references to women continued to be a subject of controversy, if only because it was raised constantly by the opposition. However, the feminists' speeches and articles increasingly relied on what the authors saw as the bedrock of authority for woman's equality: the human rights argument of Enlightenment philosophy and Revolutionary ideology. Basically in agreement with the Grimké-Brown reading of Scriptures, most feminists felt themselves on firmer ground with a more secular approach. Ernestine Rose, responding to Brown at the 1852 national women's rights convention, expressed the conviction of many that the Bible was at best so "obscure and indefinite as to admit of different interpretations." The demand for "Human Rights and Freedom" required no written authority but was based on "self-evident" moral precepts and on "the fundamental principles of the Republic." Susan B. Anthony later became a principal exponent of this secular approach and on many occasions expressed impatience with the scriptural controversy. At an 1885 convention she typically declared that she had "found long ago that the settling of any question of human rights by peoples' interpretation of the Bible is utterly impossible."[8]

Though most feminists took the Bible more seriously than Rose or Anthony did, their rhetoric tended to be based more often on the Declaration of Independence—controversial enough, when given a feminist interpretation. As patriotic granddaughters of the Revolutionary generation, the doctrine of natural, inalienable rights came easily to their minds and lips. Calling on that doctrine first to justify the emancipation of slaves, the feminist-abolitionists quickly saw the need to extend rights to women as well. God had also created women equal, they avowed, and had endowed them with natural rights which could be neither granted nor denied by men. Just as the feminists rejected the orthodox view of Christianity, so they denied that the traditional interpretation of the Christian Republic was the true one. The Declaration of Independence, like the Scriptures, needed to be stripped of the meaning given by male interpreters.

"Christian Republic," to the feminist-abolitionists, evoked images of their Yankee grandfathers and grandmothers battling to preserve representative government and natural, God-given freedoms in the face of royal despotism, British aristocracy, and "foreign" influences. In their rhetoric the women drew freely on these images, adding the "slavery of sex" and the "aristocracy of sex" to the list of oppressions, and pointing to their Revolutionary foremothers, who had been denied freedom and equality in spite of their heroic efforts for the Republic. The present oppressors were labeled the "masculine aristocracy" and the "lordly sex," but the language of the Revolution was otherwise kept largely intact.

194

In its most direct form, the rhetoric of the Revolution appeared in feminist-abolitionist protests against taxation without representation. Not a widespread tactic, such protest was nevertheless highly symbolic and effective, at least among sympathizers, in generating indignation and enthusiasm for united action on behalf of women. Harriot Hunt was probably the first to publicize this approach. Appearing at the local assessor's office to pay her property taxes in 1851, she was appalled to learn that a "simple Irish boy" had become a full citizen while she, "a Bostonian by birth, education, and life," was paying taxes without enjoying the full rights of citizenship. She subsequently submitted well-publicized protests with her taxes each year.[9]

Lucy Stone, in public addresses in the 1840's and 1850's, regularly urged women to resist taxation until they gained representation, even at the risk of losing both property and friends. She herself took Hunt's method of agitation one step further: in 1858 she refused to pay her property taxes and allowed her household goods to be sold at public auction. The property was bought by a neighbor and returned to her, but the protest was widely publicized and provided a concrete opportunity to apply Revolutionary principles to the women's cause.[10]

In the postwar years, other feminist-abolitionists also used this strategy. Lydia Maria Child filed a protest with her taxes. Abby Kelley and Stephen Foster joined with others in Worcester, Massachusetts, in the 1870's to rebel against the "masculine aristocracy" by refusing to pay their taxes. The Fosters saw their farm sold at auction, later buying it back with the help of the community. To the public they explained, "We are simply fighting over again the battles of the Revolution, only on a higher moral plane." Since the feminist-abolitionists shared with their Revolutionary forebears a dedication to the right of property ownership, these protests were not undertaken lightly. Thomas Wentworth Higginson, supporting the Fosters' action, assured them that the sales of property "are to the Woman Suffrage movement what the Fugitive Slave cases were to the Anti-Slavery movement . . . they are the nearest we can come to the blood of the martyrs!"[11]

Privately as well as publicly, the feminist-abolitionists felt responsible for carrying forward the Revolutionary struggle, as well as for maintaining the ideals of the antislavery movement. Both were viewed as part of a broader battle for human rights—the feminist struggle was only the newest battle in the larger war. Susan B. Anthony, writing in the 1850's, begged her brother to see that the "woman's revolution" was based on the same principle for which the Revolutionary fathers fought and died: that one class may not usurp the power to legislate for another. The principles of representative government and individual liberty constituted a theme which unified their many causes.[12]

The feminist-abolitionists had drawn on the "natural rights" ideology of the Revolution in the antislavery cause, and the transfer of abolitionist rhetoric to the women's movement was logical and inevitable. The "woman and slave" comparison was the most frequently used feminist argument in the antebellum period. The Grimké sisters had set a pattern for public rhetoric by linking their own rights to those of all women and all oppressed persons. As early as 1837, Angelina appealed to her white sisters to speak out against slavery in spite of the prejudice against women taking this action, and she warned them that a refusal to affirm their right to speak out would make them "the white slaves of the North." Calling on "the great doctrine of Human Rights" on another occasion, she declared that "the rights of the slave and of woman blend like the colors of the rainbow."[13]

From the human rights argument linking the denial of the rights of women and slaves, it was a short step to the declaration that women, denied their rights, were like slaves. This argument was particularly persuasive within the antislavery movement, since abolitionists were already moved by the injustice of slavery. Abby Kelley, attempting to explain women's position to a fellow abolitionist, asked him to "imagine a colored man's feelings, when kept at bay and held in contempt by his white brother." "Then," she continued, "can you have some faint conception of a woman's heart, when she awakes to a realizing sense of her true position, as a responsible being, and sees herself fenced in by the iron prejudices of centuries. . . ."[14]

The "woman and slave" parallel was partly an effective rhetorical device, to be carried to eloquent heights by the consummate skill of Elizabeth Cady Stanton. It also represented the feminists' private belief that women were oppressed, like slaves, by the denial of legal rights and by their involuntary confinement in a narrow sphere.

Though the reformers acknowledged that (as Stanton put it) woman's bondage "differs from that of the negro slave," they nevertheless viewed it as equally oppressive—it "frets and chafes her just the same."[15] Like slaves, women were treated as inferiors and forced into a state of helpless dependence and low self-esteem, resigned to a life of submission and obedience. Like slaves, they were forced to appear contented because of fear of displeasing their masters. One of the most frequently expressed goals of Stanton and other feminists was to stir in women the same hope that abolitionists had attempted to arouse in slaves—the hope of escape from bondage, and the self-respect required to work for their own emancipation.

For political reasons, public rhetoric on this issue was often softer than private language. Lydia Maria Child used a moderate voice in her public role as writer and antislavery editor, but her private correspondence revealed a fierce feminist rage. Seething at the injustice of the slave system and especially its effects on women, she wrote to a friend: "Cursed is that system of considering human beings as chattel! Whether it be because they are women, or because they are colored." To another friend she expressed her "towering indignation" for "womanhood made chattels personal from the beginning of time, perpetually insulted by literature, law, and custom." Clearly she saw the plight of slave women as part of the larger history of female bondage, linked to it by common bonds of immorality and injustice.[16]

The wife, particularly, was viewed as a slave, and marriage was considered a condition of bondage for women. From the earliest days of feminist-abolitionism, the relationship of husband and wife was most frequently compared to that of master and slave on the southern plantation. Often the subject of marriage was introduced into antislavery speeches and articles by feminists who found it difficult to speak of one form of bondage without the other. Lucy Stone, attacking slavery in an article in the *Una,* noted also: "Marriage is to woman a state of slavery. It takes from her the right to her own property, and makes her submissive in all things to her husband." The views she expressed privately were essentially the same, although in one letter, responding to a challenge from a fellow abolitionist, she admitted that marriage was "capable of being bad enough for women but slavery is a still 'lower depth.'"[17]

To the feminists, the human rights argument which was used to defend the slave carried equal weight when applied to the oppressed wife. Denied legal protection against sexual and other physical abuses, forced into total dependence because of the denial of her right to keep her own property or earnings, deprived of her birth-given name, denied legal guardianship of her children—the wife, to the feminist-abolitionists, was the epitome of woman as slave.

Equality and freedom for married women were among the most prized goals of the feminist-abolitionists, expressed early and frequently in the antebellum period. Lucretia Mott, in a "Discourse on Woman" delivered as a sermon in 1849 and published as a widely circulated pamphlet, typically applied the abolitionists' human rights argument to women who were fettered like slaves and prevented from developing their full capacities. The notion of the wife who played a perpetual secondary role, ministering to "her lord and master," was an "old-fashioned absurdity." True marriage was a union between equal and independent persons, she argued; only when women were accorded dignity and self-respect could this ideal be achieved. In keeping with this belief, Mott proselytized for changing the customary "man and wife" in the wedding ceremony to "husband and wife," because the former implied that the wife was "a mere appendage." Marriage "left a man still a man, and a woman still a woman," only now they stood in a "*new* relation to each other."[18]

Others expressed similar views. As Antoinette Brown protested in 1853, "The wife owes service and labor to her husband as much and as absolutely as the slave does to his master." Amelia Bloomer, deploring the loss of individuality in marriage, declared in a temperance speech, "How degrading the thought, that before marriage Woman can enjoy freedom of thought, but afterwards must endorse her husband's sentiments be they good or bad! Call you not this slavery?"[19]

"Slavery" was a general word subsuming a multitude of evils. Publicly, the emphasis was on the right of married women to own property and obtain guardianship of their children. Privately, the feminists felt that "the right of a wife to her own person" (i.e., the right to refuse sexual intercourse) was at the heart of her emancipation. In 1860 Abby Hopper Gibbons warned her unmarried daughters that girls were prone "to become possessed of the absurd notion that it is a wife's duty to submit even to the waywardness of her husband." "God forbid," she declared, "that our free children should *fall* into such an error!" Elizabeth Cady Stanton, the most vocal public advocate of this position, wrote in 1857 that "the present false marriage relation" was "nothing more nor less than legalized prostitution," and that "personal freedom is the first right to be proclaimed." Less well known are the similar views expressed by Elizabeth Oakes Smith in a tract on "The Sanctity of Marriage." Wives were commonly "bought with a price"; husbands were in the habit of using money to control the wife "if she fail to become in all things the subservient creature she is expected to be."[20]

The parallel between marriage and slavery was most compelling to the feminists when they considered the "right of a woman to her own body." The common principle of human freedom was seen quite explicitly. Stanton, reacting angrily to the refusal of Wendell Phillips and others to deal with the issues of marriage and divorce at the 1860 national convention, pointed out in a sharp letter to the *Liberator* that the moral principle which forbade man to hold property in man applied to marriage as well as to slavery.[21] The feminist-abolitionists were in private agreement on the importance of this grievance, but they differed widely in their willingness to deal publicly with the issue. That disagreement contributed to the ultimate division in their ranks.

Similarly, most feminist-abolitionists agreed on the need for legal protection for the wives of drunkards and for other abused wives. They also favored some kind of provision for legal separation, although they differed in their views on divorce. The most prevalent feminist view was expressed by Amelia Bloomer. Speaking of the woman unfortunate enough to be married to an intemperate husband, she said she cared little what words were used: "All we ask is that law and public sentiment forbid that any woman should live in close companionship with a creature so gross and vile."[22]

One of the clearest links between abolitionist rhetoric and the developing feminist ideology appeared in the emphasis given to the need for a married woman to retain her own name. Long before Lucy Stone made this a public issue by refusing to add her husband's name to her own, other women were defying convention in a less spectacular but significant way: their signatures appeared as "Maria Weston Chapman" and "Lydia Maria Child," never "Mrs. Henry Chapman" or "Mrs. David Lee Child." Lucretia Mott, at a women's rights

199

convention in 1852, requested that "Mrs. Stephen Smith" on a committee roster be changed to "Rosa Smith." She explained that "Woman's Rights women do not like to be called by their husbands' names but by their own."[23] Here was another example of the influence of Quaker custom, which reflected both a distaste for titles and a commitment to the spiritual equality of partners in marriage.

The symbolic gesture of retaining one's own name after marriage was always linked, in feminist rhetoric, to the parallel of woman and slave: like slaves, women took the names of their masters; like slaves, they suffered a loss of identity and were "swallowed up" in marriage. The feminist-abolitionists stressed the importance of this symbolism to slaves, who often gave up their slave names and took new ones on gaining freedom. In a letter to the 1856 national women's rights convention, Elizabeth Cady Stanton noted that the wife, like the "Southern slave," existed nameless and unrecognized. "Many people consider this a very small matter, but it is the symbol of the most cursed monopoly . . . by man of all the rights, the life, the liberty, and happiness of one-half of the human family—all womankind."[24]

Stanton's private indignation was equally intense. To a friend she expressed her "very serious objections . . . to being called Henry. There is a great deal in a name. It often signifies much, and may involve a great principle." Several years later, responding to a letter from Wendell Phillips sent to "Mrs. H. B. Stanton," she sent off a lengthy missive attempting to persuade him of "the heinousness and criminality" of his offense. (Phillips, a match for Stanton, assured her that he would hereafter always remember her first name by thinking of Queen Elizabeth: "so jealous of her looks that she forbade [by proclamation] all but two painters to attempt painting her likeness—she will exactly bring you to my mind."[25])

This sensitivity to the symbolic importance of language extended beyond the choice of names, and reflected a widespread feminist consciousness among the early "women's rights women." Maria Weston Chapman, discussing her latest plan of action in 1839, wrote, "Let us strike manful and womanful for justice and freedom." The same awareness of the masculine orientation of everyday language appeared in the correspondence of Antoinette Brown, who referred to their group of feminists as "our sisternity," and Elizabeth Comstock, who wrote from an ocean voyage that seasickness "has completely unmanned or *unwomanned* us both."[26]

This strong feminist consciousness led the women to develop a new concept of the ideal relationship between the sexes. Their views on the proper roles of women and men appear in speeches on abolitionism and women's rights, and in private letters and diaries. One can piece these fragments together to obtain a fairly coherent picture of this new ideal. The feminist-abolitionists accepted many of their society's values but modified them in significant ways to conform to their own view of women's rights and woman's sphere. These modifications reflected a commitment to the ideology of human rights and constituted still another link between abolitionism and feminism.

The feminist ideology which developed within the nineteenth-century women's movement was built on the basic acceptance of marriage and family as central social institutions. Feminists always directed their efforts toward reforming marriage (by providing equality and freedom for women) and elevating it (by eliminating society's double moral standard); they never intended to abolish the institution. All the feminist-abolitionists argued that emancipating women would produce better marriages and more stable, harmonious families, and there is no evidence that this was not their private expectation as well. As Caroline Severance explained it, giving women their rights would result in better families by changing mothers from "ignorant and enslaved" persons to "educated, harmoniously developed equals." Elizabeth Cady Stanton argued that allowing women to take part in public affairs would result in "far less nagging at the family hearth"; harmony in marriage required perfect freedom for both partners.[27] In addition, women who were trained to support themselves would not have to rush into bad marriages but would be free to marry when and whom they chose; hence the opportunity for dignified labor for women would mean the end of forced and unhappy unions. These points, which Sarah Grimké had argued in the 1830's in her *Letters*, became major themes in the antebellum speeches of Abby Kelley Foster and Susan B. Anthony, as well as in the writings of Stanton, Lucy Stone, and others.

The *Una,* a newspaper published and edited by Paulina Wright Davis in the 1850's, displays the development of antebellum feminist thought on this subject. Like Stanton, Davis saw the marriage question as the key to all reform and advocated a relatively bold and direct treatment of the subject. Much of her paper is devoted to this concern. Declaring that "the true family" was "the central and supreme institution among human societies," she argued that only by striving for pefect equality in marriage could men and women approach this ideal. Like all the feminists, Davis envisioned equality in marriage leading to superior children and a healthier, more perfect race. Ultimately, the "true family" would provide the harmony and cooperation needed to make the world better. The organization of society depended upon the character of the family: "its evils are the source of all evils, its good the fountain of all good." The correction of abuses in marriage was "the starting-point of all the reforms which the world needs."[28]

Private expressions of the desire to reform marriage reinforced the feminists' public statements. Though many of them were reluctant to marry because they feared a loss of independence, given the imperfect state of their society, virtually all feminists saw "true" marriage as an integral and essential part of their ideal society. Susan Anthony congratulated Amelia Bloomer and her husband on their fiftieth wedding anniversary by noting that their marriage stood as one of the strongest refutations of the charge that equality for women would cause "inharmony and disruption of the marriage bond." "To the contrary," she exulted, "such conditions of perfect equality are the best helps to make for peace and harmony and elevation in all true and noble directions."[29]

Though the feminists shared their society's glorification of marriage and family, they modified this belief by insisting on the right of women to remain unmarried. Their demand that unmarried women be accorded equal status in society was a significant plank in their developing feminist platform. Like their call for equality in marriage, this was an early demand, expressed publicly in the 1830's and 1840's by the Grimkés, Abby Kelley, Lucretia Mott, Lucy Stone, and others. Their private views on the subject were, if anything, more forceful than their public statements. The choice by Susan Anthony and others to remain single in order to pursue their work testified to the group's strong feelings on the lack of freedom for women in traditional marriages. That the majority of them did marry is a tribute to the feminist-abolitionist men they tended to choose, who were also committed to the ideal of equal marriage.

Abby Kelley, who finally married because she was assured of

maintaining her independence, nevertheless continued to be highly sensitive to the need of unmarried women for well-paid work, recognition, the opportunity to enjoy their own homes, and other rights and amenities accorded unmarried men. In her speeches and articles, she continued to stress that marriage was not the only means to woman's fulfillment. Seeing the importance of role models for unmarried women, she privately chastised sister reformer Louisa May Alcott for giving in to public pressure and marrying off her alter ego, Jo of *Little Women.* Alcott, apparently repentant, promised that "by and by her old maid would come."[30] In questioning one of the most sacred dogmas of their day, the women were sharpening the cutting edge of the developing feminist ideology.

The feminists' position on unmarried women was part of their broader concept of overlapping spheres and flexible, dual roles for women and men. This was a critical modification of the prevailing belief in separate spheres and rigidly defined, exclusive sex roles. Such a position was never brought forth fully developed at a given moment in time; rather, it developed naturally from the women's belief in the equal rights and responsibilities of the sexes, as well as from their acceptance of much of society's assumption of sex differences.

Women and men in the feminist-abolitionist group felt that both sexes had responsibilities in the home as well as in the community. The Reverend Samuel J. May, a strong supporter of women and an abolitionist who had been "converted" by his exposure to the woman-and-slave parallel, was a typical example. In an influential sermon on "The Rights and Conditions of Women" (1846), he explained that the rigid assignment of the sexes to separate spheres and functions was "a perfect caricature of the true business of life." Just as the father's role in the family was vital, he argued, so the influence of woman in government was also needed. All of the feminist-abolitionists agreed. As Jane Grey Swisshelm explained in a series of "Letters to Mothers" in the *Lily,* husbands and wives were equal partners: the husband's business included spending time with his children, and the wife's entailed understanding and helping in his work, at least by sympathy and advice. All felt that the rearing of children was the most sacred obligation of both sexes.[31]

Still, the spheres were not seen as identical. Women were viewed as the bearers of special moral and domestic responsibilities. There was an apparent contradiction between the demand for woman's equality and unlimited sphere, and the belief in her moral superiority and special obligations. This was justified intellectually by distinguishing between women's primary existence as human beings and citizens of the Republic, and their secondary function in social roles as wives and mothers. As Stanton explained, "Womanhood is the great fact, wifehood and motherhood its incidents."[32] As human beings, the rights and responsibilities of women and men were the same, and their spheres were identical; both had obligations to the total society, including family and community. Only in their more narrow social roles did some differentiation of sphere occur: because of divinely ordained duties and talents, woman's special function was to nurture and preserve the family, and man's to labor in the world outside.

The feminists' conception of sexual spheres can be visualized by picturing two circles overlapping so that the largest area is the one held in common. This broad area is the one shared by women and men in their primary function as human beings and citizens. The smaller, peripheral areas are assigned each to one sex; here women and men function in their unique social roles. This concept of overlapping spheres and dual natures was used to justify all the demands of the movement. It underlay all of the proposed reforms, including restructuring of the marriage relationship; furthermore, it reconciled the apparent inconsistency between the feminists' radical demand for woman's emancipation from her narrow sphere, and their conservative support of the family as the central institution of society.

Again, the earliest public defense of this concept was made by Sarah Grimké, whose *Letters on the Equality of the Sexes* foreshadowed much of the movement's ideology. She defended the right of women to speak publicly by arguing that their spheres and duties as citizens and as spiritual beings were identical with those of men; only in social roles were their responsibilities different. Angelina Grimké, in a private letter, developed this idea further: "Rights and duties depend *not* on *sex* but on our *relations* in life; as women we have *no* peculiar duties, but as mothers, wives and daughters we have." Men and women had identical freedom in regard to moral issues which affect them as human beings, but different provinces when they functioned in specific sex roles. Angelina went on to explain that the equality thus achieved would benefit men as well as women: "Woman has been used as a drudge or cared for like a spoiled child, and man has inflicted no less an injury on himself in thus degrading *us*, for some of the noblest virtues are too generally deemed *unmanly*." Equality, then, meant freedom from restrictive sex roles and stereotypes: women, like men, could develop their physical and intellectual abilities; men, like women, could be free to act in their highest moral capacities.[33]

The Grimkés' conceptualization of overlapping spheres and dual roles became an important part of nineteenth-century feminist thought. Its most eloquent expression appeared at the end of the century in Elizabeth Cady Stanton's celebrated speech, "The Solitude of Self." Here she reminded her audience that a woman could be considered in four separate ways: as an individual human soul, Protestantism granted her the right of individual conscience and judgment; as a citizen in a republic, she was due the same rights as all others; as a woman, her rights and duties were still the same as a man's—individual happiness and development. Only in her fourth role, in her "incidental relations of life, such as mother, wife, sister, daughter," did she acquire special duties and training. Similarly, Stanton argued, in discussing the sphere of man "we do not decide his rights as an individual, as a citizen, as a man, by his duties as a father, husband, brother or son. . . ."[34]

The feminists' designation of special roles derived from their partial acceptance of the popular belief that the sexes were different spiritually and psychologically, as well as physically. They were influenced, in varying degrees, by the romanticism of the mid-nineteenth century, and by the Transcendentalists' emphasis on the divinity within each human being. Dedicated to the improvement of the human family, reformers looked to humanity's innate spirituality to make this transformation. Woman, however, was seen as the more spiritual and less earthly of the sexes; her naturally higher level of innocence and purity made her the most likely leader in this moral revolution—the redeemer of the race.

The feminist-abolitionists always espoused their belief in woman's moral superiority. As early as the 1830's they argued for the expansion of woman's sphere in order that her "civilizing" influence might have broader scope. Aileen Kraditor and other historians have pointed to the "moral superiority" argument as an expedient device used to gain supporters for woman suffrage in the later period, and have contrasted that argument with the more idealistic ones used by the first generation. While the earlier feminists were indeed idealistic, they also argued that the broader world needed the purity and spirituality which women could bring to it. Similarly, the distinction made by William O'Neill and other historians between "hard-core" feminists and "social" feminists in the later movement has little relevance for the earlier generation. All were "hard-core" feminists in arguing for women's inherent human rights, and "social" feminists in seeking the social reforms that women could effect by broadening the scope of their moral influence.

Elizabeth Chandler, one of the first to defend women's public role in antislavery, wrote in the 1830's of the natural selflessness and tenderness that characterized the female, as opposed to the "grosser nature" and selfishness of her male counterpart. Woman's special mission on earth, Maria Weston Chapman wrote in an 1840's antislavery tract, was to be "a minister of Christian love . . . to keep alive in society some feeling of human brotherhood."[35] All feminists believed that woman had a special role to play in the betterment of the human family, and demanded that she be given the freedom to carry out this mission.

Not only did women deserve an equal role in public affairs, the feminists argued, but they even ought to predominate in some areas because of their special gifts. Elizabeth Stanton declared in the early 1850's that woman was especially suited for the ministry because she was "superior to man in the affections, high moral sentiments, and religious enthusiasm." While this was a politically expedient argument to use in public rhetoric, it also reflected private views. As Sarah Grimké wrote to Lucy Stone, "I feel deeply that the regeneration of this world is to be achieved through the instrumentality of Woman. . . ."[36]

Nevertheless, the feminists departed significantly from the prevailing view of innate sex differences. Most important was their belief in human pefectibility. Men and women not only *could,* but *should,* change—and in the direction of minimizing sex differences. One of the earliest and most persistent themes of the movement was the appeal for women to abandon their dependence and timidity and become more self-reliant and courageous, like men. As early as 1829, Lydia Maria Child, in her *Frugal Housewife*, urged that women be raised from an early age to be useful and independent members of society, rather than idle, vain ornaments interested only in trapping husbands. Similarly, one of the most important themes of the entire nineteenth-century movement was the need to elevate man's grosser nature to woman's higher level and, by implication, to eliminate society's double moral standard. Men ought to become more pure, pious, gentle, and sensitive; women needed to develop their intellectual and physical capacities in order to balance their moral strengths and become better-rounded, self-sufficient persons. The goal for both sexes was to develop all capabilities as much as humanly possible.

The implicit assumption behind this lifelong crusade for self-improvement seemed to be that, except for physical differences, there were few innate obstacles to either sex's self-development. Feminists also recognized that apparent differences between the sexes were often due to neglect, rather than to biology. All agreed, for example, that women had the potential for being men's intellectual equals, even though, because of lack of training, most women were not so in fact. Lucretia Mott, writing to Elizabeth Cady Stanton in the 1850's, assured the latter that she would have "hard work to prove the intellectual equality of woman with man—facts are so against such an assumption, in the present stage of woman's development." Mott applauded the effort, however, and reminded Stanton that she need not "*admit* inferiority, even tho' we may not be able to *prove* equality."[37] Neither woman harbored the slightest doubt of woman's potential ability.

This is not to suggest that the feminists were advocating an androgynous society. Though their emphasis on woman's untapped and undeveloped potential strongly suggested that the female "character" was shaped by cultural conditioning, not many pursued this intellectual direction. For one thing, it was a politically unwise tack; for another, it tended to bring into question the validity of differences which the feminists accepted. Women were seen not only as more virtuous, but also as endowed with superior endurance, compassion, gentleness, and other qualities which especially suited them for child-rearing, nursing, and other nurturing roles.[38] The spheres envisioned for women and men were not identical, because each would give priority to their distinct functions while also being free to serve in other areas.

There was divergence, of course, in the way this question was viewed within the group. From the early years of her career, Antoinette Brown emphasized the differences between the natures and interests of the sexes; women and men were equal but not identical, "two halves of a great whole." She argued that men could not therefore represent women's interests in government or any other policy-making position, later developing this argument more extensively in her *Sexes Throughout Nature*. This stance brought Brown somewhat in conflict with feminists like Clarina Howard Nichols, who countered that women and men shared identical interests and should therefore have identical spheres, duties, and rights.[39]

Although the view that women and men were equal but complementary halves of the human family predominated, occasionally one of the more skeptical feminists raised the possibility that most sex differences were due to cultural influences. Stanton, of course, constantly deplored the fact that men were taught to take a comprehensive view of life while women were trained only to deal with minutiae, "constantly concentrating our powers of vision and thought on the point of a needle," and thereby acquiring "an exactness never reached by the other sex." Lydia Maria Child on several occasions suggested that woman's apparent moral superiority and intellectual weakness, as well as other qualities, were due to the role she was forced to play; the "perfect" man or woman was one who combined both "masculine" intellect and "feminine" affection. Susan B. Anthony, in an 1854 speech on women's rights, argued that if women were given the same education as men, one might find their differences not God-ordained, but the result of "false education and conventionalisms." Women might become strong and capable of intense intellectual effort, like men, and "cease to live wholly in the affections." Anthony hastened to add that education would not change whatever differences were found to be genuinely ordained by God. Other feminists also occasionally argued that woman's "true nature" was still a "mystery" because she had been shaped by men.[40]

The feminists' departure from the norm of their society can further be seen by comparing their views with the "cult of true womanhood," the prescription for nineteenth-century female behavior described by the historian Barbara Welter. According to the "experts" of the day, the "true woman," who would also be a "true wife," was characterized by piety, purity, domesticity, and submissiveness. The feminist-abolitionists did not totally reject this view, but modified it in important ways. They retained the high value on piety and purity but conceived of piety in a nonsectarian and unorthodox way, and insisted that men meet these requirements as well. They approved of domesticity for women, with the qualification that they not be restricted to the domestic role. The "virtue" of submissiveness, however, was totally rejected, to be replaced with the concept of equality between the sexes. A letter to the *Una* from an indignant female reader spelled out this view: a woman should be submissive only to God; the "true woman" will be a good wife and mother, but when her job is done she ought to be free to enter public affairs or any other field of endeavor.[41]

The feminist-abolitionists' attitude toward sexuality also illustrates the way in which the group accepted many of the prevailing views of sex differences, while adding important modifications. Generally, these women shared the prudishness and repressive attitude toward sexuality that became an institutionalized campaign for moral reform later in the century. In this stance they were closer to society's norm than in their defense of equality between the sexes. Even here, though, they differed from contemporaries, and even from other moral reformers.

Their private letters indicate that some of the feminists were quite capable of sexual passion, and one finds, even in public statements, implicit references to the existence of a sex drive in women. Still, the feminists believed the sex drive to be far greater in men; women were seen as less prone to carnal desires and better able to control them. Even Elizabeth Cady Stanton, who in her later years wrote in her diary that a healthy woman had as much passion as a man, seemed less sure of this "great natural fact" thirty years earlier, when she told Susan Anthony that "man in his lust has regulated long enough this whole question of sexual intercourse." She was even more explicit in an earlier temperance speech, arguing that economic independence would keep women from entering prostitution because "thank God, the true woman in her organization is too refined and spiritual, to be the victim of an overpowering passion."[42]

The feminists were repelled by "excessive" sexuality and found it desirable to subordinate physical passion to the force of reason. Such sexual inhibition was certainly not limited to the unmarried feminists, though their critics often assumed this to be true. For example, there appears to be little difference between Angelina and Sarah Grimké or between Lucy Stone and Elizabeth Blackwell. All four, at least in their youths, expressed a similar aversion to physical sex and shared equally lofty moral standards; all had been exposed to the Puritan belief that salvation was endangered by placing carnal pleasure before spiritual love, and had come to maturity in a period of religious revivalism. Though they rejected many of the doctrines of their faith, the Puritan ideal of heavenly love remained part of their romantic vision.

There is no evidence, however, that the feminist-abolitionists were more sexually repressed than other middle-class contemporaries,[43] and their attitude toward sexuality was functional in the context of the period in which they lived. It reflected a feminist concern that married women, legally subject to their husbands, were vulnerable to "sexual abuse"; presumably this abuse included sexual practices or frequency that were unacceptable to the wife, though this was never made explicit. What was very clear, however, was the constant fear and danger of unwanted pregnancy and the consequent suffering endured by women. The feminists preached late marriage and "moral restraint" within marriage as a means to reduce the frequency of pregnancies, as well as to diminish women's exposure to men's "brutal lusts." These were virtually the only techniques the feminists could comfortably advocate. Contraceptive devices, when they became available in the 1840's and 1850's, were considered unnatural and probably were associated with non-marital sex and prostitution. Occasionally, especially in later years, some feminists expressed the wish that an acceptable "natural" method had been available; in their earlier child-bearing years, however, they were forced to rely on "self-control" and to urge it for others. Their demand for woman's autonomy and "control over her own body" meant the right to abstain from sex. To the feminist-abolitionists, female emancipation meant freedom *from* sex, not *for* it. The nineteenth-century movement for birth control was conducted outside the organized women's movement and was unrelated to it. Feminist ideology developed from a base of reality and was a response to felt physical and psychological needs. Given the religious milieu in which they were raised and the low level of sexual knowledge in their society, the feminists' attitude toward sexuality was not incomprehensible. Given their commitment to woman's self-development and the expansion of her sphere, it was not irrational.

Such prudishness was not only functional for women; it was also consistent with the romantic and perfectionist world-view held by feminist-abolitionists of both sexes. Sexual restraint was part of their broader program for self-improvement and the moral elevation of society, as well as for the emancipation of woman. Subordinating physical passion to spiritual and intellectual concerns would presumably bring about a number of beneficial results. Like many nineteenth-century people, these reformers believed in the conservation of sexual energy; by exercising self-control, excess sexual energy could be diverted into higher pursuits, and men could be brought to the same level of purity and morality as women. In addition, they believed that limiting sexual expression to procreation would produce a superior breed of offspring, a "nobler type of humankind." Children should be the products of love, not of "passional indulgence." Henry C. Wright wrote of "love children" in this context, and Harriot Hunt similarly praised the "love babies" that resulted from spiritual unions. Elizabeth Cady Stanton commended "those holy instincts of the woman to bear no children but those of love." Sexual restraint was seen as still another means of perfecting the race.[44]

The feminist-abolitionists continued their moral crusade with unabated vigor in the postwar period, but again they differed from most Victorian Americans by refusing to engage in the "conspiracy of silence." They objected strenuously to the common attitude, shared by much of the medical profession, that preventing discussion of sexuality would improve the general level of morality. They campaigned for sex education and public debate on moral issues in the interest of reform. Ironically, their aggressive pursuit of the subject did make useful information available, but it also served to place them in the vanguard of sexual repressiveness and social control.

The feminists' attitude toward sexuality and sex differences was clearly related, like all facets of their ideology, to their concept of woman's dual role. In her narrower function and limited sphere as wife and mother, sex differences were relevant; in her broader role as citizen and human being, woman's functions and sphere were identical with man's, and sex differences, biological and otherwise, became less important. This concept distinguished the feminists from a group of more conservative reformers who were also concerned with woman's needs but who conceptualized her only in her more limited role. A comparison between the two groups helps to clarify the shape of the developing feminist ideology.

Catharine Beecher, best known for her pioneer work in opening schools for women, is representative of a group called "domestic reformers" by the historian Anne Kuhn. Beecher and others sought increased power and dignity for women by expanding and professionalizing their domestic role, especially its maternal aspect. Beecher shared with the feminist-abolitionists the belief in woman's special role as moral guardian, and both the domestic reformers and the feminists glorified the importance of the mother in shaping the character of the child and, ultimately, of society. As Beecher explained, the mission of America was in the hands of her women, who could "turn for good or for evil the destinies of a nation."[45]

Both groups agreed on the importance of the new science of "domestic education," and on the need to train women in the profession of motherhood. Lydia Maria Child, in the first edition of her *Mother's Book* (1831), anticipated this movement for domestic reform. Like Beecher, the feminists envisioned women as the conservators of traditional New England values, a harmonizing and unifying force in a changing society. This was a conservative strain in nineteenth-century feminist thought.

Beecher, however, disagreed with the feminists' view that women ought to exert a moral influence in the public sphere as well as at home—indeed, she had a very different vision of how women would obtain power and fulfillment in the ideal society. She opposed women's participation in government and worked against suffrage. The home would be the source of woman's power, in Beecher's vision, and self-sacrifice the guiding tenet of female ideology and the key to woman's influence in society.[46] Both groups were concerned with expanding the power of women in a reformed society, but the feminists also considered the growth of the individual woman and the effect of her emancipation from a rigidly defined sphere. For feminists, female self-development was an even more important goal than self-sacrifice.

The contrast between the feminists and domestic reformers like

Catharine Beecher is illustrated by two incidents. In one, which occurred in 1846, Beecher epitomized the characteristic female submissiveness that the feminists so deplored. Invited to deliver an address on education, she conformed to custom by sitting on the platform while her brother read her speech. Eight years earlier, Beecher had publicly opposed the Grimkés' public speaking as unfeminine. Like the orthodox clergymen who had also condemned the sisters, she insisted that woman's power depended on her reliance on "peace and love," to be exerted only within the "domestic and social" circle, and on her "retaining her place as dependent and defenceless, and making no claims, and maintaining no right." Angelina Grimké, responding to this attack, cited the Bible as authority for the equal rights and duties of the sexes, and anticipated the later demand for the suffrage by arguing for woman's right to participate in the making of all laws by which she was governed.[47] The difference in direction was thus established early in the movement for women's rights. Beecher continued to work for increased educational opportunities for women, and for increased female power; but not for equal education, or equal power. The feminists continued to demand that women have equal access to all opportunities for education, work, and power in the broader public sphere.

The feminists were vocal in urging women to combine their private and public roles, but few of them dealt with concrete proposals for achieving this end, or with the special obstacles faced by working-class women. Their general assumption was that these tasks would be carried out sequentially—as domestic burdens eased, more time could be devoted to other work. Lucretia Mott, elder stateswoman of the group, served as a model for many of the younger women. Because she married early and had largely completed the raising of her five children before she began her reform work, she provided others with one type of life plan. Elizabeth Cady Stanton, who juggled speeches and children for many years, looked to Mrs. Mott for inspiration and consoled herself with the prospect of more leisure in the future. To Anthony she wrote, "You and I have the prospect of a good long life. We shall not be in our prime before 50, and after that we shall be good for 20 years at least."[48] This was a solution that worked for Stanton, but it was less practical for the woman of average health, wealth, and longevity.

Antoinette Brown Blackwell spent more time than most conceptualizing an ideal life plan for women. She advocated this plan in public and followed it successfully in private. While Mott, Stanton, and others had arrived at their "plan" more or less without previous design, Blackwell consciously ordered her life in a manner consistent with her life goals. Her plan was based on the concept of dual roles, and assumed that at different stages of her life a woman would shift between her specialized role in the home and her broader role outside. Most feminists could agree in principle on the steps she proposed: each young woman should educate herself for a profession, marry late (between twenty-five and thirty), and choose a husband carefully; twenty years would be spent dividing her time between her domestic life and her work, leaving twenty more in which she could devote her mature powers to her "noble life purpose." The choice of a partner who shared her views was especially important, since the key to the success of this plan was independence and cooperation within the marriage relationship.

Though Blackwell's plan was generally geared to middle-class women, specific ideas were applicable to all classes. She suggested that women could be freed from home duties for short periods by mutually exchanging tasks with their husbands, as well as with neighbors. She expressed the hope that "the time will come when men are more men than professional drudges and business machines." Then, she predicted, women would be "generally uniting with them in the same occupations." She later suggested, in a remarkably advanced paper on "Woman's Work" (1874), that industries set up shorter (3-5 hour) work schedules for the benefit of men and women who wished to divide their time between home and work. [49] All of her proposals were based on the feminists' concept of dual roles and overlapping spheres. Their goal was to allow both sexes to participate fully in important work both at home and in the world outside. Women and men would be developing their faculties more fully, becoming more truly equal, and at the same time helping to "make the world better."

The crusade to "make the world better" had begun in the 1820's and 1830's with the movement for the abolition of slavery. The feminist-abolitionists applied the same philosophy of human rights to the emancipation of women; the influence of antislavery ideas and rhetoric continued to be evident in the arguments for equality in marriage, as well as in demands for access to education, employment, and suffrage. All of the feminists' arguments were based on their new concept of woman's nature and role, and of her "proper" sphere. Accepting society's glorification of the family and marriage, they distinguished between the differing roles of women and men within the narrow domestic sphere, and their similar roles as citizens in the broader public sphere. Sharing society's belief in woman's moral superiority, the reformers argued for the elevation of man and for bridging the gap between the natures of the sexes, and therefore between their functions and spheres. Approving of the high value which society placed on sexual control, they advocated such discipline as a way of protecting and emancipating women, and as a means of elevating and perfecting the race. In all of these ways, the feminists departed from the prevailing views of their society. They bequeathed to future generations a coherent feminist ideology based on their belief in the innate equality of the sexes, and on their romantic faith in the perfectibility of the human race.

NOTES

1. *Aurora Leigh* (book 5, line 82) by Elizabeth Barrett Browning, much quoted by the group; *Liberator,* June 13, 1860.

2. *Anti-Slavery Bugle,* July 14, 1848; *History of Woman Suffrage,* 1:694.

3. Wyman, ed., *Elizabeth Oakes Smith,* p. 156.

4. Lucy Stone speech, *Chicago Tribune,* Nov., 1853, copy in Blackwell Family Papers, LC.

5. Sarah Grimké to Amos Phelps, Aug. 3, 1837, Amos Phelps Papers; Grimké to Mary S. Parker, July 11, 1837, Garrison Papers, BPL; Grimké, *Letters on the Equality of the Sexes.*

6. Lucy Stone speech "The Province of Woman," n.d., Blackwell Family Papers, LC; Paul's edict is in 1 Cor. 14:34.

7. *Oberlin Quarterly Review,* July, 1849; *History of Woman Suffrage,* 1:535–36; Paul's injunction is in 1 Tim. 2:12.

8. *History of Woman Suffrage,* 1:536–37; Harper, *Anthony,* 2:595.

9. Hunt, *Glances and Glimpses,* p. 293; see also *Una,* Mar., 1853, and *History of Woman Suffrage,* 1:259, 564.

10. *History of Woman Suffrage,* 1:527; Blackwell, *Stone,* pp. 195–96.

11. For Child, see *Woman's Journal,* Aug. 28, 1875; see Fosters' letter in Worcester *Evening Gazette,* Apr. 11, 1876, and T. W. Higginson to A. K. Foster, Feb. 15, 1874, Kelley-Foster Papers, AAS; also *Woman's Journal,* Feb. 17, 1872, Feb. 28, 1874.

12. Harper, *Anthony,* 1:169–70.

13. Lerner, *Grimké Sisters,* p. 162; Blackwell, *Stone,* p. 30.

14. *Liberator,* Sept. 6, 1839.

15. *History of Woman Suffrage,* 1:860.

16. L. M. Child to Marianne C. D. Silsbee, Feb. 6, 1849, Child Papers, AAS; Child, *Letters,* p. 74.

17. *Una,* Apr., 1854; Lucy Stone to H. B. Blackwell, Apr. 26, 1854, Blackwell Family Papers, LC.

18. Hallowell, ed., *Mott,* pp. 506, 350.

19. *History of Woman Suffrage,* 1:580; Bloomer, ed., *Life and Writings,* p. 105.

20. Gibbons, *Life,* 1:280; E. C. Stanton to S. B. Anthony, July 20, 1857, Elizabeth Cady Stanton Papers, LC; E. Oakes Smith, "Sanctity of Marriage," Woman's Rights Tracts No. 5, Women's Rights Collection, SC.

21. *Liberator,* June 1, 1860.

22. *Lily,* Aug., 1852.

23. *History of Woman Suffrage,* 1:528.

24. Ibid., p. 860.

25. Stanton, *Stanton,* 2:16; E. C. Stanton to Wendell Phillips, Aug. 18, 1860, and reply, Aug. 21, 1860, Elizabeth Cady Stanton Papers.

26. Margaret Munsterberg, "The Weston Sisters and 'The Boston Controversy,'" *Boston Public Library Quarterly* 10 (Jan. 1958): 38–50, quote on p. 50; Harper, *Anthony,* 1:142; Hare, ed., *Comstock,* p. 348 (emphasis hers).

27. *History of Woman Suffrage,* 1:262; Stanton, *Stanton,* 2:23.

28. *Una,* Feb., 1855; see also Feb., 1854, and Feb. 1, 1853; *History of Woman Suffrage,* 1:534–35.

29. Bloomer, ed., *Life and Writings,* pp. 312–13.

30. A. K. Foster to Alla Foster, Mar. 3, 1870, Kelley-Foster Papers, AAS.

31. Samuel J. May, *The Rights and Condition of Women* (Syracuse: Stoddard & Babcock, 1846), pp. 9–10; *Lily,* Mar., 1850; see also Sarah Grimké in *Lily,* July, 1852.

32. Paulina W. Davis, *A History of the National Woman's Rights Movement* (New York: Journeymen Printers' Co-operative Association, 1871; reprinted, New York: Source Book Press, 1970), p. 63.

33. Angelina Grimké to Amos A. Phelps, Sept. 2, 1837, Amos Phelps Papers.

34. Stanton speech, "The Solitude of Self," 1892, Elizabeth Cady Stanton Papers.

35. Chandler, *Essays,* p. 50; Chapman, *Ten Years of Experience,* pp. 26–27.

36. *Lily,* June, 1851; S. Grimké to Lucy Stone, July 13, 1853?, Blackwell Family Papers, LC.

37. L. Mott to E. C. Stanton, Mar. 16, 1855, Elizabeth Cady Stanton Papers.

38. See, e.g., Paulina Davis in *Una,* Feb. 1, 1853.

39. *Una,* Aug. 15, 1855; see also debate at 1852 convention, *History of Woman Suffrage,* 1:522–36.

40. E. C. Stanton to Elizabeth Smith Miller, ca. 1855, Elizabeth Cady Stanton Papers; *National Anti-Slavery Standard,* Oct. 30, 1869; Child, *Letters,* pp. 243–44; Anthony speech, "Woman's Rights," 1854, Susan B. Anthony Papers, RC; Celia Burleigh, in *Woman's Journal,* July 29, 1871.

41. Barbara Welter, "The Cult of True Womanhood," *American Quarterly* 18 (Summer 1966): 151–75; A. H. Price to *Una,* Feb. 1, 1853.

42. Stanton, *Stanton,* 2:210; E. C. Stanton to S. B. Anthony, Mar. 1, 1853, Elizabeth Cady Stanton Papers; *Lily,* May, 1852. See also ch. 7.

43. Cf. Ronald Walters,"The Erotic South: Civilization and Sexuality in American Abolitionism," *American Quarterly* 25 (May 1973): 177–201.

44. Henry C. Wright, *Marriage and Parentage,* 5th ed. (Boston: B. Marsh, 1866), pp. 133–35; Hunt, *Glances and Glimpses,* p. 183; *History of Woman Suffrage,* 1:720.

45. Anne L. Kuhn, *The Mother's Role in Childhood Education: New England Concepts 1830–1860* (New Haven: Yale University Press, 1947), p. 181.

46. See Kathryn Kish Sklar, *Catharine Beecher, a Study in American Domesticity* (New Haven: Yale University Press, 1973).

47. *History of Woman Suffrage,* 1:122; Catharine Beecher, *An Essay on Slavery and Abolitionism with Reference to the Duty of American Females,* 2nd ed. (Philadelphia: Henry Perkins, 1837), pp. 100–102; Angelina E. Grimké, *Letters to Catherine E. Beecher* (Boston: Isaac Knapp, 1838).

48. Lutz, *Created Equal,* p. 104.

49. Blackwell speech to 1860 convention, Blackwell Family Papers, RC; A. B. Blackwell to Olympia Brown, n.d. [probably 1860's], Olympia Brown Papers, RC; Aileen S. Kraditor, ed., *Up from the Pedestal: Selected Writings in the History of American Feminism* (Chicago: Quadrangle Books, 1968), pp. 150–59.

7

The Role of Husbands in the Women's Movement

A RECENT STUDY of the twentieth-century American woman has concluded that the most significant obstacle to sexual equality is still the prevailing attitude that woman's primary role is in the home. Women seeking careers face a profound marriage-career conflict, because society still assumes that a wife's aspirations are secondary to her husband's.[1] The "slavery of sex" which confined the nineteenth-century woman in a narrow sphere continued to oppress the next generations, despite the feminist-abolitionists' efforts. Some historians, noting this failure to abolish the customs and prejudices that enslaved women, have concluded that the institutions of marriage and family constituted the prime obstacles. The early feminists' inability to radically restructure the nuclear family, they assert, was the fatal flaw in the women's movement.[2]

A closer look at the lives of this first generation of feminists, however, reveals a special sensitivity to the need to reform the nature and underlying assumptions of the traditional marriage relationship. The women retained, and indeed glorified, the conventional domestic structures, but they also recognized the crucial importance of new roles and new arrangements within the traditional framework. An impressive number of these women chose to marry men who were also feminists; these couples shaped their own marriages into new patterns, creating egalitarian unions based on autonomy and shared responsibilities that would still be radical today. The rejection (by both husbands and wives) of the conventional view of "woman's proper sphere" was the key innovation in this new kind of marriage. The equality that such a couple achieved, though imperfect, permitted the wife to play the dual role of wife-mother and reformer, and freed her to work for radical causes of the day. Equality in marriage was not only an integral part of the feminists' belief system; it was also a personally liberating force, and was the closest they came to solving the dilemma of balancing family and work outside the home. Given their cultural milieu, it was virtually the only solution available to those women who married.

These feminist families became models for the future and suggested one significant means toward the broader emancipation of all women. As models, such families represented a pivotal reform in the feminist-abolitionist movement, one that has gone virtually unnoticed by historians. The women themselves, well aware of the importance of this reform, proselytized for equality and independence within marriage as part of their broad platform for human rights. Both the abolition of chattel slavery and the emancipation of women from the slavery of traditional marriage were high priorities in their reform agenda, although the latter ultimately provided the more formidable challenge.

Thirty-seven of the fifty-one feminist-abolitionist women in this study married, seven of them twice. They tended to marry somewhat late (average age: 24.5 years) and to bear fewer children than the norm (3.7).[3] The percentage who married is not unusual when compared with the general population,[4] but it seems surprisingly high when one considers that most of the women were active in reform before marriage, and that they married in spite of well-developed feminist views and a strong desire to continue their reform work. In addition, most were teachers or were otherwise able to support themselves. The relatively late age at marriage is at least partly explained by these women's fear that marriage would mean a loss of freedom and an end to their work (although it may also be linked to their high social class[5]). The fact that they married at all is best explained by their choice of husbands: of the thirty-seven who married (considering only the second marriages, which, in every case, were the longer and more important ones), twenty-eight had husbands who supported their feminist activity. Of the remaining nine, the husbands of only four are known to have been unsympathetic or actively opposed; the attitude of the others is not known.

The husbands of the feminists played a key role in the women's movement. They often contributed financially and gave of their time and energy, usually in secondary roles. Most important were their commitment to women's equality and their support at home, which freed their wives for important leadership positions. Though even the best marriages could not avoid tensions and conflicts, especially in the child-bearing years, those women who married feminist men were better able to weather such periods and to continue their work because of their husbands' sympathy and help. The importance of the husband's role is further indicated by the fact that the four women who married non-feminist men were unable to maintain both marriage and reform work—one or the other was sacrificed. Even their middle-class status and the servants it afforded were insufficient to insure the freedom they required. The acquiescence of her husband was crucial if a wife wished to work outside the home: this was a woman's problem that cut across class lines.

This important dimension of the women's movement needs to be explored, with attention devoted to significant and neglected questions: What kind of men became feminists and married reformers? What was the nature of marriages that afforded women freedom to become important leaders? How did such marriages, in practice, conform to feminist principles? How did children fare in such families? What happened to aspiring feminists who chose less compatible mates? How did unmarried leaders view the marriages of their co-workers?

Who were the unusual men who married "strong-minded" women and helped to create new kinds of marriages? The data on them are less complete than on their wives because, with a few exceptions, they were less well known and less important in reform. Enough is known, however, to suggest several generalizations.

These husbands tended to be remarkably like their wives' fathers, in terms of family background and economic status.[6] Many came from old New England families, though not all could point to an ancestor who arrived on the Mayflower (as could Henry Brewster Stanton). As one would expect, fewer were farmers, and more were in business and the professions. Of the thirty-seven husbands, ten were businessmen, sixteen professionals, ten farmers or artisans; the occupation of one is unknown.[7] The professionals included seven lawyers, four writers or editors, three ministers, one doctor, and one teacher (others, like Theodore Weld, who was primarily a reformer and worked a small farm, turned to teaching to earn a living). Only seven men, all lawyers and businessmen, could be considered wealthy. Five faced a constant struggle to support their families—these were all primarily reformers who worked also as farmers, artisans, and teachers. The large majority (like the preponderance of the wives' fathers) were middle class: small businessmen, ministers, teachers and writers, farmers and artisans.

A striking number of husbands supported their wives' reform work. While only eleven of these thirty-seven women received support from their fathers, twenty-eight had the sympathy of their husbands; all but three of these latter men were active reformers themselves. Four of the husbands opposed their wives' reform efforts (including Samuel Gridley Howe, himself a noted reformer); of these, three successfully ended or postponed their wives' careers, and in the fourth case the wife, Jane Grey Swisshelm, deserted her husband.[8] The views of the remaining five husbands are not clear, but one can infer from problems in two of these marriages that the men may not have been sympathetic; the other three apparently accepted their wives' work without either opposition or support.[9]

What can be surmised of the twenty-eight men who married women whom society considered to be freaks or monsters, who lived with those women in relationships of equality, and who encouraged or permitted them to spend a great deal of time away from home? The evidence, albeit impressionistic, points to one obvious generalization: the men were extraordinarily like their wives in their optimistic faith in progress and in their compulsive sense of duty. Their world-view, based on their utopian reform religion, allowed them to transcend their society's sex roles and stereotypes. Like their wives, they fit badly into conventional molds. Henry and Sam Blackwell were businessmen who wrote poetry and occasionally published it, as did lawyer and politician John Hooker. All three men, like many of the other husbands, displayed the "moral sensibilities" and romantic fervor generally associated with the female sex.

The fragmentary data suggest some answers to an important historical question: "Why do men become feminists?" Like their wives, a disproportionate number grew up in liberal religious faiths which respected women's independence and permitted greater female participation in decision-making. Others gravitated toward these smaller sects and away from orthodox churches. Eight husbands were Quakers; eleven were either Universalists or Unitarians or were unaffiliated with organized religion. (It was not uncommon for the husbands of Quaker ministers to care for their children at home while their wives traveled about the country to preach.[10]) The religious affiliation of nine husbands is not known but can be surmised to be liberal because of their compatibility with their wives. Significantly, only one feminist husband was a minister (Daniel Livermore, a Universalist). Of the four men who opposed their wives' feminism, Prudence Crandall's husband was a Baptist minister, Abby Hutchinson's was the son of a Presbyterian minister, Jane Swisshelm's was a devout Methodist, and only Howe's was a Unitarian. (The husbands of Howe and Crandall were also considerably older than their wives—nineteen and sixteen years. However, several compatible marriages also involved large age differences, including two in which the wives—Lucy Stone and Abby Hopper Gibbons—were seven and eight years older than their husbands.)

James Mott typified the Quaker reformer-husband who was taught early in life that men and women were one in Christ.[11] His religious training, combined with a natural sensitivity and intelligence, helped make him responsive to injustice of all kinds. As early as 1820 he complained that women were not given an equal voice in the administration of the Society of Friends, and he expressed the hope that "as we become more enlightened and civilized, this difference will be done away."[12]

Though the men did not experience rejection first-hand, as their wives did, they nevertheless became sensitive to injustices against women in the same way, and for the same reasons, that they responded to the plight of the slave. They took the principle of human rights seriously and were moved, by moral considerations, to protest violations of these rights. Many of the men (like their wives) left their churches in reaction to clerical antifeminism and antiabolitionism. They consistently rejected both orthodox religious views and conventional ideas of woman's role. Elizabeth Cady Stanton, who felt that equality between men and women was impossible without throwing off the restraints of religion, used the example of the "true marriage" of her cousins Gerrit and Ann Smith. The Smiths, she liked to observe, gained freedom in religion and perfect independence in marriage, despite differences of opinion.[13] Their daughter Elizabeth Smith Miller repeated this pattern in her own life.

Like their wives, the feminist husbands often came from families sympathetic to reform. Stephen Foster, for example, worked with his father for temperance, antislavery, peace, and women's rights. James Mott's grandfather was concerned with temperance and anti-slavery, and his mother was an active abolitionist. Several men had mothers who were notable for their independence and feminism. Daniel Livermore's mother was a women's rights woman who brought up her sons and daughters to share equally in household tasks. Daniel attended a coeducational college and was an advocate of woman suffrage long before his better-known wife was. When the couple married, he taught Mary Livermore to cook and to arrange their home simply, so as "not to be slaves to a house." The mother of Henry and Samuel (and Elizabeth) Blackwell was also strongly for women's rights; in 1868, though quite elderly, she joined Lucy Stone and others who attempted to vote, in order to publicize their cause. The Blackwell's father was also an abolitionist and feminist.

As with the women, the family backgrounds of the men were probably influential, but then one must explain why most of their siblings were *not* reformers. The influence of liberal theology was also important, but apparently not crucial. Theodore Weld expressed feminist views while a convert to evangelicalism; he championed the right of women to speak at revival meetings as early as the 1820's.[14] The men, like their wives, seem to have been distinguished from their contemporaries by an ability to envision a world free from evil and injustice, and by the determination to pursue that vision.[15] Their choice of unusual, strong-minded wives was not unrelated to their faith in reform. For both men and women, choosing the right mate was a reform in itself, reflecting their belief in equality and serving as a step toward self-improvement and the perfection of society. These men's religious faith enabled them to face the ridicule heaped upon them as the husbands of non-conforming women.

Probably the most common charge hurled against them was that they were "hen-pecked husbands" who "ought to wear petti-coats."[16] There must have been husbands in the movement who passively acquiesced to their domineering spouses. In this group, only Matilda Joslyn Gage was described as the "dominant" one in her marriage; very little is known of Henry Gage, who left no imprint on the movement beyond supporting his wife's career. However, the large majority of feminist husbands did leave a record of their opinions and activities. These gave evidence of vigor and independent thought, rather than weak-kneed submissiveness. Private correspondence also confirms this impression. Many of the men were as well known as their wives within reform circles, and a few, like James Mott, were revered. Most could not devote as much time and energy to the cause as their wives could, but a few made national reputations as reformers in the course of their careers in journalism and politics. This was true of Henry Stanton, John Hooker, and William Stevens Robinson, a political writer and activist known by his pen-name "Warrington." Theodore Severance, Dexter Bloomer, and Thomas Davis were less well known reformers who entered local and state politics. All were vocal about their belief in equality of the sexes, and a few wrote and lectured on the subject. Robinson's Free Soil newspaper, the *Lowell American,* ran strong statements on women's rights. In a typical editorial, Robinson argued for women's right to vote and hold office and concluded: "Who set up any man as a judge of what is woman's sphere, or what the Almighty Maker designed her to be?" The cause of woman, he wrote on another occasion, was "the movement of civilization itself."[17]

Since the large majority of the feminist husbands did not play prominent roles in reform, they faced the uncommon male dilemma of being eclipsed by their wives' fame (or notoriety). Most seemed to accept this situation with good grace and shared in their wives' successes. They were able to do so partly because they shared their wives' cause; in addition, they were unusual men, apparently secure in their masculinity and not easily threatened. David Lee Child accepted his wife's leaving home to edit the *National Anti-Slavery Standard,* and her subsequent support of him with the proceeds of her writing. He could do this because he was engaged in a cause he knew was right though unprofitable, and because he considered Maria an equal, independent person. Mrs. Child wrote to Angelina Grimké that David "despised the idea of any distinction in the appropriate spheres of human beings." In 1838 he had urged her to follow the example of the Grimkés and become a public speaker, but she disappointed him by declining to do so. On another occasion, she wrote to Abby Kelley that David had urged her to travel to a peace convention but did not "make use of his legal right to command." (As usual, she was the frugal, practical one and stayed home.[18])

Stephen Foster also faced the fact that his wife was more successful in her reform efforts. Because she was more in demand as a speaker, he often stayed home to work the farm and care for their daughter while Abby traveled on extensive lecture tours. When the child became seriously ill, he was her chief nurse. His letters reveal careful attention to his daughter's needs and education. In one letter, he assured Abby that Alla "is a great comfort to me in your absence." He also dealt with the question of their respective careers. In a letter to Abby in 1850, five years after their marriage, he congratulated her on a good tour and noted that her achievement threw him "entirely into the shade." Her "great success" might awaken his envy, he admitted, "if it were not, after all, *my own.*" As it was, he could only congratulate himself on "the good fortune which placed such a *prize* within my grasp." He may, nevertheless, have had some ambivalence in the matter of exchanging roles. Several years later, when he was on tour and she was home, he wrote that he had little confidence in her ability to manage the farm (though she was "a capital housekeeper") and added, perhaps with mixed feelings, "However, I am very glad you are having an opportunity to try your skill in that department also."[19]

The Fosters' marriage thrived in spite of their unconventional lifestyle. Their friend Aaron Powell, noting that people in the town had warned Stephen that he was being led astray by "a vile and dangerous woman," called their marriage "true and beautiful" and "a union of close sympathy." Many friends noted the independence each had managed to retain. Thomas Wentworth Higginson, who also lived in Worcester, described them as "two of the very strongest individualities united in one absolutely independent and perfectly harmonious union." Lucy Stone, whose standards for marriage were very high, wrote of the Fosters' home: "*There* was seen the beauty and the possibility of a permanent partnership of equals."[20]

Though the Fosters had a good marriage, Stephen Foster was not a typical feminist husband. His extreme tactics antagonized many in the movement and made him unpopular and controversial, though he was personally genial and good natured. A better example is

James Mott, who was looked upon as the model of a capable, well-respected, independent-minded reformer who fully appreciated his wife's superior talents and complemented her with his own quiet strength. Known for his warmth and generosity, he was also reserved and shy; it seemed natural to him that his more vivacious and energetic wife should express the views they both shared. (Though she was the better speaker, he wrote more imaginative letters and enjoyed the novels which she considered a waste of time.) The consensus among their friends was that perfect agreement existed between them, and all commented on the unique strength of purpose and will each displayed in what was considered an ideal marriage. On the Motts' fiftieth wedding anniversary, in 1861, their friends gathered to celebrate and to "joyfully record," on the reverse side of their wedding certificate, a testimonial to the couple "who have given to us, and to the world, another illustration of the beauty and glory of true marriage."[21] (Though sincere, they could not, as true reformers, resist the opportunity to propagandize.)

The many available letters give no evidence that James Mott resented or felt eclipsed by his more famous spouse. On the contrary, he did everything possible to support her, and accompanied her on extensive preaching and lecturing tours. At a time when most husbands were inclined to keep their wives at home, this was no small contribution. The Motts' lives were so intertwined that their granddaughter, preparing to write about Lucretia, found it difficult "to write of one without the other" and decided her book would be about both. In perhaps the most eloquent statement on the role of husbands in the women's movement, she wrote that it was impossible to contemplate her grandparents' lives "without realizing that *his* life made *hers* a possibility."[22]

Both James and Lucretia Mott envisioned an ideal society in which women would be free to follow their consciences and abilities without first receiving permission from their husbands. In the existing and imperfect world, though, a wife was largely dependent on the will and whim of her husband. Lucretia Mott's career as reformer and preacher, a major part of her life, was indeed made possible by her husband's enlightened view of woman's sphere. His belief in female equality enabled her to achieve the independence they both prized. This attitude was the key to the most important contribution of feminist husbands to the women's movement.

226

James Mott himself urged others to follow his happy example. To Lucy Stone, who was contemplating marriage, he wrote, "As age advances, our love, if possible, increases." Marriage was the natural state for men and women, "and when rightly entered into" would lead to an increase in happiness. Lucy was impressed with the example of the Motts, and they were a strong influence in her decision to marry.[23]

Just as Lucretia Mott was an example used in arguments to further the cause of women's rights, so James Mott was also a model. Thomas Wentworth Higginson pointed to Mott when he praised the role of "Women's Husbands" in a *Woman's Journal* article. "In the existing state of prejudice," he argued, "it may sometimes require moral courage in a man to recognize frankly the greater ability or fame of his wife." Mott, he recalled, had never made a speech, "but in his sphere of quiet sense and justice he was as self-relying and as strong as she in hers." This was "true marriage"; the kind of union in which the husband's dignity depended on overshadowing his wife was only "petty despotism in disguise."[24]

Other men also displayed James Mott's kind of quiet strength and were admired for the ungrudging encouragement they gave their wives. Charles Dudley Miller, a lawyer from a prominent New York family and the husband of Elizabeth Smith, joined his wife in signing the call to the first national women's rights convention and supported her in all her feminist endeavors, including her work for the *Revolution*. Feminists especially praised him for accompanying his wife throughout the country while she wore the bloomer dress, and for enduring the ensuing ridicule with "coolness and dogged determination." Elizabeth Cady Stanton, whose own husband never received such praise from her, said Miller had "done more to raise the women in his circle of acquaintance to self-respect, courage, thought and action" than any other man she knew.[25]

Samuel Blackwell, like his brother, was an unusual and much-admired man. As a young theology student, Antoinette Brown had not expected to find a man who would sympathize with her feelings and acquiesce in her plans to continue writing and working, so she had resigned herself to not marrying. It would "take a miracle to find a man of talent and heart to do this," she wrote Lucy Stone in 1850; five years later she avowed that "nothing but an unsought all absorbing affection can make me feel it right to waver in my plan for an untiring life-work of isolation." But the following year, having found this miracle and this affection, she married, and enjoyed one of the happiest and closest marriages on record. Later she happily admitted that her marriage had been a help, not a hindrance, to her public service because of her husband's "sustaining sympathy." On Sam's death, his niece Alice said she had never seen "such a pair of lovers," even after forty years of wedded life. The family agreed that Sam had been the symbol of everything a man should be.[26]

These examples are not conclusive, but they suggest the possibility that, given their feminist commitment, these men were able to support their wives in equal marriages of strong partners without any loss of personal dignity or self-respect. It should be noted, as a counter-argument, that few of the men were challenged in their role as primary breadwinner, a central feature of "man's sphere." Most wives either volunteered their efforts or received only small incomes from lecturing and writing. Several of the women in compatible feminist marriages were professionally employed, however: Lydia Maria Child supported her husband by her writing through most of their married life; Mary Frame Thomas and Hannah Longshore practiced medicine. Interestingly, the women who divorced their husbands (Swisshelm, Lozier) or separated from them for long periods (Anneke, Dall) all were employed in professional work, which permitted independence but may also have been threatening to their husbands. Nevertheless, the achievements of all the women, and the status and prestige they attained at least among reformers, provided a substantial challenge to their husbands' sense of importance. Most of the men were able to accept this unusual marital circumstance with grace and equanimity.

The men's moral support of their wives was most striking, but these husbands also lent the force of their personal prestige to the woman's cause. Men like Stephen Foster and Benjamin Jones, who were full-time radical reformers, carried little weight in the outside world, but others were respected businessmen whose reform work was only peripheral. The advantages this circumstance could bring to the movement can be seen in a letter from Lucy Stone to Elizabeth Buffum Chace in the late 1860's. Referring to a hostile editorial in the *Providence Journal,* Stone urged Chace to set aside all other chores and answer it immediately: "The name of Elizabeth Chace, backed by the position of Samuel Chace, gives you a vantage ground, possessed by no other person here—to give weight and respectability and wings to our cause." (Samuel Chace, in the earlier years of marriage, had also helped with household work and child care. Like James Mott, he complemented his wife's public activity and more vocal personality with his own quiet strength and integrity.[27])

Many husbands, including Chace, made substantial financial contributions. Thomas Davis supplied funds to launch the *Una* and also lent his prestige to the movement. Ernestine Rose was able to carry on an extensive campaign for a married women's property law and to give free lectures on her many speaking tours because of her husband's financial support, an advantage she fully appreciated. William Rose went further in his devotion, keeping a scrap-book of her clippings and doing minor jobs for the women's rights conventions.[28]

The importance of the husbands' role in the women's movement is even more conclusively confirmed when one looks at those women who married more conventional kinds of men. Prudence Crandall was a Quaker teacher and abolitionist who became notorious for her unsuccessful attempt to open her Connecticut boarding school to Negro girls in 1833. The following year, despite warnings from her Garrisonian friends, she married Calvin Philleo, a Baptist minister sixteen years older and a widower with three children. Fulfilling the worst fears of her supporters, her husband (though an abolitionist) opposed her efforts to keep her school open and put an end to her reform career. A thorough antifeminist, he even forbade her to read his books (an interdiction she secretly disobeyed). She retained her interest in reform, especially temperance and woman suffrage, but her husband's opposition kept her from playing an active role. After his death, she told an interviewer that there had been nothing for her soul to feed upon. "My whole life has been one of opposition," she admitted. "I never could find anyone near me to agree with me. Even my husband opposed me more than anyone."[29] There is no way of knowing how many women, not catapulted into brief fame as Crandall was, remained passive and anonymous because of their marriages.

Abby Hutchinson's experience was similar to Crandall's. As a young woman, she was part of a well-known professional singing family who toured the country for radical causes of the day. Elizabeth

Cady Stanton recalled that, when abolitionists were so hated that not even Wendell Phillips or Abby Kelley could get a hearing, people would listen to the Hutchinsons. In 1849 Abby married Ludlow Patton, a Wall Street stockbroker and son of one of the founders of Union Theological Seminary. Because of her husband's wishes (apparently his pride was involved), she gave up her career, although she sang occasionally for women's rights and in support of the Civil War. Her brothers continued without her. In one of their suffrage songs, they assured their audiences that giving women the vote would not cause them to neglect their duties: "Fear not, we'll darn each worthy stocking/ Duly keep the cradle rocking. . . ." Ironically, though Abby had no children, her own fate was domesticity without emancipation. Her private feelings on the subject were only hinted at by her biographer, but clearly her husband's attitude determined the course of her life.[30]

The other two examples of incompatible marriages are somewhat different. Jane Grey Swisshelm was a particularly independent woman from a strict Scotch-Irish Covenanter family in Pennsylvania. A teacher at fourteen, at twenty she became trapped in a marriage to a Methodist farmer with a domineering mother and conventional views about a wife's duty to submit to her husband. Better educated than he, she gave up her interest in writing and painting to devote herself to housewifery. She later noted bitterly that while her brushes "hung writhing on the cross," she spent her best years and powers cooking cabbage. Swisshelm's feminist tendencies were further reinforced in a dispute with her husband over property left to her by her mother; the trust had been a legal device intended to circumvent the law forbidding married women to own property. (Because Swisshelm had spent time away from home, nursing her mother during her last illness, her husband threatened to sue the estate for the value of his wife's nursing services.) Unable to fit herself into "woman's sphere," she began writing for antislavery papers and established her own reform paper, the *Saturday Visiter* (her spelling), in 1848.[31]

Finally, after twenty years of turbulence and conflict, Jane Swisshelm deserted her husband in 1857 (he later divorced her) and, with a young daughter, settled in St. Cloud, Minnesota, where her sister lived. There she started another paper and tangled with the most powerful state politicians on the slavery question. It is difficult to know if her sharp tongue and vitriolic manner resulted from her marriage, but in her subsequent career in politics and reform, in Washington, D.C., as well as in Minnesota, she left behind a trail of frayed male egos and irritated feminists who deplored her abrasive, one-woman crusade and her scorn for their efforts. Typically, Swisshelm charged that "dare-devil independence" was ruining American women. Amelia Bloomer bravely tried to answer by pointing to her own unusual career, but she was no match for her opponent. All the women eventually decided to praise the example Swisshelm set, and to avoid argument with her.[32]

Swisshelm was *sui generis;* the less dramatic case of Julia Ward Howe was probably more typical of exceptions that proved the rule. Coming from an aristocratic Rhode Island family, Julia Ward married Samuel Gridley Howe, nineteen years her senior, in 1848, when she was twenty-four and he was already a noted reformer. Famous for his work with the blind, Howe was also involved with abolition and other reforms and was known for his efforts with Greek revolutionaries. Though Julia was gifted and eager to share her husband's work, he was fanatically opposed to married women taking on a public role because it was contrary to tradition. However, he favored woman suffrage and was apparently not a complete antifeminist. The Howes' marriage was a stormy and unhappy one and was also troubled by financial problems. Julia wrote later that her husband had never approved of any act of hers which she herself valued. Uninterested in domestic skills, she withdrew to a life of study and writing while raising her five children.[33]

The fame gained from her "Battle Hymn of the Republic" turned Julia Ward Howe toward the outside world, but it was her involvement in the suffrage movement in the late 1860's that gave her relief from isolation and changed her life. Her husband's opposition was now less violent, though he forbade her to be a nurse during the war. She began a long, diverse reform career, the bulk of it after Samuel's death in 1876, which lasted until she died in 1910 at ninety-one. The day after his death, she wrote in her journal: "Began my new life today."[34]

Julia Ward Howe's longevity and the difference in the couple's ages permitted her to have a family and a career in succession, but she was more fortunate than other talented women in similar kinds of marriages. The experiences of these four women give credence to

Margaret Fuller's declaration that women's *lives,* even more than their ideas and writings, gave evidence of the need for new options and new institutional arrangements.[35] The unhappily married feminists were themselves trapped in the "slavery of sex" they abhorred.

The feminist-abolitionist women approached marriage cautiously, fearful of being "drowned in matrimony" and losing their prized independence and the opportunity to work for reform. They saw the family as vital in meeting social and personal needs, but they were equally sensitive to its stultifying effects on women. Most of those who chose to marry solved their own dilemma by consciously selecting husbands who would help them create the new options and new arrangements they needed, within the framework of the conventional social system. Most realized how liberating this new kind of marriage could be for all women—but they also saw what an impossible expectation this was, given the sexism of society. Each was aware of the uniqueness of her own situation, and grateful for her good fortune. The happily married feminists recognized that the egalitarianism of their marriages derived from a shared commitment to human liberation. To them, this was added proof of the rightness of their cause.

A distinction should be made between equality and freedom in marriage, and that elusive quality called happiness. This judgment was a difficult one for contemporaries to make, and is an even more conjectural one for historians. Since the women in this group were feminists dedicated to reform work, it is not farfetched to assume a high correlation between their degree of freedom and their marital satisfaction. All of the women who married non-feminist husbands gave evidence of dissatisfaction, whereas, of the twenty-eight couples who shared a feminist commitment, only five are known to have had some conflicts or periods of separation.[36] Since information on five couples is too scanty to allow even tentative conclusions, we can infer that eighteen of the twenty-eight feminist couples seem to have been unusually compatible.

The new models created by these feminist couples reflected their belief in human rights as well as their concept of overlapping spheres, a departure from the prevailing doctrine of separate spheres. In their primary role as human beings and citizens of the Republic, men and women would ideally occupy the same sphere and enjoy identical rights. In marriage, this meant the freedom of each to participate equally in the family's decision-making process, as well as in government and other aspects of the public sphere; both the burdens and privileges of family life were to be shared equally. Child-rearing, especially, was the responsibility of both parents.

However, equality did not mean androgyny. Reflecting their belief in natural sex differences, the feminists envisioned that women, in their specialized roles as mothers and wives, would have greater involvement in the home, especially during the child-rearing years. This domestic activity would be matched by the husbands' greater efforts, outside the home, to provide for the family. Neither spouse would be restricted to these special and somewhat temporary roles. In practice, the feminist husbands were unusual in encouraging their wives' activities outside the home, and in helping them with family responsibilities. On a day-to-day basis, however, most of the women still bore the major housekeeping burden. In spite of their travels and speaking engagements, a good part of their time was spent supervising servants, doing chores, and caring for their children. (Household help of some kind was common even for lower-middle-class families.)

During the early years of most of these marriages, income was low and household help minimal or absent. When both husband and wife were full-time reformers, life was particularly difficult. Jane Elisabeth Jones, reared in a wealthy family, lived on her husband's $400 annual salary as an antislavery agent, plus a small income from her writings. They married in 1846 while co-editing the *Anti-Slavery Bugle* and set up housekeeping in two rooms; one was used for parlor, office, and bedroom, and the other for kitchen and dining room. Their letters tell of financial troubles and doubts about the future. By 1848, contemplating the birth of their first child, they were considering opening a shop so he could pursue his trade and they could acquire a home. In 1856 they were still living frugally. Elisabeth told Abby Kelley Foster that she had become "more of a philosopher" and was now accustomed to doing her own work. Though she had declared her intention of staying home with her child and had criticized Abby for not doing so, she lectured regularly in this period and probably left her daughter with her husband and family, as Abby did.[37]

During their child-rearing years, the domestic responsibilities of all the women were naturally the heaviest. All but four of the thirty-seven wives had children—Child, Rose, Crandall, and Hutchinson were the exceptions. Of the thirty-four who continued their reform work after marriage, all but two—Child and Rose —had children. The thirty-three mothers averaged 4.1 children each, including several who died in infancy. A number of the women married late and had only one child—Foster, Stone, Jones, Comstock, Lozier—while others had large families. Blackwell had seven children (in spite of marrying late), as did Stanton and Wright. Frances Gage had eight; Mott, Gibbons, and Howe had six each. All of these women managed to devote part of their time to their own work. Antoinette Blackwell, highly disciplined and able to work amid a chaotic household, spent several hours a day at scholarly study. Others dashed off articles and speeches when they could, and left their children with husbands, servants, and relatives when it was necessary to attend a convention or address a state legislature.

All of the women put a high value on good housekeeping. Ten years before her own marriage, Lucy Stone gave her younger sister detailed instructions about the care of her husband's wardrobe and urged her to have a regular plan for keeping the house clean. The feminists also tended to be efficient and well organized, partly because they were conscientious, but also because they had important things to do with the time thus saved. The order and regularity of Lucretia Mott's household was legendary, even at the height of her reform activities and with a constant stream of visitors to look after. Mrs. Mott explained how she accomplished so much: she performed only *necessary* housekeeping duties and skipped the nonessentials, "the self-imposed labors under which so many women struggled." She did no fancy sewing or light reading, and all entertainment was kept simple. The reminiscences of the feminist-abolitionists contain many references to dining at the Motts while attending a convention; visitors noted that Mrs. Mott brought a cedar tub of hot water and a snowy cloth to the table after each meal, and washed the silver and china without any interruption in her brilliant conversation.[38]

Such extraordinary efforts to excel at housekeeping were good tactical strategy—the women's journals were filled with stories proving that strong-minded women could be good wives and mothers, and their pages contained lengthy descriptions of the feminists' well-ordered homes and well-mannered children. The reformers also had a personal need to compensate for not devoting themselves exclusively to their families, though their guilt was diminished by the worthiness of their cause. Basically, though, they believed that both jobs were important, and saw one as an extension of the other. Elizabeth Smith Miller saw no contradiction in working for the *Revolution* and, shortly after, publishing a popular book with recipes and advice on entertaining graciously. She also combined both interests by putting up preserves for market and donating the proceeds to good causes.

Though domesticity was important in principle, equality in marriage was even more so. Many couples—including the Stantons, Bloomers, Fosters, Welds, and Joneses—began life together by omitting the customary "obey" from the marriage vows. Several, like Lucy Stone and Henry Blackwell, publicly protested the legal slavery of marriage and established their own rules. The Stone-Blackwell protest, published by the couple in 1855, was the first to be well publicized. Blackwell renounced all privileges which the law conferred on the husband, and the whole system by which "the legal existence of the wife is suspended during marriage." Personal independence and equal human rights, the two declared, could never be forfeited. This statement stood for a long time as an inspiration to budding feminists. In 1894 the national NAWSA convention held a memorial service for Lucy Stone and praised that marriage contract as the "grandest chart of the absolute equality of man and women that has ever been made." In a eulogy that Lucy would have approved, the speaker added that their contract "throws a new halo of consecration and sanctity around the institution of marriage." The following year, Henry Blackwell reaffirmed that his and Lucy's marriage had been "a noble and life-long partnership of equals," and he later officially declared this fact in a written endorsement on their original protest.[39]

Others also made marriage contracts and issued declarations of mutual obligation. At the Quaker wedding ceremony of Angelina Grimké and Theodore Weld, each spoke spontaneously of love and devotion, and Weld took the opportunity to denounce the laws giving men control over their wives' property. Abby Kelley and Stephen Foster, married in a similar ceremony, on their handwritten marriage certificate made a "public declaration of our mutual affection, and a covenant of perpetual love and fidelity, of our purpose

to perform faithfully, all the relative duties of husband and wife."
They also agreed that they would retain their independence and
could withdraw whenever they chose. In accordance with their
principles, the farm they subsequently purchased was deeded to
them jointly. Antoinette Brown and Sam Blackwell also contracted
at the time of their marriage to be "joint owners of all properties,
real estate and moneys."[40]

Behind these legal pronouncements there was a genuine commitment to what Antoinette Brown described as "independent
thought and keen feeling for justice between men and women." In a
letter to his fiancée, Sam Blackwell expressed concern that marrying
him might mean giving up a great deal for his sake. Antoinette
replied, "Only leave me free, as free as you are and everyone ought to
be, and it is giving up nothing." She looked forward to "a dear quiet
own home with one's husband to love and be loved by, with his big
heart full of sympathy and an active spirit ready to cooperate in
everything good." He might sigh for a more domestic wife, she
predicted, but added that having her preach occasionally or go on a
tour of a few days or weeks "won't be so very bad, will it?"[41]

The Brown-Blackwell arrangement worked remarkably well for
almost fifty years, and letters written after their marriage were, if
anything, even more loving. Abby Kelley was also completely
satisfied with the independence and support she enjoyed; in
fact, she regretted that she had postponed marriage for fear that it
would interfere with her work. "A whole man and a whole woman,"
she assured Stephen, "are far better than a half man and a
half woman."[42]

All the feminist-abolitionists described "true" marriage as union
involving "completeness," "mutuality," and a sharing and blend-
ing of "lives and interests into a common harmony."[43] In practice,
their marriages were characterized by shared responsibilities and
decision-making. Not only did the husbands help with home duties
and women's rights activities, but the wives often shared in their
husbands' work as well. Mary and Daniel Livermore worked closely
together, for example; she contributed to his books and preached at
his pulpits, whereas he helped with her lectures and preserved the
notes and letters she later used for her autobiography. They shared
the editorship of his *New Covenant* in the 1860's, and he helped her to
establish her suffrage paper, the *Agitator*. In his book *Women Suffrage*

Defended, he argued that "The responsibilities of the home need not conflict with the duties one owes to humanity, to society and the State." He practiced what he preached, and urged his wife to use her talents outside the home. When she had qualms about leaving for her first lecture tour, he declared that it was preposterous for her to continue doing housework when "work of a better and higher order" was waiting for her. He assured her that she would not be forsaking home and family, and that she would return from her occasional absences fresher and more interesting. While the Livermores had servants and relatives to care for the house and children so that her absences were not burdensome to him, he was nevertheless expressing a most atypical attitude.[44]

Furthermore, in what must have been an unusual move even in this group, Daniel Livermore gave up his paper and his pastorate in Chicago in 1870 and moved the family back to the Boston area. This move enabled his wife to merge her paper with the *Woman's Journal* and to take over the editorship. For more than ten years he traveled from Melrose, seven miles north of Boston, to a pastorate in Hingham, about twenty-five miles away on the south shore. After retirement, he devoted himself to helping his wife by doing research for her lectures and accompanying her on tours. A writer who interviewed the couple in 1871 found him a "proud and happy husband." Their granddaughter recalled that he "always stood behind her and urged her on," and often stayed home to look after household matters so that Mary could go out and speak. Like many feminist husbands, Daniel Livermore had apparently accepted his wife's greater fame without feeling personally threatened or resentful.[45]

Other couples also put their beliefs into practice. Dexter Bloomer shared his job as postmaster with his wife, encouraged her to write for his paper and then to start her own, and shared the facilities of his paper with her. He also took faithful care of her letters and articles, and he published her *Life and Writings*. Bloomer obviously considered his wife's work important, in addition to respecting her rights as an individual; this attitude explains much of the harmony in their relationship. The two collaborated on other newspapers and many reform projects in their happy fifty-four-year marriage, and they raised two adopted children with the same degree of cooperation.

Clarina Howard Nichols edited the Vermont newspaper which her husband published, and in fact took over its complete management when George Nichols became seriously ill shortly after their marriage in 1843. She had managed the paper for six years before this fact was announced publicly. Though her husband had been against this deception, she explained, she felt it necessary to labor "under my husband's hat" in order to establish her competence and to lay a better foundation for requesting support for the reforms she advocated. George Nichols also encouraged Clarina to leave home for lecture tours. His sympathy and support, she later recalled, gave her the courage to engage in what was then an unheard-of activity for a woman. He had come to value his own rights, she observed, and wished to have women gain them also.[46]

Harriet Hanson Robinson also worked with her husband on his antislavery paper in the 1850's and, like the Fosters and the Joneses, lived frugally on less than $400 a year. In 1852, after three years of marriage, her diary recorded that she was learning to read proof and "can do it and plenty of housework and sewing besides." (She also had one child at this time.) The couple's relationship was unusually close and affectionate: in 1852 she wrote, "My heart still leaps when I hear his step." Four years later, when he was away on a trip to raise funds for the antislavery effort in Kansas, she confided to her diary that they were still in love and that she missed him terribly: "Willie is kind and good and makes all life burdens easy to me." In another entry she noted that he was "the crowning joy" of her life.[47] Their marriage continued to be a warm and collaborative enterprise. They worked together on women's rights campaigns, and Harriet edited a book of William's writings.

The record of the feminist-abolitionist marriages leads one to the inescapable conclusion that a shared commitment to reform strengthened these relationships, in spite of the financial problems and other difficulties that such a commitment may have caused. It was not only the shared belief in woman's equality, but also the common sense of a broader mission which reinforced their initial attraction and provided a continuing source of inner strength and mutual respect. Reform work also provided such couples with a focus for family activities and with a circle of close friends who shared their cause, both factors adding to marital stability.

The reality of these marriages reinforced the ideal that all the women believed in and talked about in their feminist speeches: in the true marriages of the future, women and men would work side by side in love and equality to rear their children and work for a better world. This dream was held even by feminists who rejected marriage because of its present state of imperfection. It was said, for example, that Susan Anthony carried with her everywhere, for inspiration, the following quotation from Elizabeth Barrett Browning's *Aurora Leigh,* a verse that could well have been written for her married friends:

> The world waits
> for help, Beloved, let us work so well,
> Our work shall be better for our love
> And still our love be sweeter for our work.

Lucretia Mott understood this phenomenon and told a young couple that she owed the happiness of her wedded life to the fact that she and her husband "were one in a deep interest in the sacred cause of wronged humanity."[48]

This shared cause was inherited by many of the feminist-abolitionists' children, although adequate information is available only for those few who became well known. The pattern of achievement that one expects from the children of educated and highly motivated parents also seems to exist. The unsuccessful offspring left few traces, but at least six of the feminists had daughters who became nationally known. Alice Stone Blackwell and Harriot Stanton Blatch were noted suffragists, the latter an activist in England as well as in the United States. (Theodore Stanton was also active in the women's cause.) Harriette Robinson Shattuck was a suffrage leader as well as a writer and expert on parliamentary law. She assisted her father when he served as clerk of the Massachusetts House of Representatives in 1871–72, the first and only woman to hold the position in that century. Julia Ward Howe's daughters, Laura Richards and Maud Howe Elliott, were noted writers who won a Pulitzer prize for their biography of their mother. One of Hannah Longshore's two children, Lucretia Blankenburg, was a suffragist and civic reformer who married another noted reformer. Julia Thomas Irvine, the daughter of Mary Frame Thomas, became a professor of Greek at Wellesley College and later served as that school's fourth president. Interestingly, of this group of career women only Alice Stone Blackwell remained unmarried. The children of other feminists were also reformers and educators. Martha Wright's two daughters were both suffragists, and one of her three sons became a noted prison reformer. One of Elizabeth Chace's daughters was a writer, and her son Arnold was chancellor of Brown University. Caroline Dall's only son, William Healey Dall, was an eminent naturalist.

A chief source of pride among the feminist-abolitionists was the fact that these strong-minded women were able to marry and continue their work without loss of either domestic virtue or reform commitment. This was true in all but one of the twenty-eight feminist marriages under consideration. One of the most compatible and dedicated couples proved to be the exception to the rule. Ironically, Angelina Grimké and Theodore Weld, because they married in the midst of the furor over her public speaking, saw their union as an experiment. They had felt an attraction for some time, but he had repressed his feelings. Weld was a man with enormous passion and physical energy (and a fierce and striking appearance which belied his gentleness). Nevertheless, he had, with his friend Whittier, pledged not to marry until slavery was abolished, and he lived a spartan, self-disciplined life. In 1838, after wrestling with himself "like a blind giant" for many months, Weld finally confessed his love to Angelina and was accepted.[49]

Some of Weld's associates felt that he showed great moral courage in marrying a "notorious" woman who had been utterly "spoiled" for domestic life. Because even friends held this opinion, the couple decided their marriage would be a test of their belief in equality, and proof that a woman could be both an abolitionist and a good wife. Angelina wrote to Theodore: "May the Lord Jesus help me for thy sake and for *woman's* sake to prove that well regulated minds can with equal ease occupy high and low stations and find *true happiness* in both." In his letters he acknowledged the "peculiar responsibility" resting on her because of her "*doctrine and practice* touching the sphere of woman." She was, he reminded her, "the FIRST woman everywhere known to be on this ground, to whom in the Providence of God the *practical test* of married life will be applied."[50]

Both expected that she would continue to write, and lecture occasionally. Though they achieved personal equality in marriage, that union meant virtually the end of the Grimkés' public career, and it halted most of Weld's work as well. Both Angelina and Sarah (who lived with the couple for most of her life) became bogged down in child-rearing, financial difficulties, and Angelina's health problems. They lived a plain, spartan life, eschewing servants. Weld himself described them as "a strange trio, different from all the world." They participated only occasionally in reform work, Theodore more than the sisters.[51]

Just as successful marriages were a source of inspiration, so the failure of the Grimké-Weld experiment acted as a deterrent to other feminists. Abby Kelley asked Sarah if she and Angelina had been "swallowed up and utterly annihilated in Theodore?" Abby lamented to Anne Weston a year after the marriage: "How many changes have come over 'the spirit of the dream.'" In the early years, at least, the sisters insisted that they were doing as much for the cause of woman by staying home and proving they were not "ruined as domestic characters." Sarah explained that her task had been "simply to open doors, or do the first rough work"; she no longer felt called to the work. The Lord had brought Angelina into the domestic sphere, according to her sister, "that she may vindicate the character of female lecturers from the aspersions with which we have been loaded." Angelina wrote to her friends describing their happy domestic life, "serving one another in love," and sharing housekeeping burdens among the trio. Theodore explained to Henry Blackwell that they had given up the work because there was "a fighting era in everyone's life," but now they had reached "another and a higher view."[52]

At least one historian has seen the Grimkés as symbols of the movement's failure to recognize that the institutions of marriage and family were the chief obstacles to sexual equality.[53] The conventional nineteenth-century marriage was certainly incompatible with equality, because most men (and many women) expected wives to play a subservient role. What is most striking about the feminists, however, is the number who were able to solve woman's dilemma, at least for themselves, by molding their marriages into new shapes. the Grimkés were exceptional cases, rather than the norm. Most of their colleagues not only retained their independence in spite of marriage; indeed, they achieved independence *because* of the kinds of marriages they made. The Grimkés were also atypical in that Weld, too, was preoccupied with family needs and was able to do only a little more for reform than the women. Theirs was not solely a female dilemma.

A few feminist marriages were marked by some conflict or tension, but such difficulties were rarely caused simply by the career-versus-home dilemma. Although the Stantons remained affectionate and respected each other's separate careers, these occupations were not shared, and there were some resentments expressed in otherwise friendly letters, especially when the children were young. Elizabeth felt that her husband was away from home too much, and envied his freedom; he often complained that she was too preoccupied with the cause. This union of two unusually strong personalities might have been stormy under any circumstances. More important, Elizabeth Cady Stanton did achieve a degree of independence in marriage, and was regarded by her husband as an equal partner in spite of her opposing views on many personal and political issues. She was limited more by her children than by her husband, and did enjoy a great deal of freedom after they were grown.

The Childs also maintained a deep affection and were considered a devoted couple, but their marriage was marred by serious disappointments. David's impractical idealism and chronic business failures, and later his poor health, kept him dependent on his wife. For Maria, this situation provided an unsatisfactory substitute for the child she never had. Her "good David," she wrote plaintively at sixty, "serves me for husband and 'baby and all.'"[54] This unhappiness, however, was not directly related to her career as writer and reformer.[55] She was also more subject to internal conflict than most feminists—a temperamental characteristic that preceded her marital troubles.

In at least one case, the marriage of two devoted feminists was so threatened by strong personalities and career conflicts that separation was the only solution. Although Mathilde and Fritz Anneke shared deep affection, mutual respect, and a commitment to radical social change, they pursued independent careers, for the most part in separate places. Their daughter affectionately called them "two flaming spirits." Their emotional letters during frequent separations and estrangements reveal their personal devotion, but their relationship suffered under the constant strain of financial troubles, health problems, and isolation from the European intellectual community. Added to this was the blow of losing three of their six children in a single epidemic in 1858, an emotional setback from which neither parent ever recovered. Mathilde Anneke also felt the constant need to assert her independence, although her husband was not the cause of her rebellion. All of these difficulties were greater than the strength they gained from their shared beliefs.[56]

No matter how compatible their marriages, all of these women suffered the conflict between private and public duties—a difficulty endemic among all reformers, but especially so among women. Despite their own efficiency and their husbands' help, their lives were constant balancing acts. In allocating their time and energy, they were constantly forced to choose between their two jobs—child-rearing and housekeeping in the domestic sphere; work for women's rights, abolition, temperance, and other reforms in the public sphere. At times, the urgency of one or the other was particularly overwhelming, but usually both seemed compelling. Maternal responsibilities made the choice especially difficult. Lucy Stone's letters home often expressed guilt about leaving her child and neglecting her domestic duties. (Her husband chastised himself regularly for not doing enough for the cause.) Her conflict was greatest during the few years after Alice's birth, when she withdrew from her work. Attending a lecture during this period, she was inspired to believe "all things were possible to me" and was tempted to rejoin the battle. When she came home "and looked at Alice's sleeping face, and thought of the possible evil that might befall her if my guardian eye was turned away, I shrank like a snail into its shell."[57]

Abby Kelley Foster, torn by the same conflict of duties, continued her work but kept up an active correspondence with her child, with the help of her husband and family. To four-year-old Alla she wrote that she wished she could come home—"Do you begin to think I shall never get ready to keep house?"—but explained that the little slave girls needed her even more than Alla did. She added: "Do you often think of the little slave girls who can never see their dear mothers again?"[58]

Elizabeth Cady Stanton was often the "caged lioness," torn between her joy in motherhood and the demands of the women's cause. In 1857 Susan Anthony described Stanton as a soul on fire who vowed to escape "this *bondage* to *babies* and *children* and *house* cares."[59] Lydia Maria Child, childless but burdened with caring for both her father and her husband, and usually without servants, divided her time between her writing and her diligent and sometimes frantic efforts to keep up with the cooking, food preserving, sewing, mending, and cleaning.

The conflicts in feminist marriages arose not from differences in ideology, but from the difficulty of making the reality conform to the ideal. This conflict was probably most evident in the area of sexuality, where the feminists' attitudes were closer to the mainstream than were their views on equality. Though much is known of their rhetoric and little of their sexual practices, one can infer that the feminists' sexual feelings were often at war with the tenets of their reform-religion, which stressed purity and self-control for both sexes.

Though the feminists shared the general view of women as the more spiritual sex, their private correspondence indicates that they themselves, though not generally sophisticated on the subject, were not "unsexed." Angelina Grimké, in a series of courtship letters, wrote with both excitement and anxiety about the "restless longings" of her heart and the strange new feelings which "have returned with increased strength." Both "alarmed and confused," she asked Theodore: "Why pants my *soul* after *thee*, and sighs and mourns because tho' present in mind thou art absent in body?" Her sexual feelings were a "mystery" to her, and she asked with the innocence of a child: "I want to know why those of our own sex *cannot* fill the void in human hearts."[60]

The correspondence between the Fosters both before and after marriage indicates great passion, especially on Stephen's part but also on Abby's. In accepting his proposal, she wrote that as the thirsty traveler in the desert longs for the cool spring,"so does my heart pant to stand before the world the wife of Stephen S. Foster." In the same letter, she explained that her wish to postpone the marriage did not signify lack of affection: "My arm of flesh is eager to follow the promptings of the spirit, and to encircle you *to poison or the stake,* if need be. . . ." Their meetings were apparently intense as well, because Stephen wrote the following month that if she wanted him to come to work in her area, she could not expect to receive him in "a cool business-like way . . . have you forgotten Syracuse?" In the same letter, he wrote ardently and at great length of his desire to clasp her in his arms (but assured her that his conscience was "unsullied" by "an unworthy motive, or an improper desire"). He had no idea, he wrote, "of spending another *cold winter* alone." Though the idea of premarital sexual intercourse between them was unthinkable, they vowed to belong to each other and be spiritually man and wife. Two years later, still unmarried, Abby wrote of the difficulties of separation: "I frankly confess I cannot again be an old maid—I want to see my other half more than ever before. . . ."[61]

Their love letters continued after marriage as well. In an interesting letter written five years after the wedding and during a long separation, Stephen wrote: "I never felt more like a lover than at the present time." Recalling their courtship, he promised that their reunion would be a "new marriage" in which the experience of the last years would enable him to conduct himself "with somewhat more facility and grace" than the first time. In a similarly ardent letter, he wrote of their separation as "a sensation which has no parallel in the experience of an old bachelor."[62]

Antoinette Brown and Sam Blackwell also exchanged letters that were often passionate. During their courtship, she wrote that she had belonged to no one before, but that his love filled a void in her life and "they grew together." She felt "more ready to nestle quietly into his heart and rest there." Several years after their marriage, she wrote from a lecture tour: "The truth is I fall in love with you anew every time we separate." "There is only one luxury that I long for," she wrote, "and that is yourself. . . . Even the babes are not wanted here." With a slight tinge of guilt, she added: "I always think of you and very little of them."[63]

With self-control as the ideal, there were inevitable conflicts even in the best feminist marriages. Those who were most intense and compulsive about fulfilling their divine mission were undoubtedly most plagued with guilt about feelings that were physical, not spiritual. A letter from Abby Kelley Foster indicates how this dilemma may have been resolved: "My thoughts are *too much* with thee," she told her husband. "I fear I love the creation more than the creator, but in analyzing my feelings, I believe it is only the *image* of the creator which I love in the creation."[64]

Grimké and Weld were similarly torn between the (to them) unaccountable force of their passion and their guilt at being distracted from the path of duty. Their lengthy courtship letters constitute an excellent and unusual record of the torments and rationalizations experienced by reformers with their cultural background. In the first expression of his love, Theodore admitted that he had been "stifling by violence all the intensities of my nature." He was careful to remind Angelina, and himself, that though she had his whole heart, "I *do* love the Lord our righteousness *better* than I love *you*." "And it is *because* I love him *better*," he added, "that I love you *as* I do." He expressed the constant fear that he would lose the self-restraint he prized so highly. His stormy feelings were kept in subjection "only by the *rod of iron* in the strong hand of con- science and reason and never laid aside for a moment with safety." The phrase "warring against nature" appears again and again in his letters.[65]

Angelina assured him that "the springs of Womans love [are] as deep as those of man," but she was obsessed with guilt about her sexual feelings and with fear of divine punishment. "Am I putting *thee* in the place of Jesus?" she asked him, and *"Am I sinning. . . .?"* "The conflict is great," she admitted, *"for I want to know where* I am. . . ."[66]

Weld and Grimké struggled with the mysteries of their feelings and the weight of their conflicts. After some months had elapsed, they decided that their "affinities" for each other were part of the "law of our nature sublimely assigned by God." As added assurance that he and Angelina would be doing the right thing by marrying, Theodore speculated that perhaps God had brought them into this state for a special mission. The relations of husband and wife were among "the most horrible perversions" of the age, he wrote; by the example of their own union, they could help to redeem marriage from these perversions. "We marry," he told Angelina, "not *merely* nor *mainly* nor *at all comparatively* to ENJOY, but . . . together to toil and testify and suffer . . . to crucify the flesh with its affections and lusts and to keep ourselves and each other unspotted from the world. . . ."[67] They were finally able to accept their physical desires by subsuming them within a higher and nobler purpose, making their marriage a test of their faith.

The shared commitment to "purity" and self-control, and a belief in egalitarianism and mutuality in marriage, may have made it easier for these reformers to control the size of their families, and may help to explain their below-average family size. Cooperation between husband and wife was especially important, since the only means of contraception they were likely to use were the "natural" methods of withdrawal and abstinence. It seems likely that, given the demands of their public work, these couples were anxious to control the size of their families. Undoubtedly there also was more agreement on mutual goals in the feminist families. Unfortunately, prudishness probably prevented both husbands and wives from referring to the matter in letters, if they discussed it at all. Since their correspondence leaves no clues, the historian can only speculate.

On the whole, the feminist-abolitionists' marriages came remarkably close to their ideal "partnership of equals." These couples believed that marriage should embrace autonomy, equality, and shared responsibilities, and they were generally successful in implementing these goals. The wives retained primary responsibility for the home, in keeping with their own beliefs, and rarely challenged their husbands as breadwinners. The commitment of both to the ideal of overlapping (rather than separate) spheres meant, however, that the women were free to continue their reform work; such freedom few nineteenth-century wives enjoyed. The husbands also contributed their own prestige and financial support to the women's movement and, most important, helped to create models of egalitarian marriage for others to emulate. The feminists themselves cited these successful marriages, hoping to prove two points: to show the world that women could play a public role without neglecting domestic responsibility or losing "femininity," and to prove to their sister reformers that women could marry without losing independence. Evidence indicates that younger feminists were indeed influenced by these examples.

Feminist husbands and wives tended to come from the same cultural background and followed similar paths away from religious orthodoxy and toward greater freedom of thought. They shared a world-view which embraced the concept of universal reform and the emancipation of the human family. They saw the choice of a proper mate and the reform of marriage as a key step toward their ideal society. In these marriages, egalitarianism coexisted with a repressive attitude toward sexuality; both were consistent with the reformers' campaign for the moral elevation of home and family, and the ultimate regeneration of the race. Because human rights and self-improvement were cornerstones of their program to make the world better, their idea of marriage incorporated both concepts.

Many questions about this dimension of the women's movement remain to be investigated. The effect of a feminist and reformist milieu on the family, and especially on the children of such marriages, has only been suggested here. From the available evidence, however, one can infer that a shared commitment to reform was a source of strength in the family as a whole. The reformers' common cause enabled them to overcome many of the difficulties caused by their efforts to combine the duties of both family and reform. In a striking number of cases, the feminists' work was indeed better for their love, and their love sweeter for their work. The strong ideological bonds between husband and wife reinforced their emotional ties to provide a personal existential base from which to launch reformist crusades; furthermore, the satisfying reality of their own lives strengthened their belief that the perfect society would ultimately be realized. Though the reform of marriage was a politically impossible goal in the nineteenth century, these feminist families stand today as a reminder of important directions not taken.

NOTES

1. William H. Chafe, *The American Woman: Her Changing Social, Economic, and Political Role, 1920–1970* (New York: Oxford University Press, 1972).

2. See William L. O'Neill, *Everyone Was Brave: The Rise and Fall of Feminism in America* (Chicago: Quadrangle Books, 1969); Ellen DuBois, "Struggling into Existence: The Feminism of Sarah and Angelina Grimké," *Women: A Journal of Liberation* (Spring 1970).

3. Cf. Yasukichi Yasuba, *Birth Rates of the White Population in the United States, 1800–1860* (Baltimore: Johns Hopkins University Press, 1962), p. 45.

4. Ibid., p. 114.

5. See Daniel Scott Smith, "Parental Power and Marriage Patterns: An Analysis of Historical Trends in Hingham, Massachusetts," *Journal of Marriage and the Family* 35 (Aug. 1973): 419–28.

6. Unlike the exceptional women cited by Alice S. Rossi in "Feminist History in Perspective: Sociological Contributions to Biographic Analysis," in *A Sampler of Women's Studies,* ed. Dorothy Gies McGuigan (Ann Arbor: Center for Continuing Education of Women, 1973), pp. 85–108, esp. p. 99.

7. Almost nothing is known of Clemence Lozier's second husband.

8. Swisshelm's marriage (also Lozier's second marriage and Nichols's first) ended in divorce.

9. Lozier and Caroline Dall had problems; the others are Elizabeth Oakes Smith, Matilda Joslyn Gage, and Hannah Tracy Cutler.

10. Calvo, "Quaker Women Ministers," esp. pp. 84–85. Cf. Michael Gor-

don and M. Charles Bernstein, "Mate Choice and Domestic Life in the 19th Century Marriage Manuals," *Journal of Marriage and the Family* 32 (Nov. 1970): 665–74.

11. Mary Grew, *James Mott, a Biographical Sketch,* undated pamphlet, Garrison Family Papers, Smith College.

12. Hallowell, ed., *Mott,* p. 74.

13. See, e.g., *Revolution,* Aug. 6, 1868.

14. Benjamin Platt Thomas, *Theodore Weld: Crusader for Freedom* (New Brunswick, N.J.: Rutgers University Press, 1950), p. 16.

15. See Rossi, "Feminist History in Perspective," esp. pp. 88–89.

16. *New York Herald,* Sept. 12, 1852, in *History of Woman Suffrage,* 1:854.

17. Harriet H. Robinson, ed., *"Warrington" Pen-Portraits* (Boston: By the Editor, 1877), pp. 547, 562.

18. Weld et al., *Letters,* 2:702, 544; L. M. Child to Abby Kelley, Oct. 1, 1838, Kelley-Foster Papers, AAS.

19. S. F. Foster to A. K. Foster, July 27, 1851, Sept. 11, 1850, Sept. 15, 1855, Kelley-Foster Papers, AAS.

20. Aaron M. Powell, *Personal Reminiscences* (New York: Caulon Press, 1899), pp. 8, 10; Pease, "Freshness of Fanaticism," p. 84; newsclipping on Foster's death, Harriet Hanson Robinson Scrapbook, RC.

21. Hallowell, ed., *Mott,* pp. 89, 271, 400 and *passim.*

22. Ibid., Preface and p. 89.

23. James Mott to Lucy Stone, June 29, 1853, Blackwell Family Papers, LC.

24. *Woman's Journal,* Sept. 27, 1873.

25. Stanton, *Eighty Years and More,* p. 202; *Revolution,* Aug. 4, 1870.

26. Antoinette Brown to Lucy Stone, "1850," and Brown to Samuel Blackwell, 1855?; Blackwell Autobiography, Blackwell Family Papers, RC; Hays, *Extraordinary Blackwells,* p. 298.

27. Wyman and Wyman, *Chace,* 1:312.

28. Davis Reminiscences, *History of Woman Suffrage,* 1:283–89; for Rose, see *Agitator,* June 25, 1869, ibid., 1:95–96.

29. Edwin W. Small and Miriam R. Small, "Prudence Crandall, Champion of Negro Education," *New England Quarterly* 17 (Dec. 1944): 506–29; quotation on pp. 528–29.

30. Brink, *Harps in the Wind;* song is in *History of Woman Suffrage,* 2:934.

31. Swisshelm, *Half a Century,* quotation on p. 49; see also Jane Grey Swisshelm, *Crusader and Feminist; Letters of Jane Grey Swisshelm, 1858–1865,* ed. Arthur J. Larsen (St. Paul: Minnesota Historical Society, 1934).

32. *History of Woman Suffrage,* 1:844–45; cf. Stanton in *Lily,* July, 1851; Davis in *Una,* 1855.

33. *Notable American Women,* 2:226; Richards and Elliott, *Howe,* p. 78.

34. Richards and Elliott, *Howe,* p. 194; see also Howe, *Reminiscences.*

35. See Rossi, "Feminist History in Perspective," p. 106.

36. Stanton, Child, Anneke, Jones, Griffing.

37. Jane E. Jones to Abby Kelley and Stephen Foster, Jan. 23, Apr. 18, 1848, Nov. 4, 1856, Jan. 23, 1848, Kelley-Foster Papers, AAS.

38. Lucy Stone to Sarah Stone, Mar. 31, 1845, Blackwell Family Papers, LC; Hallowell, ed., *Mott,* p. 251.

39. The eulogy is in *History of Woman Suffrage,* 4:226; H. B. Blackwell to Elizabeth Blackwell, Sept. 11, 1895 (this and the protest in Blackwell Family Papers, LC).

40. Weld et al., *Letters,* 2:678–79; Fosters' marriage certificate is in Kelley-Foster Papers, WorHS; see also Zelotes W. Coombs, *Stephen Symonds and Abby Kelley Foster* (Worcester, Mass.: Worcester Historical Society, 1934); Antoinette Brown to Samuel Blackwell, Dec. 14, 1855, Blackwell Family Papers, RC; Hays, *Extraordinary Blackwells,* p. 122.

41. Antoinette Brown to Samuel Blackwell, Dec. 14, 1855, Blackwell Family Papers, RC.

42. Pease, "Freshness of Fanaticism," p. 83.

43. See, e.g., *History of Woman Suffrage,* 1:164.

44. Livermore, *Story of My Life,* p. 486; Daniel Parker Livermore, *Woman Suffrage Defended* (Boston: Lee & Shepard, 1885), p. 75.

45. Virginia Townsend, "A Night at the Home of Mary A. Livermore," *Melrose Journal,* Nov. 11, 1871; interview with Mrs. M. D. Barrows, Feb. 10, 1916, in Livermore Scrapbook, both in Melrose, Mass., Public Library.

46. Gambone, ed., "Forgotten Feminist," p. 14, note 8, 246–47; *History of Woman Suffrage,* 1:171–200.

47. Diary of William Stevens Robinson and Harriet Hanson Robinson, her entries, 1852, 1856, 1855, Robinson Papers.

48. Rossi, ed., *Essays on Sex Equality,* p. 44; Hallowell, ed., *Mott,* pp. 379–80.

49. Weld et al., *Letters,* 2:555.

50. Ibid., pp. 649, 638.

51. Ibid., p. 629; see also *History of Woman Suffrage,* 1:392.

52. S. Grimké to Abby Kelley, June 15, 1838, Kelley-Foster Papers, AAS; A. Kelley to A. W. Weston, May 29, 1839; S. Grimké to A. W. Weston, July 17, 1838; A. G. Weld to A. W. Weston, July 15, 1838, all three in Weston Family Papers; H. B. Blackwell to Lucy Stone, June 13, 1853, Blackwell Family Papers, LC.

53. See DuBois, "Struggling into Existence," p. 11.

54. Child, *Letters,* p. 140; see also Lydia Maria Child Autobiography, Child Papers, CU.

55. Cf. Kirk Jeffrey, "Marriage, Career, and Feminine Ideology in Nineteenth-Century America: Reconstructing the Marital Experience of Lydia Maria Child, 1828–1874," *Feminist Studies* 2, nos. 2/3 (1975): 113–30.

56. Henriette M. Heinzen and Hertha Anneke Sanne, "Biographical Notes in Commemoration of Fritz Anneke and Mathilde Franziska Anneke" (1940), typescript in Mathilde and Fritz Anneke Papers, State Historical Society of Wisconsin.

57. Lucy Stone to Antoinette Brown Blackwell, Feb. 20, 1859, Blackwell Family Papers, LC.

58. Abby Kelley Foster to Alla, Apr. 17, 1852, Kelley-Foster Papers, WorHS.

59. Susan B. Anthony to Lucy Stone, July 18, 1857, Blackwell Family Papers, LC.

60. Weld et al., *Letters,* 2:537, 625, 569.

61. A. Kelley to S. Foster, July 30, 1843, Feb. 2, 1845, S. Foster to A. Kelley, Aug. 10, 1843, Kelley-Foster Papers, AAS.

62. S. Foster to A. K. Foster, Sept. 26, 1850, July 27, 1851, Kelley-Foster Papers, AAS.

63. A. Brown to S. Blackwell, Dec. 30, 1855, and n.d., Blackwell Family Papers, RC.

64. A. K. Foster to S. Foster, Sept. 28, 1847, Kelley-Foster Papers, AAS.

65. Weld et al., *Letters,* 2:555, 532, 560.

66. Ibid., pp. 566, 625, 554.

67. Ibid., pp. 583, 637, 601.

8

The Feminist-Abolitionists
in Perspective

THIS STUDY BEGAN with abolitionist Elizabeth Chandler defending her right to leave her "proper" sphere in order to work against slavery; it closed with an examination of feminist marriages and the role of husbands in the nineteenth-century women's movement. These seemingly disparate subjects are linked by an important historical development: the rise of a distinctive group of feminist-abolitionist women who dedicated themselves to emancipating the human family from all fetters, but especially to freeing women from the slavery of sex. Their movement differed from the parent antislavery crusade in that these women brought a feminist perspective to their varied causes: an intense, personal awareness of the social injustices that were harmful to women, and a commitment to abolishing these inequities. This group was distinct also from the postwar suffragist generation because it was rooted in the romanticism and religious fervor that inspired so much antebellum social reform. Jane Elisabeth Jones, writing to Lucy Stone in 1848, spoke of "the holy nature of our enterprise"; both women personified the spirit of the feminist-abolitionists.[2]

Their antislavery heritage remained an important influence in the movement and in their lives, especially the perfectionism of the Garrisonian group. A radical offshoot of the evangelicalism of the day, that perfectionism also bore the imprint of eighteenth-century Enlightenment ideas. The resultant millennialism embodied secular and religious elements. Inheriting the human rights

252

ideals and liberal religious tendencies of their revolutionary forebears, the feminist-abolitionists also felt "called" to a sacred mission.
Abolitionism and feminism became mere battles in a larger crusade
which embraced all good causes and would lead to the perfect
society. This "reform religion" became their life's work. To truly
understand this particular group of feminists is to know that divine
guidance was as important a source of their inspiration as the call of
sisterhood. To see them in their own perspective is to understand
much which is otherwise obscure. Their romantic optimism (which
often bordered on otherworldliness) and their involvement with
diverse and often seemingly irrational "isms" stemmed from their
search for knowledge and their faith in the ultimate perfectibility of
the human race.

Though these women were moved by religious promptings, their
lives clearly indicate that theirs was an eclectic and nonconformist
faith. Emancipation, to them, meant liberation from the religious
orthodoxy so oppressive to women, as well as from other aspects of
women's enslavement. Virtually all of these reformers followed
strikingly similar paths to religious liberalism. Though the influence of Transcendentalism and the liberal religions of the day was
strong, the role of the Quakers in their "conversion" process (as well
as in their lives as a whole) is especially notable. The tenets and
members of the Society of Friends provided examples of moral
independence and reliance on inner conscience, as well as a guide to
survival as a righteous but unpopular minority. They also offered
models of women playing relatively equal roles in church and family,
and a theology which at least partially justified this equality.

The religion of the feminist-abolitionists was unorthodox in still
another way: the women's perfectionism was tempered, for the most
part, by a pragmatic sense that some compromises were necessary in
the immediate, imperfect world. Moral suasion as a tactic was never
abandoned, but the need for laws and other external controls was
quickly recognized. The feminists' working philosophy, in fact,
represented a transitional state between the earlier emphasis on
salvation through individual moral regeneration and the social and
institutional approaches taken by a later generation of reformers and
professional social workers. Their rejection of Calvinism was accompanied by the conviction that people could be improved by environ-
mental changes, as well as through their own efforts (although the

women saw this progress to be limited by natural differences of class and race, as well as by individual capacities).

Another theme, apparent in their collective biographies, concerns the opportunities and frustration experienced by a new class of urban, middle-class women in this era of enormous social change. Though the particular work they chose was determined by their religious idealism, many of them probably would have sought to expand the boundaries of "woman's sphere" even without this motivation. Unusually intelligent and strong minded, they were persistent in their efforts to acquire education and eager to make their mark in a society that seemed to promise greater fulfillment for the individual. The clash between their youthful dreams and this same society's determination to keep women in their "proper" place was inevitable. Because the feminist-abolitionists were sensitive to injustice and were moved by moral concerns, and in many cases received encouragement from their families, it seems logical that their personal efforts were turned to the larger cause of universal emancipation, and especially to the liberation of women. In turn, the feminist-abolitionist movement provided them with the powerful driving force of a human rights ideology, and with the unifying strength of like-minded reformers and a struggling sisterhood.

A representative type of feminist-abolitionist emerges from the collective portrait, though diversity within the group is also apparent. Lucy Stone—and Mary Livermore, Elizabeth Buffum Chace, Amelia Bloomer, and others—were in the mainstream: naively optimistic, self-righteous, humorless, morally rigid; but also compassionate, courageous, and determined. Sharing the radical goal of female emancipation, they were more conforming in personal style and moderate in tactics than their somewhat daring or flamboyant sisters. The less representative feminists seem more interesting simply because they deviate from the pattern. The brilliant and irreverent Elizabeth Cady Stanton, the free-thinking Ernestine Rose, and the gifted, unhappy Lydia Maria Child are unique; Lucretia Mott and Antoinette Brown Blackwell achieved breadth and maturity that gave them special standing in the sisterhood; Susan B. Anthony, with her peculiar blend of passion and level-headedness, is also distinctive; others could be cited. Virtually none in the group fits the popular stereotype of the suffragist as embittered, aggressive spinster. Most were maternal in manner and "feminine" in appearance, indistinguishable from their more conventional middle-class sisters.

Because they were rooted in their society, the feminist-abolitionists were imperfect people like the rest of their human family. Their social vision was limited by their elitism and the class and race consciousness with which they were raised. Even their ideal of sisterhood had its limitations in practice—women who were socially or sexually deviant were not accepted into the ranks; lower-class women were treated as causes, rather than as equals. The reformers' views on the economic questions of their day were as conservative as their social beliefs were radical. These women were prudish in sexual matters, and many were willing to resort to censorship and other illiberal tactics to impose their moral standards on others; however, these repressive attitudes were closely related to their realistic efforts to protect women from sexual abuse and unwanted pregnancies.

In spite of these and other imperfections, the feminist-abolitionists were an inspiring lot. While they were limited by the alternatives available in their society, their achievements remain impressive. They raised the question, decisively and permanently, of a woman's right to define her own sphere and created the first organizations to act on this issue. Influenced by their antislavery experience, they were sensitive to discrimination's psychological effects on women and were the first to raise this issue publicly, as part of their campaign. They pioneered in opening up "male" professions, and were among the first to establish women's colleges and edit women's newspapers; they were the vanguard of the movement to meet women's health needs.

More important than the short-range effects of such gains were the models created by the first generation of feminists, and the ideology they espoused to justify their actions. They represented, in effect, a new type of woman who claimed the right to be an independent public person as well as an equal in the private sphere. They set new styles of leadership in public and created new kinds of unions based on equality and shared responsibilities at home. Apparently conservative in their defense of home and family, the feminists were actually radical in advocating a new type of marriage as the basis for domestic life. Although they appeared to conform in their espousal of woman's moral superiority, they were actually daring in their hope of raising both sexes to the same high level of morality. Their rejection of the doctrine of separate spheres opened the way for new arrangements and practices in marriage and child-rearing, as well as in government and social institutions. The possible shapes of some of these innovations were evident in their own marriages and careers; indeed, the diverse ways in which the feminists managed to function both in the family and in the outside world suggest "life plans" that remain relevant today.

These women provided models for the future. In the course of their own lives, they made waves among only a small circle; hence their main goal eluded them. Like the Garrisonians, who helped to end slavery but who failed to achieve their dream of a racially equal society, the feminists helped win suffrage and other legal gains but failed in their broader goal of abolishing the prejudices and practices which enslaved women. They realized the ambitious scope of their undertaking and viewed their cause as a radical one, precisely because it struck at the heart of human relationships. In 1891 Mary Livermore explained that woman suffrage had been delayed because of "the magnitude of the change contemplated by this reform." Aware that more was involved than simply granting women the vote, she further noted that transforming the leadership of society from one of men alone to one of both sexes involved "a radical reconstruction of social ideas and usages all along the line of human relations."[3] The radical changes that she and others were able to achieve within their own domestic spheres seem to confirm Elizabeth Cady Stanton's lifelong maxim that creed and custom, even more than laws, created the "slavery of sex."

NOTES

1. Mary A. Livermore's recollection of her antislavery associates in *Story of My Life*, p. 586.

2. Jane Elisabeth Jones to Lucy Stone, July 1, 1848, Blackwell Family Papers, LC.

3. *North American Review* (Sept. 1891), p. 294.

Bibliography

MANUSCRIPT COLLECTIONS

American Antiquarian Society (AAS), Worcester, Mass.
    Kelley-Foster Papers
    Lydia Maria Child Papers

Boston Public Library (BPL), Manuscript Division, Antislavery Collection
    American Anti-Slavery Society Papers
    Boston Female Anti-Slavery Society Papers
    Lydia Maria Child and David Lee Child Papers
    Garrison Papers
    Higginson Correspondence
    Livermore Correspondence
    Amos Phelps Papers
    Weston Family Papers (includes Maria Weston Chapman Papers)

Cornell University (CU), Olin Library, Manuscript Division, Ithaca, N.Y.
    Antislavery Papers (includes Lydia Maria Child Papers)
    Emily Howland Papers

Library of Congress (LC), Manuscript Division, Washington, D.C.
    Susan B. Anthony Papers
    Blackwell Family Papers (includes Lucy Stone Papers)
    Elizabeth Cady Stanton Papers
    Western Anti-Slavery Society Papers

Melrose Public Library (MelPL), Melrose, Mass.
    Mary Livermore Collection

New York Public Library (NYPL), Manuscript Division, New York.
  Smith Family Papers
  Caroline Soule Papers

Radcliffe College (RC), Schlesinger Library on the History of Women in America, Cambridge, Mass.
  Susan B. Anthony Papers
  Blackwell Family Papers
  Olympia Brown Papers
  Lydia Maria Child Papers
  Loring Family Papers
  Alma Lutz Collection
  Harriet Hanson Robinson Papers

Smith College (SC), Sophia Smith Collection, Northampton, Mass.
  Garrison Family Papers (includes Wright Family Papers)
  Women's Rights Collection

State Historical Society of Wisconsin (WisHS), Madison, Wis.
  Mathilde and Fritz Anneke Papers

Worcester Historical Society (WorHS), Worcester, Mass.
  Kelley-Foster Papers

NEWSPAPERS AND MAGAZINES

Agitator
Anti-Slavery Bugle
Arena
Lily
Liberator
Melrose (Mass.) *Journal*

Melrose (Mass.) *Reporter*
National Anti-Slavery Standard
North American Review
Revolution
Una
Woman's Journal

UNPUBLISHED MATERIAL

Blackwell, Antoinette Brown. "Antoinette Brown Blackwell, the First Woman Minister." Ed. Claude U. Gilson. 1909. Typescript in Blackwell Family Papers, RC; foreword added, 1921.

Cooper, Sheila M. "Quaker Women and the 19th Century Women's Movement: A Social-Historical Perspective." Paper given at Thomas More College Conference on Women in World and American History, Apr. 24, 1976.

Fischer, David Hackett. "America as Social History." Unpublished MS.

Giele, Janet Z. "Social Change in the Feminine Role: A Comparison of Woman's Suffrage and Woman's Temperance, 1870–1920." Ph.D. dissertation, Radcliffe College, 1961.

Heinzen, Henriette M., and Sanne, Hertha Anneke. "Biographical Notes in Commemoration of Fritz Anneke and Mathilde Franziska Anneke." 1940. Typescript in Anneke Papers, WisHS.

Hersh, Blanche Glassman. " 'The Slavery of Sex': Feminist-Abolitionists in Nineteenth-Century America." Ph.D. dissertation, University of Illinois, 1975.

James, Janet Wilson. "Changing Ideas about Women in the United States, 1776–1825." Ph.D. dissertation, Radcliffe College, 1954.

MacGilvray, Daniel. "Stephen Symonds Foster." N.d. Typescript in WorHS.

Melder, Keith. "The Beginnings of the Women's Rights Movement in the United States, 1800–1840." Ph.D. dissertation, Yale University, 1964.

Pease, Jane H. "The Freshness of Fanaticism; Abby Kelley Foster: An Essay in Reform." Ph.D. dissertation, University of Rochester, 1969.

Riley, Glenda Lou Gates. "From Chattel to Challenger, the Changing Image of the American Woman, 1828–1848." Ph.D. dissertation, Ohio State University, 1967.

Swerdlow, Amy. "Abolition's Conservative Sisters: The Ladies' New York City Anti-Slavery Societies, 1834–1840." Paper given at Third Berkshire Conference on the History of Women, June 9–11, 1976.

Warbasse, Elizabeth B. "The Changing Legal Rights of Married Women, 1800–1861." Ph.D. dissertation, Radcliffe College, 1960.

BOOKS AND ARTICLES

Adams, James Douglass, ed. *A Collection of Letters of Ephraim and Elisabeth Douglass Adams.* 2 vols. Berkeley, Calif.: By the Author, 1973.

Alcott, Louisa May. *Louisa May Alcott; Her Life, Letters and Journals.* Ed. Ednah Dow Cheney. Boston: Roberts Brothers, 1889.

Baer, Helene G. "Mrs. Child and Miss Fuller." *New England Quarterly* 26 (June 1953): 249–55.

Banner, Lois W. "Religious Benevolence as Social Control: A Critique of an Interpretation." *Journal of American History* 60 (June 1973):23–41.

Beard, Mary. "Lucretia Mott." *American Scholar* 2 (Jan. 1933): 4–12.

Beecher, Catharine E. *An Essay on Slavery and Abolitionism with Reference to the Duty of American Females.* 2nd ed. Philadelphia: Henry Perkins, 1837.

Birney, Catherine H. *The Grimké Sisters, Sarah and Angelina Grimké.* Boston: Lee & Shepard, 1885; reprinted, Westport, Conn.: Greenwood Press, 1969.

Blackwell, Alice Stone. *Lucy Stone, Pioneer of Woman's Rights.* Boston: Little, Brown, 1930.

Blackwell, Antoinette Brown. *The Sexes Throughout Nature.* New York: G. P. Putnam's Sons, 1875.

Blackwell, Elizabeth. *Counsel to Parents on the Moral Education of Their Children.* New York: Brentano's Literary Emporium, 1881.

———. *How to Keep a Household in Health.* London: Ladies' Sanitary Association, 1870.

Blatch, Harriot Stanton, and Lutz, Alma. *Challenging Years, the Memoirs of Harriot Stanton Blatch.* New York: G. P. Putnam's Sons, 1940.

Bloomer, D. C., ed. *Life and Writings of Amelia Bloomer.* Boston: Arena Publishing 1895; reprinted, New York: Schocken Books, 1975.

Breault, Judith Colucci. *The World of Emily Howland.* Millbrae, Calif.: Les Femmes, 1976.

Brink, Carol. *Harps in the Wind: The Story of the Singing Hutchinsons.* New York: Macmillan, 1947.

Calvo, Janis. "Quaker Women Ministers in Nineteenth Century America." *Quaker History* 63 (Autumn 1974):75–93.

Cassara, Ernest. *Universalism in America, a Documentary History.* Boston: Beacon Press, 1971.

Chace, Elizabeth Buffum. *Anti-Slavery Reminiscences.* Central Falls, R.I.: E. L. Freeman & Son, 1891.

———, and Lovell, Lucy Buffum. *Two Quaker Sisters; From the Original Diaries of Elizabeth Buffum Chace and Lucy Buffum Lovell.* Ed. Malcolm R. Lovell. New York: Liveright, 1937.

Chafe, William H. *The American Woman: Her Changing Social, Economic, and Political Role, 1920–1970.* New York: Oxford University Press, 1972; paperback ed., 1974.

Chandler, Elizabeth Margaret. *Essays, Philanthropic and Moral.* Philadelphia: L. Howell, 1836; reprinted, Philadelphia: T. E. Chapman, 1845.

———. *Poetical Works, with a Memoir of Her Life and Character by Benjamin Lundy.* Philadelphia: L. Howell, 1836.

Chapman, John Jay. *Memories and Milestones.* New York: Moffat, Yard, 1915; reprinted, Freeport, N.Y.: Books for Libraries Press, 1971.

Chapman, Maria Weston. *Right and Wrong in Boston.* Boston: Annual Reports of Boston Female Anti-Slavery Society, 1836–39.

———. *Right and Wrong in Massachusetts.* Boston: Dow & Jackson's Anti-Slavery Press, 1839; reprinted, New York: Negro Universities Press, 1969.

———. *Ten Years of Experience: Ninth Annual Report of Boston Female Anti-Slavery Society.* Boston: Oliver Johnson, 1842.

Child, Lydia Maria. *An Appeal on Behalf of That Class of Americans Called*

Africans. New York: John S. Taylor, 1836.

————. *Letters of Lydia Maria Child, with Biographical Introduction by John G. Whittier and Appendix by Wendell Phillips.* Boston: Houghton Mifflin, 1883.

————. *Letters from New York,* 3rd ed. New York: C. S. Francis, 1845.

Colman, Lucy N. *Reminiscences.* Buffalo: H. L. Green, 1891.

Coombs, Zelotes W. *Stephen Symonds and Abby Kelley Foster.* Worcester, Mass.: Worcester Historical Society, 1934.

Crocker, Lucretia, and May, Abby W. *Memoirs of Lucretia Crocker and Abby W. May.* Ed. Ednah Dow Cheney. Boston: By the Editor for the Massachusetts School Suffrage Association, 1893.

Cromwell, Otelia. *Lucretia Mott.* Cambridge: Harvard University Press, 1958.

Dall, Caroline H. *Alongside.* Boston: T. Todd, 1900.

————. *The College, the Market, and the Court.* Boston: Lee & Shepard, 1867; reprinted, Concord, N.H.: Rumford Press, 1914.

Davies, John D. *Phrenology, Fad and Science; A Nineteenth Century American Crusade.* New Haven: Yale University Press, 1955.

Davis, David Brion. "Some Ideological Functions of Prejudice in Antebellum America." *American Quarterly* 15 (Summer 1963): 115–126.

Davis, Paulina W. *A History of the National Woman's Rights Movement.* New York: Journeymen Printers' Co-operative Association, 1871; reprinted, New York: Source Book Press, 1970.

DuBois, Ellen. "Struggling into Existence: The Feminism of Sarah and Angelina Grimké." *Women: A Journal of Liberation* (Spring 1970); reprinted as pamphlet by New England Free Press, Boston.

————. "The Radicalism of the Woman Suffrage Movement: Notes toward the Reconstruction of Nineteenth-Century Feminism." *Feminist Studies* 3 (Fall 1975): 63–71.

Edwards, Herbert. "Lydia Maria Child's 'The Frugal Housewife.'" *New England Quarterly* 26 (June 1953): 243–49.

Filler, Louis. *The Crusade against Slavery, 1830–1860.* New York: Harper & Row, 1960; Harper Torchbooks, 1963.

Fladeland, Betty. *Men and Brothers: Anglo-American Antislavery Cooperation.* Urbana: University of Illinois Press, 1972.

Flexner, Eleanor. *Century of Struggle; The Woman's Rights Movement in the United States.* Cambridge: Belknap Press of Harvard University Press, 1959; New York: Atheneum, 1970.

Foner, Philip S., ed. *The Factory Girls.* Urbana: University of Illinois Press, 1977.

Foote, Edward Bliss. *Medical Common Sense.* New York: By the Author, 1863.

Gambone, Joseph G., ed. "The Forgotten Feminist of Kansas: The Papers of Clarina I. H. Nichols, 1854–1885." 8 installments. *Kansas Historical Quarterly* 39–40 (Spring 1973–Winter 1974).

Garrison, William Lloyd. *Letters of William Lloyd Garrison; Vol. 1: I Will Be Heard, 1822–1835*. Ed. Walter M. Merrill. Cambridge: Belknap Press of Harvard University Press, 1971.

———. *Letters of William Lloyd Garrison; Vol. 2:1836–1840*. Ed. Louis Ruchames. Cambridge: Belknap Press of Harvard University Press, 1971.

Garrison, W. P., and Garrison, F. J. *William Lloyd Garrison 1805–1879, the Story of His Life Told by His Children*. 4 vols. Boston: Houghton Mifflin, 1894.

Gibbons, Abby Hopper. *Life of Abby Hopper Gibbons. Told Chiefly Through Her Correspondence*. 2 vols. Ed. Sarah Hopper Emerson. New York: G. P. Putnam's Sons, 1896–97.

Gordon, Linda. "Voluntary Motherhood: The Beginnings of Feminist Birth Control Ideas in the United States." *Feminist Studies* 1 (Winter-Spring 1973): 5–22.

Gordon, Michael, and Bernstein, M. Charles. "Mate Choice and Domestic Life in the 19th Century Marriage Manuals." *Journal of Marriage and the Family* 32 (Nov. 1970): 665–74.

Greven, Phillip J., Jr., ed. *Child-Rearing Concepts, 1628–1861*. Itasca, Ill.: F. E. Peacock, 1973.

Grimké, Angelina E. *An Appeal to the Christian Women of the South*. New York: American Anti-Slavery Society, 1836.

———. *An Appeal to the Women of the Nominally Free States*. Boston: Isaac Knapp, 1838.

———. *Letters to Catharine E. Beecher*. Boston: Isaac Knapp, 1838.

Grimké, Sarah M. *Letters on the Equality of the Sexes, and the Condition of Woman*. Boston: Isaac Knapp, 1838; reprinted, New York: Source Book Press, 1970.

Gusfield, Joseph R. *Symbolic Crusade: Status Politics and the American Temperance Movement*. Urbana: University of Illinois Press, 1963.

Gutman, Herbert G. "Work, Culture, and Society in Industrializing America, 1815–1919." *American Historical Review* 78 (June 1973): 531–88.

Hallowell, Anna Davis, ed. *James and Lucretia Mott. Life and Letters*. Boston: Houghton Mifflin, 1884.

Hare, C., ed. *Life and Letters of Elizabeth L. Comstock*. London: Headley Brothers, 1895.

Harper, Ida Husted. *Life and Work of Susan B. Anthony*. 3 vols. Indianapolis: Bowen-Merrill, 1898–1908.

Haviland, Laura S. *A Woman's Life-Work*. Cincinnati: Walden & Stowe, For the Author, 1881; 5th ed., Grand Rapids, Mich.: S. B. Shaw, "c. 1881."

Hays, Elinor Rice. *Morning Star; A Biography of Lucy Stone, 1818–1893*. New York: Harcourt, Brace & World, 1961.

————. *Those Extraordinary Blackwells*. New York: Harcourt, Brace & World, 1967.

Hersh, Blanche Glassman. "A Partnership of Equals: Feminist Marriages in Nineteenth-Century America." *University of Michigan Papers in Women's Studies* 2, no. 3 (1977): 39–62.

Higginson, Thomas Wentworth. *Common Sense about Women*. Boston: Lee & Shepard; New York: C. T. Dillingham, 1882.

————. *Contemporaries*. Boston: Houghton Mifflin, 1899.

————. *Letters and Journals of Thomas Wentworth Higginson, 1846–1906*. Ed. Mary Thacher Higginson. Boston: Houghton Mifflin, 1921; reprinted, New York: Da Capo Press, 1969.

History of Woman Suffrage. 6 vols. Vols. 1–3 ed. Elizabeth Cady Stanton, Susan B. Anthony, Matilda Joslyn Gage. New York: Fowler & Wells, 1881–87. Vol. 4 ed. S. B. Anthony and Ida Husted Harper. Rochester, 1902. Vols. 5–6 ed. I. H. Harper. New York: National American Woman Suffrage Association, 1922.

Hogeland, Ronald W. "Coeducation of the Sexes at Oberlin College: A Study of Social Ideas in Mid-Nineteenth-Century America." *Journal of Social History* 6 (Winter 1972/3): 160–76.

Holley, Sallie. *A Life for Liberty; Anti-Slavery and Other Letters of Sallie Holley*. Ed. John W. Chadwick. New York: G. P. Putnam's Sons, 1899.

Hooker, Isabella Beecher. "The Last of the Beechers: Memories on My Eighty-third Birthday." *Connecticut Magazine* 9 (Apr. 1905): 286–98.

Hooker, John. *Some Reminiscences of a Long Life*. Hartford, Conn.: Belknap & Warfield, 1899.

Howe, Daniel Walker. *The Unitarian Conscience; Harvard Moral Philosophy, 1805–1861*. Cambridge: Harvard University Press, 1970.

Howe, Julia Ward. *Reminiscences, 1819–1899*. Boston: Houghton Mifflin, 1899.

————, ed. *Representative Women of New England*. Boston: New England Historical Publishing, 1904.

Hunt, Harriot K. *Glances and Glimpses*. Boston: John P. Jewett, 1856; reprinted, New York: Source Book Press, 1970.

Jeffrey, Kirk. "Marriage, Career, and Feminine Ideology in Nineteenth-

Century America: Reconstructing the Marital Experience of Lydia Maria Child, 1828–1874." *Feminist Studies* 2, nos. 2/3 (1975): 113–30.

Kraditor, Aileen S. *The Ideas of the Woman Suffrage Movement 1890–1920.* New York: Columbia University Press, 1965; Garden City, N.Y.: Anchor Books, 1971.

———. *Means and Ends in American Abolitionism.* New York: Pantheon Books, 1969.

———, ed. *Up from the Pedestal: Selected Writings in the History of American Feminism.* Chicago: Quadrangle Books, 1968.

Krueger, Lillian. "Madame Mathilde Franziska Anneke, an Early Wisconsin Journalist." *Wisconsin Magazine of History* 21 (Dec. 1937): 158–67.

Kuhn, Anne L. *The Mother's Role in Childhood Education: New England Concepts 1830–1860.* New Haven: Yale University Press, 1947.

Le Duc, Thomas H. "Grahamites and Garrisonites." *New York History* 20 (Apr. 1939): 189–91.

Leopold, Richard W. *Robert Dale Owen, a Biography.* Cambridge: Harvard University Press, 1940.

Lerner, Gerda. *The Grimké Sisters from South Carolina.* Boston: Houghton Mifflin, 1967. New York: Schocken Books, 1971.

———. "The Lady and the Mill Girl: Changes in the Status of Women in the Age of Jackson." *Mid-Continent American Studies Journal* 10 (Spring 1969): 5–15.

———. "Placing Women in History: Definitions and Challenges." *Feminist Studies* 3, nos. 3/4 (Fall 1975): 5–14.

———, ed. *Black Women in White America.* New York: Pantheon Books, 1972; Vintage Books, 1973.

Lewis, E., ed. "Letters of Wendell Phillips to Lydia Maria Child." *New England Magazine* 5 (Feb. 1892): 730–34.

Livermore, Daniel Parker. *Comfort in Sorrow.* Chicago: New Covenant, 1866.

———. *Woman Suffrage Defended.* Boston: Lee & Shepard, 1885.

Livermore, Mary A. *My Story of the War.* Hartford, Conn.: A. D. Worthington, 1889.

———. *The Story of My Life.* Hartford, Conn.: A. D. Worthington, 1899.

Lovell, Lucy Buffum. *See* Chace, Elizabeth Buffum.

Lutz, Alma. *Created Equal, a Biography of Elizabeth Cady Stanton, 1815–1902.* New York: John Day, 1940.

———. *Crusade for Freedom: Women of the Antislavery Movement.* Boston: Beacon Press, 1968.

―――. *Susan B. Anthony: Rebel, Crusader, Humanitarian.* Boston: Beacon Press, 1959.

McPherson, James M. "Abolitionists, Woman Suffrage, and the Negro, 1865–1869." *Mid-America* 47 (Jan. 1965): 40–47.

―――. *The Struggle for Equality: Abolitionists and the Negro in the Civil War and Reconstruction.* Princeton, N.J.: Princeton University Press, 1964.

Martineau, Harriet. *Harriet Martineau's Autobiography.* Ed. Maria Weston Chapman. Boston: J. R. Osgood, 1877.

Massachusetts Anti-Slavery Society. *Annual Reports, 1833–1853.* Published by the Society in Boston; reprinted, Westport, Conn.: Negro Universities Press, 1970.

Massey, Mary Elizabeth. *Bonnet Brigades.* New York: Alfred A. Knopf, 1966.

May, Abby W. *See* Crocker, Lucretia.

May, Samuel J. *Memoir of Samuel Joseph May.* Ed. T. Mumford. Boston: American Unitarian Society, 1876.

―――. *The Rights and Condition of Women.* Syracuse: Stoddard & Babcock, 1846.

―――. *Some Recollections of Our Antislavery Conflict.* Boston: Fields, Osgood, 1869.

Melder, Keith. "Ladies Bountiful: Organized Women's Benevolence in Early Nineteenth Century America." *New York History* 48 (July 1967): 231–54.

―――. "Woman's High Calling: The Teaching Profession in America, 1830–1860." *American Studies* 13 (Fall 1972): 19–32.

Mott, James. *Hints to Young People on the Duties of Civil Life.* New York, 1826; pamphlet in Garrison Family Papers, Smith College.

Mott, Lucretia Coffin. *Slavery and "The Woman Question," Lucretia Mott's Diary of Her Visit to Great Britain to Attend the World's Antislavery Convention of 1840.* Ed. Frederick B. Tolles. Haverford, Pa.: Friends Historical Association, 1952.

Munsterberg, Margaret. "The Weston Sisters and 'The Boston Controversy.'" *Boston Public Library Quarterly* 10 (Jan. 1958): 38–50.

Notable American Women, 1607–1950: A Biographical Dictionary. 3 vols. Ed. Edward T. James, Janet Wilson James, and Paul S. Boyer. Cambridge: Belknap Press of Harvard University Press, 1971.

O'Neill, William L. *Everyone Was Brave: The Rise and Fall of Feminism in America.* Chicago: Quadrangle Books, 1969.

Osofsky, Gilbert. "Abolitionists, Irish Immigrants and the Dilemmas of Romantic Nationalism." *American Historical Review* 80 (Oct. 1975): 889–912.

Parton, James, et al. *Eminent Women of the Age.* Hartford, Conn.: S. M. Betts, 1868.

Pickard, John B. "John Greenleaf Whittier and the Abolitionist Schism of 1840." *New England Quarterly* 37 (June 1964): 250–54.

Pillsbury, Parker. "Stephen Symonds Foster." *Granite Monthly* 5 (1882): 369–75.

Pivar, David J. *Purity Crusade: Sexual Morality and Social Control, 1868–1900.* Westport, Conn.: Greenwood Press, 1973.

Powell, Aaron M. *Personal Reminiscences.* New York: Caulon Press, 1899.

Proceedings of the Woman's Rights Conventions Held at Seneca Falls and Rochester, N.Y., July and August, 1848. New York: Robert J. Johnston, 1870; reprinted, New York: Arno Press, 1969.

Richards, Laura E., and Elliott, Maud Howe. *Julia Ward Howe, 1819–1910.* Boston: Houghton Mifflin, 1915.

Riegel, Robert E. *American Feminists.* Lawrence: University of Kansas Press, 1963.

————. "The Introduction of Phrenology to the United States." *American Historical Review* 39 (Oct. 1933): 73–78.

————. "The Split of the Feminist Movement in 1869." *Mississippi Valley Historical Review* 49 (Dec. 1962): 485–96.

Robinson, Harriet H. *Massachusetts in the Woman Suffrage Movement. A General, Political, Legal and Legislative History from 1774, to 1881.* 2nd ed. Boston: Roberts Brothers, 1883.

————, ed. *"Warrington" Pen-Portraits.* Boston: By the Editor, 1877.

Eugene H. Roseboom. *The Civil War Era: 1850–1873.* History of the State of Ohio Series, vol. 4, ed. Carl Wittke. Columbus: Ohio State Archaeological and Historical Society, 1944.

Rossi, Alice S., ed. *Essays on Sex Equality by John Stuart Mill and Harriet Taylor Mill.* Chicago: University of Chicago Press, 1970.

————. "Feminist History in Perspective: Sociological Contributions to Biographic Analysis." In *A Sampler of Women's Studies,* pp. 85–108. Ed. Dorothy Gies McGuigan. Ann Arbor, Mich.: Center for Continuing Education of Women, 1973.

————, ed. *The Feminist Papers.* New York: Columbia University Press, 1973; Bantam Books, 1974.

Scott, Anne Firor. *The Southern Lady: From Pedestal to Politics 1830–1930.* Chicago: University of Chicago Press, 1970.

Severance, Caroline M. *The Mother of Clubs: Caroline M. Seymour Severance.* Ed. Ella Giles Ruddy. Los Angeles: Baumgardt, 1906.

Sinclair, Andrew. *The Better Half; The Emancipation of the American Woman.* New York: Harper & Row, 1965.

Sklar, Kathryn Kish. *Catharine Beecher, a Study in American Domesticity.* New Haven: Yale University Press, 1973.

Small, Edwin W., and Small, Miriam R. "Prudence Crandall, Champion of Negro Education." *New England Quarterly* 17 (Dec. 1944): 506–29.

Smith, Daniel Scott. "Family Limitation, Sexual Control, and Domestic Feminism in Victorian America." *Feminist Studies* 1 (Winter-Spring 1973): 40–57.

————. "Parental Power and Marriage Patterns: An Analysis of Historical Trends in Hingham, Massachusetts." *Journal of Marriage and the Family* 35 (Aug. 1973): 419–28.

Smith, Timothy L. *Revivalism and Social Reform in Mid-Nineteenth Century America.* New York: Abingdon Press, 1957; Harper Torchbooks, 1965.

Smith-Rosenberg, Carroll. "Beauty, the Beast and the Militant Woman: A Case Study in Sex Roles and Social Stress in Jacksonian America." *American Quarterly* 23 (Oct. 1971): 562–84.

————. "The Female Animal: Medical and Biological Views of Woman and Her Role in Nineteenth-Century America." *Journal of American History* 60 (Sept. 1973): 332–56.

————. "The Hysterical Woman: Sex Roles and Role Conflict in 19th-Century America." *Social Research* 39 (Winter 1972): 652–78.

Solomon, Barbara Miller. *Ancestors and Immigrants: A Changing New England Tradition.* Cambridge: Harvard University Press, 1956.

Speare, Elizabeth G. "Abby, Julia, and the Cows." *American Heritage* 9 (June 1957): 54ff.

Stanton, Elizabeth Cady. *Eighty Years and More: Reminiscences 1815–1897.* European Publishing, 1898; reprinted, with new introduction by Gail Parker, New York: Schocken Books, 1971.

————. *Elizabeth Cady Stanton as Revealed in Her Letters, Diary and Reminiscences.* 2 vols. Ed. Theodore Stanton and Harriot Stanton Blatch. New York: Harper & Brothers, 1922; reprinted, New York: Arno Press, 1969.

Suhl, Yuri. *Ernestine L. Rose and the Battle for Human Rights.* New York: Reynal, 1959.

Swisshelm, Jane Grey. *Crusader and Feminist; Letters of Jane Grey Swisshelm. 1858–1865.* Ed. Arthur J. Larsen. St. Paul: Minnesota Historical Society, 1934.

————. *Half a Century.* 2nd ed. Chicago: Jansen, McClurg, 1880.

Thistlewaite, Frank. *America and the Atlantic Community.* New York: Harper & Row, 1959, 1963.

Thomas, Benjamin Platt. *Theodore Weld: Crusader for Freedom.* New Brunswick, N.J.: Rutgers University Press, 1950.

Thorp, Margaret Farrand. *Female Persuasion; Six Strong-Minded Women.* New Haven: Yale University Press, 1949.

Tolles, Frederick B. *Quakers and the Atlantic Culture.* New York: Macmillan, 1960.

Tyler, Alice Felt. *Freedom's Ferment.* Minneapolis: University of Minnesota Press, 1944; New York: Harper Torchbooks, 1962.

Waite, Frederick C. "The Three Myers Sisters—Pioneer Women Physicians." *Medical Review of Reviews* (Mar. 1933), pp. 114–19.

Walters, Ronald G. "The Erotic South: Civilization and Sexuality in American Abolitionism." *American Quarterly* 25 (May 1973): 177–201.

———, ed. *Primers for Prudery: Sexual Advice to Victorian America.* New Jersey: Prentice-Hall, 1974.

Weld, Theodore Dwight et al. *Letters of Theodore Dwight Weld, Angelina Grimké Weld and Sarah Grimké, 1822–1844.* 2 vols. Ed. Gilbert H. Barnes and Dwight L. Dumond. New York: D. Appleton-Century for the American Historical Association, 1934.

Welter, Barbara. "The Cult of True Womanhood." *American Quarterly* 18 (Summer 1966): 151–75.

———. "The Feminization of American Religion: 1800–1860." In *Insights and Parallels, Problems and Issues of American Social History.* Ed. William O'Neill. Minneapolis: Burgess, 1973.

Willard, Frances E. *Glimpses of Fifty Years.* Chicago: Woman's Temperance Publishing Association, 1889.

Wood, Ann Douglas. " 'The Fashionable Diseases': Women's Complaints and Their Treatment in Nineteenth-Century America." *Journal of Interdisciplinary History* 4 (Summer 1973): 25–52.

———. "The War within a War: Women Nurses in the Union Army." *Civil War History* 18 (Sept. 1972): 197–212.

Woody, Thomas. *History of Women's Education in the United States.* 2 vols. New York: Science Press, 1929.

Wright, Henry C. *Marriage and Parentage.* 5th ed. Boston: B. Marsh, 1866.

Wyman, Lillie Buffum Chace. "Reminiscences of Two Abolitionists." *New England Magazine* (Jan. 1903), pp. 536–50.

———, and Wyman, Arthur Crawford. *Elizabeth Buffum Chace, 1806–1899, Her Life and Its Environment.* 2 vols. Boston: W. B. Clarke, 1914.

Wyman, Mary Alice, ed. *Selections from the Autobiography of Elizabeth Oakes Smith.* Lewiston, Me.: Lewiston Journal, 1924.

BIBLIOGRAPHY

Yasuba, Yasukichi. *Birth Rates of the White Population in the United States, 1800–1860.* Baltimore: Johns Hopkins University Press, 1962.

Index

DATE DUE

AP 27 '84	APR 29 '84		
OCT. 1 9 1993	OCT 10 '93		

DEMCO 38-297